FIRE
MAGIC

©Kylie Moroney Photography

Josephine Winter is a writer and Pagan community builder who has spent the last two decades working in Wiccan and Pagan spaces. She is a founding member of the Pagan Collective of Victoria, a nonprofit, statewide organisation dedicated to providing networking and fellowship to witches and Pagans of all walks of life. Josie holds qualifications in literature, education, and the arts, and is the Australian correspondent for *The Wild Hunt*. She lives in provincial Victoria, Australia, with her family.

△

JOSEPHINE WINTER

FIRE MAGIC

ELEMENTS OF WITCHCRAFT

FIRST EDITION
Third Printing, 2023

Cover design by Shannon McKuhen

Llewellyn is a registered trademark of Llewellyn Worldwide Ltd.

Library of Congress Cataloging-In-Publication Data

Names: Winter, Josephine, author.
Title: Fire magic : element of witchcraft / Josephine Winter.
Description: Frist edition. | Woodbury, MN : Llewellyn Worldwide, Ltd,
    [2021] | Includes bibliographical references and index.
Identifiers: LCCN 2021008660 (print) | LCCN 2021008661 (ebook) | ISBN
    9780738763736 (paperback) | ISBN 9780738764092 (ebook)
Subjects: LCSH: Fire—Miscellanea. | Witchcraft. | Magic.
Classification: LCC BF1623.F57 W56 2021 (print) | LCC BF1623.F57 (ebook)
    | DDC 133.4/3—dc23
LC record available at https://lccn.loc.gov/2021008660
LC ebook record available at https://lccn.loc.gov/2021008661

Llewellyn Worldwide Ltd. does not participate in, endorse, or have any authority or responsibility concerning private business transactions between our authors and the public.

All mail addressed to the author is forwarded but the publisher cannot, unless specifically instructed by the author, give out an address or phone number.

Any internet references contained in this work are current at publication time, but the publisher cannot guarantee that a specific location will continue to be maintained. Please refer to the publisher's website for links to authors' websites and other sources.

Llewellyn Publications
A Division of Llewellyn Worldwide Ltd.
2143 Wooddale Drive
Woodbury, MN 55125-2989

www.llewellyn.com
Printed in the United States of America

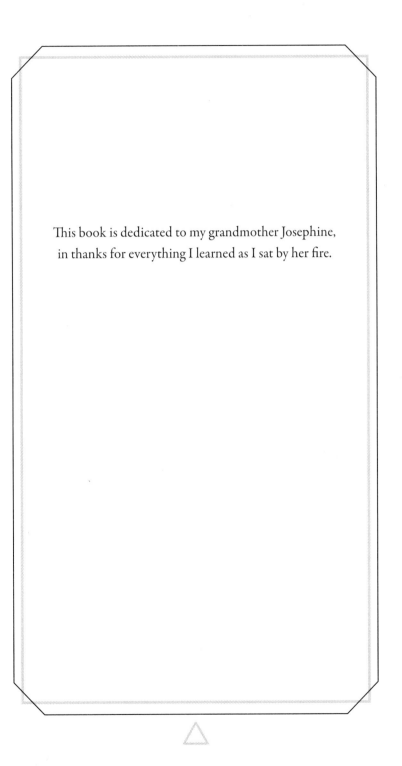

This book is dedicated to my grandmother Josephine,
in thanks for everything I learned as I sat by her fire.

CONTENTS

Contents

Part 2:
Working with the Element of Fire

Part 3:
Recipes, Rituals & Spellcraft

DISCLAIMER

The advice in this book is intended to educate and assist people on their quest to learn and become stronger practitioners of fire magic. There are no absolute guarantees of outcomes, as much is outside of our control. Please ensure your personal safety at all times. For example, don't meditate and drive or operate heavy machinery at the same time. Be cautious when using oils and herbs—don't ingest essential oils, don't use undiluted essential oils on your skin, and be cautious in the use of herbs and essential oils in case an allergic reaction or a contraindication with medicine could occur. Consult a doctor, therapist, or another health care provider before ingesting any herbs or if you have any medical or mental health concerns.

Although this book contains information about several religions, cultural practices, deities, and more, it is not meant to be a complete resource or an instruction manual. If additional information is desired, it should be sought from a proper primary source.

FOREWORD

For centuries and through many esoteric practices, the elements have been the cornerstones of magical work. Whether it's astrology or modern witchcraft, these four basic elements create the boundaries and the structures within larger multidimensional spiritual frameworks. They can bring concepts home and make them more readily understandable.

Earth is the ground we walk on, quite literally. It is the rocks, the mud, the mountains. Earth is also our body and the physical manifestation in this life. It is our center and our stability. Fire is the flame in the hearth. It is the candle, the bonfire, the sun.

Fire both warms and destroys. It has the power to transform and incite. Its flame is our passion and our will to go on.

Water is the rain from the skies. It is the world's oceans and lakes, the comforting bath, the morning dew. Water is our blood and sweat, as well as our memories. It rules our emotions and manifests as tears.

Air is all around us. It is our breath, the sounds we hear, and the wind that touches our faces. Air carries seeds and pollen, scents that warn and delight, and songs of culture. Air is our voice, our thoughts, and our ideas.

While every esoteric system applies these basic concepts differently, the elements are there, helping to structure practice and develop a greater understanding of self. For modern witches, the elements are often represented in their magical tools; for example, the chalice might be water and the pentacle earth. For Wiccans more specifically, the elements help raise the magical circle and empower the protective quarters. In tarot the elements flow through the symbolic imagery of the pip cards, and in astrology each element is represented by three signs. For others, the elements provide spiritual guidance for daily meditations, visualizations, spell work, or life lessons. One might ask, "What element do I need to get through today?"

The following book is the third in a special series that dives deeply into the symbolism and magical use of the elements. Each book focuses on one element and covers everything associated with that element, from spiritual places and deities to practical spells and rituals. For the witch who wants to envelop themselves in elemental practice or for someone who needs a resource on each element, this book and its sisters will provide everything you need.

Written by four different authors from around the globe, each book in the Elements of Witchcraft series shows just how wide and deep the esoteric understanding of the elements goes and how to make that concept work for your own magical and spiritual needs. Join us on a deep exploration of the magical use of the four elements.

By Heather Greene
Acquisitions Editor, Llewellyn Worldwide

INTRODUCTION

The ways that fire and flame are crucial to the work and practices of modern witches and Pagans are virtually countless. From huge balefires at festivals down to simple tealight candles, we've been known to use fire to represent a sacred element, a turning of the seasons, important points in the cycles of our gods, loved ones who have passed away, the sun or stars, and many more. Year round, sunshine or snow, indoors or out, fire is almost always a key part of our workings and celebrations.

It is my aim with this book to explore not only the modern and historical uses of fire throughout witchcraft communities, Pagandom, and occulture, but to also pay tribute to the ways in which it is important to our very existence as humans and a community.

Just like the kitchen hearthfire was the centre of households for centuries, so too are the bonfire, campfire, and candle flame an integral part of Pagan rituals, gatherings, and workings. The group I work with usually works outside, and fire plays a big part, usually in the form of a bonfire or candles, if Australia's fire restrictions allow.

If you think back to a Pagan festival you've attended—especially one that required you to camp—you'll probably find that many of your good memories of the time centre around fire: socialising by a campfire, dancing by a bonfire, or even just using lanterns, torches, or candles. Some of the most poignant community ritual experiences I've had have had a lot to do with looking across the circle to see the faces of my friends and loved ones illuminated in flickering yellow light and knowing that what we're working for, we're working for together. While fires aren't the only thing that make these times special, they're certainly a cornerstone of how we experience and participate in this community.

Fire has its destructive and dangerous side, too. We can forget this sometimes, cushioned as we are in the first-world luxuries of life in the twenty-first century. I completed this book as the worst bushfires in Australia's recorded history burned around me: I had friends lose their homes. Thousands of hectares of forest and fields were burned, and millions of native animals were killed. The news and all of our social media feeds were crowded with the yellows and reds of burning bush and structures and the sickening black of animals burned to death. The town of Mallacoota was completely circled by enormous forest fires that turned the morning skies black as stranded residents had to be rescued by the Navy.

The fear that hit us all this summer came with the realisation that this is an element over which we have a lot less control than we sometimes like to think. The same fire that warms our chilly fingertips and brings people together can also destroy and kill in the right circumstances.

The Element of Fire

If you've been reading about or practicing modern witchcraft for any amount of time, you will have come across the elements of earth, air, fire, water, and—sometimes, depending on your tradition—spirit. You might acknowledge them as you cast a circle or prepare sacred space, or have representations of them on your altar.

Why Four Elements?

Most of the "witchy" books that my eager teenage self read at the turn of the century (gods, I feel old writing that) insisted that having balanced representation of the elements in any ritual is essential, but none really went into the reasons why, or where this notion came from.

The idea of four (sometimes five) elements being the essential "building blocks" for all things in the natural world was a widely held belief in many ancient cultures: there were similar lists of elements in ancient Babylonia, Greece, Persia, Japan, and India to name a few. The ancient Chinese system Wu Xing (a shortened form of *wŭ zhŏng liúxíng zhī qì*—"the five types of *chi*, or energy force, dominating at different times"[1]) had wood listed as a fifth element.

For centuries these concepts were considered mostly in philosophical terms; as well as being used to explain or analyse naturally occurring things, the elements were used to explain cosmological and mythological events, too. It wasn't until the rise of science and scientific study, such as the Islamic Golden Age (800 to 1400 CE) and Europe's Scientific Revolution in the 1600s, that scientists began to study this theory more closely: experimenting, verifying, and classifying many more elements along the way.

But what does any of this have to do with witchcraft, and how did the elements get into our rituals and Books of Shadows and onto our altars? The answer lies partly in the European grimoires and grimoire traditions.

---

1   Zai, *Taoism and Science*, 133.

Grimoires, Witchcraft, and the Four Elements

The word *grimoire* comes from an old Frankish word meaning "mask" or "sorcerer" and is related to the modern word *grammar*. Grimoires are books often thought of as "books of spells" or "textbooks" of magic. These books, some of which were believed to have been imbued with magic powers, often include instructions on how to create magical objects like talismans and amulets; how to perform magical spells, charms, and divination; and how to summon or invoke supernatural entities such as angels, spirits, deities, and demons.

I want to pause here for a moment to point out that some modern witches use the terms *grimoire* and *Book of Shadows* interchangeably, but often the two terms are different: the term *Book of Shadows* is less than a century old. It was coined by British witch Gerald Gardner, the founder of Wicca, in the early 1950s and originally was used to describe the handwritten book of oath-bound material given to Gardnerian witches once they were initiated. In her book *The Rebirth of Witchcraft*, Doreen Valiente, one of Gardner's priestesses, claimed that he found the term in a 1949 occult magazine: it was the title of an article printed on the facing page to an advertisement for Gardner's novel *High Magic's Aid*.[2]

Just as witchcraft has evolved and expanded in the half century and more that followed, the definition for a Book of Shadows (or BoS, for short) has grown to include a witch's more personalised books of magical instructions and records, spells, dream journals, and more.

While grimoires had been used by some religious and spiritual sects since ancient times, they saw a sharp rise in popularity during the Renaissance, the transition period between the end of the

---

2   Valiente, *The Rebirth of Witchcraft*, 51.

Middle Ages around the fourteenth century CE and the beginning of the Age of Enlightenment in the seventeenth century CE.

The Renaissance was a time of great change and "rebirth" in much of society. Science, art, and logic became valued far more than they had in the Middle Ages, as did an interest in history and historical texts. During this time, interest in grimoires rose, and it became fashionable to own or study them: the older and more mysterious, the better.

Much of the work and commentaries on the grimoires from this time was adopted later by ceremonial magic orders such as the Golden Dawn, which in turn were drawn upon by Gerald Gardner as he pieced together fragments of a witchcraft tradition he had received and sought to "fill in the gaps" with existing material.

And the rest is history. Gardner started writing and publishing about witchcraft and Wicca in the 1950s, after the last of the laws outlawing witchcraft were repealed in England. Wicca and other forms of witchcraft made their way to America, Australia, and other parts of the world, where they met and mingled with the ideas that were coming to the fore during the sixties and seventies—environmentalism, feminism, sexual liberation, and more—and the infant forms of some of today's established Pagan traditions and ideas were born. Now there are more and more traditions and trailblazers every decade, and the Pagan "tent" grows bigger and more vibrant every decade. It's marvellous.

And still, in all kinds of ways and means, the four elements feature heavily in many rituals and in a lot of material—witchcraft and otherwise. They probably wouldn't be so prevalent if there wasn't something to them: the stability and fecundity of earth; the intelligence and creativity of air; the strength and passion of fire; the emotion and dreaming of water, and so on.

The element of fire is especially unique, in that it is the only one of the four that can be created: by lighting a match, rubbing some sticks together, or even flicking a switch on a heater or furnace. So too is it the only element that can be destroyed by the other three: you can pour water over a blaze, heap earth over a campfire, or blow out a candle.

Using This Book

In the first four chapters of this book, I'm going to look at fire veneration and magic throughout history and in folklore and mythology. Chapters 5 to 8 outline some common correspondences and associations with fire today, before we bring everything together in the later chapters, which are more hands-on and discuss fire and candle magic, ritual fires, fire festivals, and more.

It may be tempting to skip ahead to these chapters first, but as these draw heavily on historic and folkloric accounts of fire in some cases, I promise you won't get as well-rounded a picture of this fascinating element and how it fits into your witchcraft and mine.

PART
1
◈

HISTORY,
FOLKLORE & MYTH

*Mythologies act as keys to the
lucid awakening of the spirit.*

—KRISTOFFER HUGHES,
FROM THE CAULDRON BORN

Chapter 1

THROUGH HISTORY AND TIME

What we do as witches and Pagans with fire and flame is in no way new. Fire has been present in human culture since the earliest parts of the Stone Age, and there is evidence that it has been used ceremonially since then.

Prehistory

The earliest evidence of humans being able to control fire for these purposes—fragments of burned wood, seeds, and flint shards—is almost eight hundred thousand years old.[3] Fire kept our ancestors alive, providing cooking and heat for hundreds upon thousands of winters. Little surprise, then, that worship, reverence, and deification of fire is thought to date back just as far.

Most Indo-European languages—the family of languages that by 1000 BCE were spoken throughout Europe and in parts of southwestern and southern Asia—had two separate concepts for fire:

*egni: and its variants described animate fire. This is the root of the Sanskrit word for fire, *agni* (which is also the name of a Hindu

---

3   Goren-Inbar, et al. "Evidence of Hominin Control of Fire."

fire deity) and the Latin *ignis*, which is where modern English gets words such as *ignite*.

*__paewr:__ and its variants described inanimate fire. Here is where we get the Greek *pyr* (the root of words such as *pyre* and *pyromaniac*), and the great-great-granddaddy of the modern English word *fire*.[4]

Some of the earliest evidence of fire used for ceremonial purposes include:

- Fired clay "Venus" figurines dating back around eleven thousand years. These small female figures make up some of the oldest fired pottery ever discovered. The most well-known figurine, the Venus of Willendorf, is actually carved out of limestone, but others, such as the Venus of Dolní Věstonice, are fired clay and have been dated to somewhere around 25,000 to 29,000 BCE.
- The earliest evidence of ritual cremations, dating back to around 1500 BCE, in western Europe.
- Evidence of ritual fires at early Hindu altars in southern India from around the same time.

600 BCE

Zoroastrianism

The term "fire-worshipper" is sometimes associated with the Zoroastrianism, a system of religion founded in Persia in or around the sixth century BCE by Zoroaster (or Zarathustra). The first major religion to worship a single deity rather than many gods, Zoroastrianism began in what is now northeast Iran and southwestern Afghanistan.

---

4   Etymology Online, "Fire."

In Zoroastrianism, both fire (*atar*) and water (*aban*) are considered agents of ritual purification, and as such feature prominently in many rituals, which in ancient times often took place in fire temples or "houses" of fire.

Greece and Rome

In Graeco-Roman culture, there were two main types of fire worship: fire of the hearth (with deities such as the Roman Vesta and her Greek equivalent Hestia), and fire of the forge (with the Roman Vulcan and the Greek Hephaestus). The story of the Greek Titan Prometheus, who stole fire from the gods and gave it to humans, is a well known tale. You can read more about these deities in chapter 3.

1500 CE to 1700 CE

Europe: The Burning Times

I don't think I could get away with writing a book about witches and fire without mentioning the Burning Times—the period between 1500 and 1700 when people accused of witchcraft were burned at the stake in Europe—in some way.

Burning at the stake was the execution of choice for heretics at this time. This is a practice that has its origins in Babylonia and ancient Israel and was later adopted by Europeans. Fire as baptiser or purifier features heavily throughout the Bible, and executing heretics in this way was considered by many a means to rid wrongdoers of their sins or "evil"... with the convenient side effect of doing away with the wrongdoers themselves in the process.

Like others who came to witchcraft and Paganism in the late 1990s and early 2000s, I was exposed constantly to tales of the Burning Times: of the nine million or more witches who were burned during the witch trials of the Middle Ages, of the unbroken line of witches dating back to that time who have carried on the Old Religion, and so on.

It was mentioned—without any references or citations of primary sources whatsoever—in almost every witchy book I read as a baby witch. The "nine million women" figure was accepted as gospel truth by just about every witch and Pagan I knew, and it became a part of our own mythology. And who could blame us? The romance of helping revive a religion almost lost to Christian oppressors centuries ago is too much for even the hardest heart to resist.

The problem, though, was that this wasn't entirely true.

The notion of an unbroken line of witches in highly organised covens dating back to the Burning Times was first made popular by Dr. Margaret Murray in the 1920s. While a very romantic idea, this theory was quickly discredited by historians and archaeologists alike: as well as there being no physical evidence whatsoever, we know that language, literacy, dialect, travel, distance, and financial limitations would have prevented a network of witches—or of anyone, really—from existing the way Murray claimed they did in pre-industrial times.

Despite being discredited, Murray's theories were later picked up by Gerald Gardner, the first witch to "go public" after the last of the old anti-witchcraft laws were repealed in England in the 1950s. Gardner referenced these theories heavily in much of his work, which became the building blocks for a lot of the witchcraft and Paganism that we practice today.[5]

Gardner's interpretation of Murray's theories was in turn built upon by influential early ecofeminist witches of the 1960s and

---

5   American author Jason Mankey does a great unpacking of Murray
     and Gardner's contributions to modern witchcraft in his book,
     Transformative Witchcraft.

1970s, which is where we get much—not all—of the "nine million women" rhetoric we still see today in some witchy material. This number was further cemented in a 1990 Canadian documentary called *The Burning Times*, featuring several of these authors.

But when we look objectively at some of the claims made by witchy and Pagan authors about the Burning Times, it's important not to ignore what Professor Ronald Hutton described as the "tidal wave" of research that points out, in no uncertain terms:

- **Far fewer than nine million people were executed in Europe during this time.** There is no "official" number, but scholars estimate it to be somewhere between forty and sixty thousand.[6] The myth of nine million originates in a 1784 pamphlet by German scholar Gottfried Christian Voigt. In this pamphlet, Voigt estimated—again, unsupported by any evidence—the number of people executed for witchcraft *over a period of more than one thousand years*. This figure has been used out of context by countless others ever since.

- **Witch crazes were not systematic or even well organised.** Cultures varied greatly across Europe during the Middle Ages. Attitudes towards gender roles, "witchcraft"/magic, and the Church were vastly different from country to country or even city to city. The Church, too, had differing ideas in different countries and towns about the acceptability of folk-magics, superstitions, and so on, even after the publication of Kramer's *Malleus Maleficarum*, the most well-known treatise on witches

---

6 Adler, "A Time for Truth."

and witchcraft (first published in Germany in the late 1400s).[7]

- **The *Malleus Maleficarum* was not a universally accepted text for witch-hunters or the Church.** Despite it being popular with some religious extremists at the time, many considered the *Malleus Malificarum* to be degrading to the piety of men and to the works of nuns and female saints.[8] Others pointed out that it ignored much of what was already established lore about witchcraft and demonology. Many inquisitors and clergy alike dismissed and disdained it as overly paranoid and misogynist.[9]

Don't get me wrong: this was certainly a travesty and a tragedy. Tens of thousands lost their lives in the most barbaric ways and in utter misery and agony. These people were often women, they were often poor and usually disadvantaged or marginalised in some way. But this wasn't, as some call it, "the witches' holocaust." The vast majority of those accused and executed did not identify as witches or as anything that we would consider to be similar to witches as we know them today.

And does all this mean that we as witches and Pagans shouldn't be learning or reading about the witch trials? Absolutely not. Witch crazes of any kind form an important part of our history and one worth looking into if you have the inclination to. Many modern witches I know have a section of their bookshelves dedicated to this topic. Others have explored at an academic level the extent to which these trials and the confessions of the accused have informed modern understandings and interpretations of witchcraft.

---

7   Waldron, *The Sign of the Witch*, 180.
8   Hutton, *Triumph of the Moon*.
9   Waldron, *The Sign of the Witch*, 182.

What's important is that we don't help perpetuate a misnomer and an attitude that lives on in modern Pagandom to this day: every Christmas and Easter I see memes doing the rounds of social media about the "Pagan" traditions that Those Horrible Christians™ stole, and every Halloween I see twaddle about all assertive women being the "granddaughters of witches they couldn't burn." For the record, I don't need to be the granddaughter of a witch to be able to stand up for myself, and I sure as shit don't need to constantly mock others' religion to justify my own.

It might have been all right in the early days of Neopaganism to have had a vociferous beef with all Christians and to treat witchcraft as a way of rebelling against the dominant culture. It was probably fun, too. But attitudes and ideologies that base themselves on problematic stories that we now know to be untrue are unhelpful, they're embarrassing, and they detract attention from the hard work done by Pagan priests everywhere, not to mention from harmony and beauty that so many seekers have found when they came to this religion.

50 CE to the Present

Europe and the British Isles: Wicker Men

Hang around witches and Pagans long enough, and you'll probably watch the 1973 British cult horror film *The Wicker Man* at least once. Love it or loathe it (and hey, from my experience, most Pagans seem to have strong views either way), this film is what has inspired the resurgence of wicker men—great looming figures made of wood, grass, or reeds and set alight—in contemporary Pagan culture.

I've seen some bloody brilliant wicker men at Pagan festivals here in Australia. In the early 2000s, the Geelong Pagans put on a "burning man" festival in the Otway rainforest each year, which culminated in the lighting of a huge figure that we would build as a community the day before. Theirs was a clever design: he was a huge skeleton (with a ribcage and everything) made of iron pieces that locked together. All we needed to do was gather bundles of sticks to fasten to the structure to flesh him out. Once these all burned away in the ritual, the skeleton remained, glowing red-hot in the darkness.

Many folks attribute wicker men to "Celtic" culture and as an ancient Celtic practice. But it's unclear whether or not they were actually a thing. Accounts of them used in druidic human sacrifice can all be traced back to Julius Caesar's 50 CE work, *Commentaries on the Gallic War*. In this, Caesar mentions "state" sacrifices made by the Gallic people—Celtic tribes who lived in the ancient region of western Europe that included what is now northern Italy, France, Belgium, and part of Germany and the Netherlands—to appease their gods.[10]

According to Caesar, these rites were overseen and orchestrated by the Druids, and involved "colossal images, the limbs of which, made of wickerwork, they fill[ed] with living men set on fire; and the victims perish[ed], encompassed by the flames."[11]

This was, Caesar claimed, mostly used to execute criminals, although innocents were rounded up and sacrificed to make up numbers as needed. But while we know that the Druids did practice human sacrifice, there has been no archaeological evidence found that confirms Caesar's account.

Historians speculate that this story was invented by Caesar to be used as a propaganda of sorts to help justify the Gallic wars by

---

10   Symes, *Willow*, 50.
11   Caesar, Julius. *Commentaries*, 183.

illustrating that the "barbaric" Gauls and Britons needed some Roman "civilisation."[12]

Caesar's account was referenced and repeated by many other ancient writers, but it was neither questioned nor illustrated until 1676, when English historian Aylett Sammes published *Britannia Antiqua Illustrata* (Latin: "The Antiquities of Ancient Britain"). Sammes more or less quoted Caesar's account of wicker men verbatim, then added a few embellishments of his own, saying that the limbs of the man were "weaved together in the nature of Basket-ware," and so on.[13]

Along with this description, Sammes included an engraving of what he imagined the Gallish wicker men might have looked like. This image—a fair-haired character looking off into the distance with a naturalistic face, symmetrical arms and legs made of straight willow stakes formed into cages to hold miserable prisoners—became the basis of all visual representations of wicker men ever since.[14]

But even though it's getting increasingly unlikely that these improbable structures actually existed in ancient times, accounts of more modest, human-sized effigies do exist here and there.

Before the nineteenth century, burning *mannequins d'osier* or wicker figures was fairly common in France. This practice was similar to lighting a midsummer bonfire in other parts of Europe: it was thought to drive away bad spirits. In Rue aux Ours in Paris, people used to make a large wicker-work figure that they dressed as a soldier and carried around the streets for a few days, burning it on the third of July. *Le geaunt de la Rue au Ours* was burned every year until 1643 and was overseen by a local person chosen as

---

12   Hutton, *Blood and Mistletoe*, 3–5.

13   Symes, *Willow*, 51.

14   Symes, *Willow*, 51.

"king" for the occasion. The king had the honour of setting the figure ablaze with a lit torch, and as the fire died out locals scrambled for leftover fragments.[15] Some stories claim that this was to commemorate the burning of a blasphemous soldier in 1418, but most scholars disagree, saying it's more likely that this was just a regional quirk in what was a pretty commonplace tradition at the time.[16]

Regardless of whether they're a true historical practice or a product of ancient Roman propaganda that's been embellished upon ever since, thanks to the 1970s filmmakers' reimagining, and inspired by the imagery of Sammes and others, wicker men are somewhat common at today's larger fire festivals, both Pagan and otherwise.

1850 CE to 1890 CE

Fire and water made the steam that powered the Industrial Revolution in the Victorian era, changing the way humans have lived ever since. Fire lit the way for the miners of the Australian and American gold rushes that drastically changed our landscapes and populations, and fire flickered in the candles of practitioners of an ever-growing number of occult and spiritualist traditions that formed during this time.

• • • •

Burn Marks and Magical Protections in Colonial Australia

Dr. David Waldron is an historian, a folklorist, and an active researcher in local history and folklore studies. He is the author of *Snarls from the Tea Tree: Australia's Big Cat Folklore* (ASP, 2012), *Shock the Black Dog of Bungay: A Case Study in*

---

15   Frazer, *The Golden Bough*, 38.
16   Symes, *Willow*, 58.

Local Folklore (Hidden Publishing, 2010) and *Sign of the Witch: Modernity and the Pagan Revival* (CAP, 2008). Most recently he has made contributions to and edited the anthology of nineteenth century south east Australian folklore *Goldfields and the Gothic: A Hidden Heritage and Folklore* (ASP, 2016). He has written extensively on the origins of contemporary Neopaganism and its relation to mediaeval and early modern beliefs in the supernatural, romanticism, and Western modernity. He has also written extensively on British folklore as linked to local identity and community, and on the Australian folklore of Bunyips, Big Cats, and Yowies in relation to environmental and social history. A current research focus is on the use of ghost stories as a vehicle for memorialising community trauma through both story-telling and hoaxing. David Waldron is the researcher and co-writer of the Goldfields History podcast *Tales from Rat City*.

IN THE REAR of an unassuming country pub in the town of Guildford, about 130 kilometres northwest of Melbourne, is an unassuming outbuilding. A heritage remnant from Australia's gold rush of the 1850s, it was once the stables of the famous Cobb and CO Coach lines which stretched across the frontier of white civilization as the population surged by the hundreds of thousands in the hunt for gold. Upon the central beams of the stables are a range of unassuming marks, which for many would pass unnoticed or be mistaken for the residue of candles, but on closer inspection reveal themselves to be quite deliberate. Thirteen circular thumb-sized marks at eye level surround the center of each beam, many of which have been considerably dug out with a spoon and reburned into the timbers, a process which would have taken some time and effort. Perhaps most spectacular of all, and unique in Australia, is a vast display of symbols and letters drawn in soot deep underground below the 1860 Mechanics Institute on the main street of the regional city of Ballarat. These symbols and letters were first carefully etched then painstakingly traced in soot upon the roof and are both extensive and detailed. It would have taken many hours alone by candlelight to cover such an enormous space in soot-stained images, yet they were, with only ambivalent references to "the Fallen" and the date of 1882 to give any clue as to their original purpose.

Yet these marks are also found all over the British Isles, in mediaeval homes and castles, and on the walls of churches dating back to before the Norman conquest. What do they mean? Why are they so carefully placed on the thresholds of buildings and places where they are meant to be seen? What they represent is the survival of folk magical practices—the rituals and protective marks made by the cunning men and women of colonial Australia continuing the practices of their forebears from Europe. The gold rush of the 1850s and '60s brought hundreds of thousands of people to Australia from the British Isles alongside immigrants from Asia, the Americas, Africa, and the rest of Europe, and they brought their rich legacy of folklore and beliefs with them. The people who came to seek their fortune were commonly from the poor, disenfranchised, and dispossessed who were compelled by the enclosure movement, the Highland clearances, and the potato famine to seek their fortune across the world.

Historian Jill Blee, in her research into the Irish immigration to Australia, found the pervasive belief that the rural Irish immigrants had brought the "little folk" with them across the seas, that the Fae were with them on the goldfields of Australia along with a host of new spirits from a strange new land. In one recording was the belief that "the *bean sidhe* sat herself at the bow and combed her hair all the way from Cork to Botany Bay."[17] Even more than the pervasiveness of the literal belief in spirits, Blee argues that perpetuating the beliefs and customs of home allowed the Irish Catholics to survive in a new land where their very identity put them at odds with their Protestant English overlords.[18] So too it was for the poor immigrants of Cornwall, Scotland, York, and East Anglia. Wrestling with preserving their heritage and identity in what was, to them, an alien land in which their customs, beliefs, and even identity were a threat to be eradicated by the Protestant English establishment.

So, what did these symbols, so carefully placed in the walls of these outbuildings, mean to those who made them? While, for many of these people, their status as poor and uneducated prevented their voice from being heard, we do have fragments which remain in the historical record. In the newspapers of the mid-nineteenth century there are records of cunning men and women plying their trade in the cemeteries, taverns, and bushlands of colonial Australia. The Australian Ritual Magic Research Project, an endeavour supported by the University of Hertfordshire, the Society for Vernacular Architecture, and both Federation and La Trobe University, found numerous examples of surviving folk magic across Australia during the Victorian era. While sites were found in wealthy homes, police stations, coach houses, lighthouses, and squatter stations, by far the majority were in outbuildings and servants' quarters inhabited by the poor. Yet for all this, only three practitioners of magic were clearly identified, largely due to the absence of records for those who were outside of the economic

---

17　Blee, J., "The Banshees" in Waldron, D.(Ed.) *Goldfields and the Gothic: A Hidden Heritage and Folklore.* Australian Scholarly Publishing: Melbourne, 2014, 43–54.

18　Blee, J. "The Banshees," 51.

and social elite. These people offered their magical skills for hire, offering to find lost property and livestock, heal the sick, create protective charms, release people from evil magic and spirits, and predict the future. Of the two men, both were publicans and we have the good fortune of their magical practices to be recorded for posterity and available for viewing online. In his almanac, publican William Allison detailed cures, remedies, curses, protective charms, witch bottles, and other magical practices. We are also fortunate that his colleague, another publican and cunning man Benjamin Noakes, also gave his notes to William Allison to copy into his almanac.[19] This gives us some indication of what the practices and beliefs of colonial Australian magical practitioners were.

Burn Marks

Burn marks are, by far, the most numerous examples of folk magic practices in colonial Australia. In many, if not most, stables which have survived with timbers intact from the early to mid-nineteenth century, these teardrop shaped holes the size of one's thumb are prolific in the central beams of stables. Painstakingly created by holding a candle on an angle to a single point, then digging out the ash until a depression occurs, these holes took considerable time and effort. Folklorists Dean and Hill attempted to replicate the effect and were able to categorically state they are quite deliberately and systematically made. Experimenting with candles, tapers, and timber they found the marks were created by burning at 45 percent and digging out with a small spoon to remove the ash and allow for deeper digging. This would

---

19   For a digitized view of William Allison's magical almanac see here
      http://stors.tas.gov.au/NS261-1-1.

take approximately fifteen minutes to produce a sizeable mark.[20] Whilst the full significance of the burn marks is clouded, much of the research indicates they played a role in rituals inoculating buildings against fire and purifying them against evil spirits.[21]

Soot Stains

Spectacular in their scale and complexity, the soot stains on the roof of the Ballarat Mechanics Institute basement are a remarkable example of folk magical practice. Today only sixteen examples of this practice survive in the British Isles. They remain mysterious in their application to this day and the examples in Ballarat are unique in Australia. Easton suggests that the fear of witchcraft may have been a factor in their use. In one extensive example, he argued that they were, in part, used to ward off evil spirits that led to persistent nightmares. In the British context, often a sacred flame from a church was carefully carried to the site and used to draw protective marks and symbols on ceilings in vulnerable areas of buildings. Candle smoke marks are common in British medi- aeval churches, scattered across ceilings seemingly at random. Initials and symbols including stylized crosses and demon traps (geometric mandalas) are common. The marks in Ballarat, with their dating at 1882 and references to the Fallen, may well have been referring to the Great Australasian Mine disaster in which two dozen miners drowned in a breach into an underground river

20   John, Dean and Nick Hill, "Burn marks on buildings: accidental or deliberate?" *Vernacular Architecture*. 45 (1): 1–15 (12 December 2014).

21   Hutton, Ronald, and SpringerLink. "Physical Evidence for Ritual Acts, Sorcery and Witchcraft in Christian Britain: A Feeling for Magic." *Palgrave Historical Studies in Witchcraft and Magic*. London: Palgrave Macmillan UK: Imprint: Palgrave Macmillan, 2016, 56.

in nearby Creswick. However, with little references as to the cause one can only speculate.

Conclusion

The goldfields of Australia were a dangerous place for many, in a strange new land with new threats and the call of the spirit of the land from home feeling very distant in people's minds. In this new world then, it is little wonder that the traditions of the old world were brought with them and that the rituals of the past remained strong. They brought comfort, both in the believed protection they could bring, but also in the powerful emotional links to a distant homeland on the other side of the world. Yet those legacies remain written on the thresholds and hidden within the walls.

David Waldron
• • • •

Present Day
Judaism, Islam, and Christianity

The burning bushes, pillars of fire, and menorah flames are all examples of sacred fire, sometimes used as a personification of God himself.

In Judaism, Chanukah (sometimes spelled Hanukkah) is a festival held around November and December. The holiday lasts eight days, and celebrates a miracle that occurred during the reestablishment of the holy temple in Jerusalem after it was conquered by the Assyrian Greeks in the second century BCE. Of all the oil stored to be used in sacred lights, only a single vial remained untouched by the sacking. It burned for eight days, which was taken to be a miraculous sign that the people of the temple could continue their spiritual lives and have a relationship with God. At a functional level, this also meant more time to press and process more olive oil before the last of it was burned.

Chanukah is celebrated in a variety of ways all over the world, but one common tradition is to light candles in a menorah—a seven-light lampstand—and face them towards the outside world, sometimes in a window or prominent place in the house. In Hebrew, this tradition is called *pirsuma d'nisa*, "publicising the miracle."

Candles, incense, and fire also feature prominently in Catholicism, including at Easter, when Easter bonfires are still lit to this day across Europe and other parts of the world. Sacred flame or fires are often lit to signify the end of *Paschal Triduum*, the three holy days of Easter that begin on Good Friday and end on Easter Sunday.

Hinduism

Fire has long been a part of some Hindu traditions, too, with rituals often performed in front of sacred fires, sometimes with the chanting of mantras or offerings made to the gods. Flame and fire make up a key component of many different rituals, including marriages, where Agni (a Hindu fire deity, sometimes a personification of fire itself) is sometimes asked to witness the union of two people.[22]

Ancient Fire in the Everyday

While we use fire less today than we would have even twenty years ago, many fragments of ancient or folkloric practices still linger in practices most people would consider mundane.

Look at candles on birthday cakes, for example. Some people believe that the tradition of a round cake decorated with lit candles originates with celebrations for the goddess Artemis in ancient

---

22   Hazen, *Inside Hinduism*, 34.

Greek culture. And even if they don't (we do know that round "cakes" were certainly a thing in ancient Greece and Rome, and that candles were used in the worship of Artemis, but it's not clear whether lit candles on a cake were used specifically), there are records of burning candles atop cakes in Germany as early as the 1700s to celebrate *Kinderfest*, or the birthday of a child.[23]

Conclusion

There are more examples of fire worship and sacred fire throughout history than I have the space to fit them all here. Suffice to say that fire has been a part of the ceremonies of many cultures since the beginning of recorded time, and it continues to be a part of many human religions and cultures today: in cremation and bonfires; in the candles used in various religious ceremonies; and in the eternal flames that are used to remind us of significant occasions.

---

23   Nowak, "The Fascinating History of the Birthday Cake."

Chapter 2

MYTHICAL FIRE
BEASTS AND PLACES

Like the element of fire itself, fire beasts from mythology are often unpredictable, mysterious, and multifaceted. Interestingly, mythical realms and places associated with fire are often related to the act of creation and change, or with ruin and destruction in some way. In this chapter, I've included some history, contemporary beliefs, and other information about some mythical creatures and places commonly associated with fire.

Mythical Beasts

We explored a bit about the element of fire and how and why it is involved in witchcraft in the introduction to this book, but I thought it was important to point out in this chapter that the idea of ethereal creatures being associated with specific elements—such as gnomes from Earth, sylphs from Air, salamanders from Fire, and undines from Water, and so on—has been around for centuries. Some occult traditions maintain that fire elementals were the first to befriend humans, and they taught early people how to create and use campfires and torches.[24]

But one of the first mentions of elementals specifically in connection with witchcraft was in works such as the *Compendium Maleficarum,*[25] a witch-hunter's manual written by Italian priest Francesco Maria Guazzo and published in 1608. Conceived during his time in Milan, which had something of a reputation for the practice of witchcraft and sorcery, Guazzo's book made many claims about witches and their dealings with different demons and spirits, including those of earth, air, fire, and water. His writings have influenced much of what was written afterwards about these creatures in relation to magic and witchcraft.[26]

Djinn

The djinn (or jinn, genn, or genies) are spirits of Arabian tradition, considered to be a higher order of creatures than humans and created of matter that is much more subtle.[27]

Djinn were believed to have supernaturally enhanced architectural skills, and were believed to have been employed by King Solomon to help build his magnificent temple.[28] In the folklores of many countries, they are said to live or at least congregate around doorways, thresholds, and other liminal spaces, and are the root of many superstitions related to these.[29]

According to Islamic belief, the djinn ruled the earth before the creation of humans, and were considered to be an intermediate

---

24 Grimassi, *Encyclopedia of Wicca and Witchcraft*, 116.
25 Grimassi, 115.
26 Grimassi, 80.
27 Drury, *The Watkins Dictionary of Magic*, 113.
28 Drury, *Watkins*.
29 Illes, *The Encyclopedia of Spirits*.

race of beings, between angels and people.[30] By most accounts, the djinn are most active at night, and love heat, deserts, and hot climates best of all, especially natural springs, ruins, and wild places in warmer regions.

Many folklores maintain that the djinn cannot resist a good story. Telling a story or singing a song are just a couple of the many ways some modern witches make offerings or pay tribute to these spirits. Another traditional method is to pour oil over a bowl of flour. When it comes to food offerings, it is widely held that they will refuse anything with salt. Food for the djinn is usually served outside, rather than inside the home. It's believed that harmful or mischievous djinn can be repelled with salt or iron, especially beads made from iron.[31]

Dragon

These huge, serpentine creatures appear in the legends and folklore of cultures the world over. Dragons' appearance and other details change vastly from place to place, but since the High Middle Ages dragons in Western culture have often been portrayed as fire-breathing beasts with four legs, wings, and horns. The popular Western image of a dragon seems to be a combination of portrayals of earlier dragons from different traditions, and of inaccurate or incomplete early drawings of snakes.

In Western cultures, dragons are portrayed as monsters to be tamed or slain, usually by saints or culture heroes (think Saint George and the Dragon). They are often said to have insatiable appetites and to live in caves, where they hoard treasure. This flavour of dragon appears frequently in Western fantasy literature,

---

30   Drury, *Watkins*, 113.
31   Illes, *The Encyclopedia of Spirits*.

including *The Hobbit* by J. R. R. Tolkien and the series A Song of Ice and Fire by George R. R. Martin.

The dragons of Eastern cultures are often depicted as wingless, serpentine creatures who are highly intelligent. The word "dragon" has also come to be applied to the Chinese traditional character *lung* (龍), which is associated with good fortune and thought to have power over rain. Dragons and their associations with rain are the source of the Chinese customs of dragon dancing and dragon boat racing. Many East Asian deities are commonly depicted with dragons. In Imperial China, dragons were also associated with the emperor, who, during later Chinese imperial history, was the only one permitted to have dragons on his home, clothing, or possessions.

Dragons commonly have a mix of avian, feline, and reptilian traits, such as snakelike features, reptilian scaly skin, four legs with three or four toes on each, spinal nodes running down the back, a tail, and a serrated jaw with rows of teeth. It's been suggested by some modern scholars that huge extinct or migrating crocodiles bear the closest resemblance, especially when encountered in forested or swampy areas, and are most likely the template of modern dragon imagery.[32] This also fits with the ancient words *draco* and *drakon* ("large [sea] serpent").

Firebird

There are firebirds—birds made or born from fire—in the mythologies of several different cultures around the world.

BENNU

The bennu bird is a mythological Egyptian bird who is linked with the sun, creation, and rebirth, and is considered in Egyptian mythology to have played a part in the creation of the world. It's

---

32   Stromberg, "Where did the Dragons Come From?"

been proposed that the bennu might have been the inspiration for the phoenix in Greek mythology.

Firebirds in Folklore and Fairy Tales

Firebirds also appear in a number of folk and fairy tales, the most famous probably being *Die Goldene Vogel* ("the golden bird"), which was first recorded by the Brothers Grimm in the early 1800s. The eponymous bird of the story visits a king's orchard every year to steal fruit, and is hunted by a young prince. Different versions of this tale exist across many cultures and lands in Europe and farther afield. My favourite firebird is Lantern, who appears in Catherynne M. Valente's *Orphans Tales* books.

Huma

The Huma (or sometimes Homa) appears in a few different Iranian myths and folktales; it also appears as a common motif in Sufi and Diwan poetry, and in the art and architecture of several countries. While the Huma certainly bears many of the same traits as firebirds in other mythologies, one of the key differences is that its splendid, fiery form is often depicted alongside water in some way. One of many interpretations of the name comes to us from Inayat Rehmat Khan Pathan, a teacher of Universal Sufism and the founder of the Sufi Order in the West, who suggested that *hu* "represents spirit," while *ma* originates from the Arabic *ma'a,* or water.[33]

Phoenix

Appearing in the mythologies of many countries, a phoenix is a mythical bird, usually resembling an eagle or other large bird, that dies in fire and is reborn from its own ashes. Many versions of the legend have the phoenix's rebirth only happening every five hundred years.

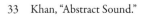

33   Khan, "Abstract Sound."

In Arabian legend, the phoenix sits on a nest that is ignited by the rays of the sun and burns to death. In this version of the myth, a worm rises from the ashes of the burned bird and grows into a new phoenix.

The phoenix is also traditionally associated with the sun in China, where it was regarded as a messenger from the heavens, appearing whenever the gods were benevolent. In mediaeval Europe, the phoenix appeared in Christian cosmology, where it was considered a symbol of the triumph of life over death; and in alchemy, where it was seen as a symbol of both the Philosopher's Stone and the Elixir of Life.[34]

Some stories associate the phoenix with frankincense, which was thought to be carried in its massive talons.[35] Heady, spiced scents such as cedar and cinnamon are also common tributes. Magical correspondences for phoenixes include beauty; beginnings; destruction; endings; happiness; hope; knowledge longevity; happy marriages; the otherworld and the underworld; rebirth and renewal; and self-work.[36]

Lampads

In Greek mythology, the Lampads (or Lampades) are nymphs of the underworld. The Romanised version of their name is *nymphae Avernales,* or "infernal nymphs," named for Avernus, a volcanic crater and the entrance to the underworld (see Mythical Places later in this chapter).

The Lampads were companions and servants of the goddess Hekate, and were given to her by Zeus as a reward for her loyalty throughout the *Titanomachy*, the decade-long war against the

---

34   Drury, *Watkins*, 232.
35   Illes, *Spells*, 625.
36   Kynes, *Correspondences*, 307.

Titans. They are usually depicted as bearing torches, the flames of which were thought to drive mortals to madness if they looked upon them. At their whim, the Lampads can turn this torchlight to the darkness to reveal lost, hidden, or necessary information.[37]

The ancestry of the Lampads is uncertain; some accounts claim they are daughters of Nyx, the goddess of night, while others say they are the offspring of one of the various river deities of the Greek underworld.[38]

In modern witchcraft, the Lampads are considered to be spirits associated with prophecy and justice. They obey Hekate and may be venerated alongside her, and some modern devotees of Hekate call upon them in ancestor work, or rites relating to death and grieving, often during the season of Samhain, the modern Pagan festival that is sometimes associated with Halloween. In works such as this, they are thought to be fiercely loyal.[39]

The Lampads are also associated with the afterlife; the subconscious; cycles; darkness; divinations; dream work; enchantment; favour and favours; hope; illumination; luck; nightmares; protection (especially for lost children); rebirth and renewal; release; revenge; strength; travel; and visions. Common offerings include black or silver candles; sprigs/pieces of dandelion, lavender, feverfew, monkshood, anise, belladonna, cardamom, galangal, or mandrake; or fires of cypress, palm, rowan, or willow wood.[40]

Salamanders

In mediaeval alchemy and magic, salamanders reside in the ethereal, sometimes otherworldly, elemental essence of fire. A salamander playing in fire is a classic symbol of energy in alchemy, and

---

37 Illes, *Spirits.*
38 Illes, *Spirits.*
39 Moss, *Hekate.*
40 Kynes, *Correspondences*, 322.

it's thought that they can be compelled to bestow gifts and good luck. According to some writings it is only through their activity that fire exists and can be used at all.[41]

Ancient writings on elementals say that salamanders appear to humans in the shape of small, lizard-like flames. The first known reference to salamanders as an elemental being comes from Greek philosopher Aristotle, who in the fourth century BCE wrote that the salamander "…not only walks through the fire but puts it out in doing so."[42] Much later, Leonardo da Vinci proposed that the salamanders might put out fires because they absorbed them for energy.[43]

Salamanders are not to be confused with the real species of amphibians that bear the same name, although it has been put forward by a few that perhaps "real" salamanders, given their fondness for rotting logs in woodlands, were inadvertently thrown into fires with the firewood of ancient peoples, and their figures were seen as they tried to escape the flames.[44]

Much of the material featuring salamanders claims that they are most active at night, sometimes appearing as balls of light drifting or bobbing across bodies of water, or in the weather phenomenon known as St. Elmo's Fire.[45]

Salamanders are often associated with action, control, and transformation,[46] and are linked by some occult writers to the human body and its ability to regulate temperature and temperament: "warm-blooded" and "hot-headed" people act in ways that are con-

---

41   Kynes, *Correspondences*, 116.
42   D'Este et al., *Practical Elemental Magick*, 74.
43   D'Este et al., *Practical Elemental Magick*, 75.
44   Chauran, *Faeries & Elementals*.
45   Grimassi, *Encyclopedia*, 117.
46   Kynes, *Correspondences*, 364.

sistent with qualities of salamanders and the element of fire, for example.

Mythical Places

Of the many theories about who the first non-indigenous people to see Australia were, I think my favourite is that about ancient Chinese explorers who, long before the idea occurred to any European folks, set out to map the uncharted oceans at the bottom of the world. Featuring on some of the maps they brought back from one expedition was a vast stretch of coastline still thought by many to be the west coast of Australia, labelled by the explorers as "the Land of Fire and Parrots." It's a pretty apt name, really: the summers here in Oz can be baking hot and dry, and we do have lots of amazing native birds.

But what I like best about this story is that there is no evidence that the explorers were able to find this coastline again, at least not straight away. And while logically we can look at the long stretch of coast and say that yes, it probably *was* the edge of Australia that these explorers had seen, there's no way of knowing for sure, and for a while there, there was a mythical *land of fire and parrots* hidden somewhere in the southern oceans of the world ... a world that nobody other than those who lived there could be sure was even actually there. I like to think that for sailors and explorers during this time, the mystery surrounding this land would have generated more stories and supposings about it, in turn.

For some of the places I've written about in this section, it's the liminality that appeals to me most: these are actual places that we can see and touch and breathe, but the stories and history attached means they also exist partly in the unknown, in the other. And in many cases this otherness is brought on by or connected to the element of fire: in transformation, in rebirth, or even in total destruction and ruin.

Avernus

Avernus is the name of a poisonous lake which was said in Roman mythology to be the entrance to the underworld. In the *Aeneid,* an epic poem written in Latin around the years 29 to 19 BCE by the Roman poet Virgil, the hero Aeneas descends to the underworld via a cave next to Lake Avernus:

> Deep was the cave; and, downward as it went
> From the wide mouth, a rocky rough descent;
> And here th' access a gloomy grove defends,
> And there th' unnavigable lake extends,
> O'er whose unhappy waters, void of light,
> No bird presumes to steer his airy flight;
> Such deadly stenches from the depths arise,
> And steaming sulphur, that infects the skies.
> From hence the Grecian bards their legends make,
> And give the name Avernus to the lake.[47]
> *Aeneid, Book 6.*

The lake itself is situated in a volcanic crater near what was once the Roman city of Cumae, but is now the much smaller village of Cuma, which lies west of Naples on Italy's coast. The name Avernus comes from the ancient Greek *aornos,* meaning "without birds."[48] Many historical and literary accounts mentioned that birds flying over the lake would fall down dead. This is probably because of the toxic volcanic fumes emitted via the lake from the still-active cra-

---

47   Virgil, *The Aeneid.*
48   "Averni," *Cyclopædia.*

ter beneath it. From time to time, volcanic vents in the lake and in nearby hillsides also open and emit sulphurous fumes.[49]

The Romans adopted a lot of Greek mythology and culture, and the underworld is similar in both mythologies. Souls travelling to the Roman underworld must first cross the river Styx, also known as the hateful waters, before being "sorted" into different districts of the underworld on the far banks.

One nearby hilltop has the ruins of a temple of Apollo. Farther down towards the lake, a trapezoidal tunnel known as the "cave" of the Sibyl runs beneath the hillside. There were many sibyls, or prophetesses who lived in caves, in the ancient world. The Sibyl at Cumae—a priestess who guarded the nearby temple of Apollo—was one of the best known.[50] It was the Sibyl at Cumae who warned the hero Aeneas about the difficulty of finding one's way back out of the underworld:

> Trojan, Anchises' son, the descent of Avernus is easy.
> All night long, all day, the doors of Hades stand open.
> But to retrace the path, to come up to the sweet air of heaven,
> That is labour indeed.[51]
> *Aeneid, Book 6.*

The area around the lake was first settled by ancient Greek colonists around the eighth century BCE.[52] In Roman times, Roman houses dotted parts of its shores, and there was a large bath house, too. The personification of the lake, the *deus Avernus*, was worshipped in lakeside temples.

While the Roman underworld isn't the dark, fiery place from Christian mythology, Avernus is still related to the element of fire

49 Paxson, *The Way of the Oracle*.
50 Drury, *Watkins*, 261.
51 Virgil, *The Aeneid*.
52 Paxson, *Oracle*.

because of its physical entrance being formed volcanically, and because of the great initiations and changes that must occur for those who seek to enter or try to leave.

Dinas Affaraon

Dinas Affaraon, sometimes written Dinas Ffaraon ("fortress of pharaoh") or Dinas Ffaraon Dande ("fortress of fiery pharaoh") is the name of a place mentioned in mediaeval Welsh literature. It is said to be an old name for the iron-age hillfort in Snowdonia, Wales, called Dynas Emrys, which is sometimes anglicised as the Ambrosial City.[53]

The place is mentioned in the twelfth- or thirteenth-century tale *Lludd and Llefelys* (*Cyfranc Lludd a Llefelys*), which is included in the Welsh collection of tales known as the *Mabinogion*. The tale tells the story of Lludd, who has just inherited the crown of Britain from his father. Soon after, he helps his brother Llefelys marry the princess of France and become king of that country. Lludd's reign starts off well, but it isn't long before three plagues disrupt the peace, the second of which is a scream that comes every May Day and is so horrible and piercing that it causes all pregnant women in Britain to miscarry and all men to lose their "hue and strength."[54]

Lludd's brother Llefelys gives him advice that helps him deal with the three plagues. The king goes to deal with the eldritch scream, which is caused by a red dragon that is locked in combat with a foreign white dragon. Lludd must set a trap for them at the exact centre of the island called Oxford, put them to sleep with mead, and then bury them underground at Dinas Emrys in a stone chest.

---

53   Hughes, *From the Cauldron Born*.
54   Gwyn Jones and Thomas Jones, transl., *The Mabinogion*.

It is in *Lludd and Llefelys* that we learn about the renaming of the site:

> [Lludd] saw the dragons fighting; and when they were worn and weary they descended on top of the covering, and dragged it with them to the bottom of the tub. And when they had made an end of drinking the mead they fell asleep. And in their sleep Lludd wrapped the covering about them, and in the safest place he found in Eryri he hid them in a stone coffer. The form by which that place was known thereafter was Dinas Emreis, and before that Dinas Ffaraon Dandde.[55]

The name Dinas Emrys is a nod to Myrddyn Emrys, or Merlin from Arthurian mythology, who was only a boy when he helped King Vortigern, a fifth-century warlord and king mentioned in many myths and stories of the time, who sought to build his tower on the site, only to have it topple over as the ground shook every night.[56]

Merlin knew of the two buried dragons, and prophesised that the red dragon was symbolic of the Britons and the white dragon the Saxons. If they were to be dug up so that they could fight, he said, the red dragon would win and the Britons would be victorious over the Saxons. The Celts often referred to their leaders as dragons (draig), so Merlin's prophecy could also be interpreted as saying the leader of the Britons would be victorious over the leader of the Saxons: something which would later take place through Uther Pendragon and then Arthur himself.[57]

So, five hundred years after they were first buried, the dragons were disinterred by Merlin and Vortigern's men. The horrible

---

55 Gwyn Jones and Thomas Jones, transl., *The Mabinogion*.
56 Squire, *Mythology of the Celtic People*, 380.
57 Woodbury, "Dinas Ffareon (Dinas Emrys)."

scream was heard again when the two creatures recommenced fighting, and the red dragon drove the white one out of Britain.[58]

Modern archaeology has revealed that Dinas Emrys was occupied in the late Roman period, though parts of its walls were built at a later time.[59] The site is on a wooded hill near the village of Beddgelert in Gwynedd, northwest Wales.

Hell

It was difficult to research mythical places associated with fire without constantly stumbling over references to the Christian hell and the history, mythology, and literature from the last thousand years and beyond that has shaped much of what some modern people consider to be its various qualities. There has been so much already written about all this that I don't feel the need to rehash it all here.

Simply put, many religious cultures including Christianity describe a fiery, harsh place where people are punished for their sins and wrongdoings. Both Christian and Egyptian mythologies describe underworlds with a lake of fire that is used to destroy, punish, or judge those who have not lived piously.

Muspelheim

Muspelheim—or Muspell, or Muspellheimr—is a realm of fire and one of the nine realms in Norse cosmology. According to Snorri Sturlusson's thirteenth-century *Younger Edda,* Muspelheim and the realm of Niflheim, a place of icy mists and glaciers, were the first two realms in existence. When rime from Niflheim met with sparks from Muspelheim, they created the other seven realms.[60]

---

58   Squire, *Mythology*, 381.
59   Ford, "Dinas Emrys: Vortigern's Hideout?"
60   Paxson, *Essential Asatru*, 133.

The realm of Muspelheim is described in the Eddas as being bright and hot—too hot for humans to set foot in. It is guarded by the *jotun* (a nature spirit with supernatural powers, sometimes a giant) called Surtr, who carries a bright, flaming sword.[61]

As well as being a creator of worlds, Muspelheim is also said to play a part in their destruction. The Eddas tell us that in the final battle of Ragnarok, the "doomsday" of the gods, the fire-giant sons of Surtr, along with many powerful allies, will go to war against the gods of Asgard, breaking the rainbow bridge of the Bifrost as they cross it. While this battle will end in a draw, the world itself will be destroyed:[62]

> In the midst of this clash and din the heavens are rent in twain,
> and the sons of Muspell come riding through the opening.
> Surtr rides first, and before him and after him flames burning fire.
> He has a very good sword, which shines brighter than the sun.
> As they ride over Bifrost it breaks to pieces, as has before been stated.
>
> *Prose Edda*

Sources vary on the exact layout of the nine realms in Norse cosmology within Yggdrasil, the world tree, apart from that Asgard, the home of the gods, is usually at the top, and Midgard, the realm that both is and is not our own realm, is in the middle. Fiery Muspelheim is usually said to be "in the south," usually interpreted as being south of Midgard.[63]

• • • •

The Monster

Ambriel is a Gardnerian and Alexandrian HPS who runs a coven with her partner. She was initiated over 25 years ago and

---

61   Paxson, *Essential Asatru*, 133.

62   Jones, Gwyn, *A History of the Vikings*, 318.

63   Paxson, *Essential Asatru*, 135.

has been involved in various Pagan organizations ever since. She lives in a small country town in southeastern Australia where she works full time and raises a family of both human and furry children. Her interests, among other things, include folklore, history, gardening, conservation, and reading lots of books.

> *The pines were roaring on the height,*
> *The winds were moaning in the night.*
> *The fire was red, it flaming spread;*
> *The trees like torches blazed with light.*
> *The bells were ringing in the dale*
> *And men they looked up with faces pale;*
> *The dragon's ire more fierce than fire*
> *Laid low their towers and houses frail.*
>
> J. R. R. Tolkien, *The Hobbit*

FIRE BRINGS LIGHT in the cold winter, they say. Without fire mankind would not survive, they say. And on it goes, the Eurocentric rhetoric which Southern Hemisphere Wiccans, Pagans, and witches have inherited. But for us that is not the case. Fire is not a friendly source of warmth and light to help us through the great cold and darkness of the winter. Fire is something to be feared, not celebrated.

All the traditional Wiccan and folkloric texts brightly claim that the summer solstice is a fire festival—so make your bonfire and celebrate the longest day! In over 30 years of being a witch, I can only remember one summer solstice bonfire. It was a very unusual summer, when there had been enough rain to make an outdoor fire safe and the fire burned merrily on a raised piece of land while the warm water ran across our bare toes. For once we could relax—no need for emergency buckets of water "just in case." We even made a sun wheel out of an old bicycle wheel and straw, and the men carried it, spitting gouts of flames, across the clearing. The burnt spots in the robes are still present, like foxing on an old newspaper, a reminder of a dying age. We celebrated that one glorious year, as our ancestors in those far northern countries must have done with bonfires, and it felt good—but strange. For us it was such an anomaly, an atypical event in an unnatural season and one that would never come again.

For most of us in the southern part of rural Australia, fire is not a life-giving, saving force, but rather an unpredictable, untamed explosion of regular and deadly proportions. Every summer we fear the puffs of smoke on the horizon and dread the wailing of the fire sirens, calling the volunteers to fight the fires. Fight them, as if we are waging a war against this most unpredictable of enemies. And for many of us it is a battle with deadly consequences. Summer rituals are at the mercy of not so much rain, but high fire danger. Each time, we carefully consult the oracles of the Bureau of Meteorology regarding their weather prophecies and make our decisions of a place based on them. High fire danger rating? Too dangerous to hold an outdoor ritual, let alone have any kind of outdoor fire. Too dangerous to even go into national or state parks, as fire spreads so quickly on a high fire rating day, like a plague through mediaeval towns.

In some ways I wonder if we are connecting with the Yule rituals celebrated at the same time by our Northern Hemisphere brethren. Feeling that reverberation of the reenactment of the dark night of the soul where primitive humans thought that the longest night might not end, and where they stared death in the face in the form of cold and starvation. Perhaps the summer solstice is our own dark night of the soul where we face our own existential crisis in the form of an excess of heat and light. At the very least, it's an interesting spiritual connection, and we certainly have experienced that fear over many summers.

In 2009 we had all been due to meet up on the Saturday to celebrate Lammas. A bit late that year for some reason, but at the last minute we decided to cancel because the word was that it was going to be the most disastrous fire day in history. The predictions turned out to be horrifyingly true, with 173 people burnt to death in one terrifying day that later came to be known as Black Saturday. One of the fires actually came to within twenty kilometres of us, a fact we were unaware of as we hunkered inside to shelter from the 45-degree heat with a 100-kph hot north wind blowing red dust at us, listening fearfully to the emergency radio. Because despite what we tell ourselves, being in a developed nation counts for nothing when the element of fire is let loose from Crow's kangaroo-skin bag. Communications go down, mistakes are made, senses are blinded by the dust and smoke. We did actually meet the next day, both to mourn the destruction and also to celebrate our survival—this time. And on it goes each summer.

However, while fires have always been a part of Australian landscapes, they have become increasingly dangerous and damaging. Part of the reason for this is of course climate change—the window for controlled burns is becoming smaller as summer comes earlier and fire restrictions are enforced almost as soon as winter finishes. And so, forest growth builds up and what could have been controlled in a slow burn becomes a raging wildfire. Temperatures are rising and drought is becoming increasingly common. Parts of the country are burning that never burned before. Here in the southeastern part of Australia the increasing prevalence of uncontrolled bushfires is our symbol of how Earth has become unbalanced and rages back at the humans who destroy her forests and animals, and pollute her waterways, and who are increasingly encroaching on the wild parts of Her country.

MYTHICAL FIRE BEASTS AND PLACES

A Monster, is how people described the fires this summer. We could hear the Monster coming, we felt the Monster's breath, we heard the Monster roar like a freight train. The metaphor shows the extent of the human fear of this most dangerous of the elements. Unpredictable, deadly, we humans have never really been sure of our mastery of fire. We use it and pretend we have tamed it but at the least provocation it stampedes over our homes and lives like a herd of brumbies let loose from a corral, leaving blackness and destruction in its wake. Even though life does spring from the ashes, that's of small consolation when day turns to night and then to a red glow and the Monster comes to visit.

In consequence our summer solstice rituals, especially of late, are not about celebrating fire, but rather about fearing it, placating it, desperately attempting to right a balance in an increasingly unbalanced world. In recent years we have created fire dragons which we have appeased with gifts to encourage the element to spare us from the worst of the summer fires. We have created rituals to balance out all the elements to try to restore harmony to our environment. And of course, we have acted in more practical ways to reduce the harm on our landscape through more conscious living, donating to environmental organizations, and promoting sustainability.

But each time summer rolls around again, we fear the element of fire, and as the years go on, we fear it more. And each time we vibrate the names of the fire quarter, and it comes through more strongly than the rest, we shiver, and wonder if it is our turn to face the Monster.

Ambriel

• • • •

Conclusion

While unpredictable, fire can be an agent of great change. These changes can be brought about by a creative force or one that destroys all in its path. Many of the mythical beings we've looked at in this chapter embody the different facets of change, while in many cases the mythical places only came about because of fire's creative or destructive qualities.

Chapter 3

FIRE AND THE DIVINE

For humans, using fire was (and is) such a crucial part of life across all parts of the world since prehistoric times. Little wonder, then, that fire deities and spirits appear in some form in the mythologies of most cultures worldwide. These deities tend to represent one or more of several different aspects relating to the element of fire:

- **Rebirth and transformation**: gods and spirits of change, or of transforming into something new out of chaos or destruction.

- **Inspiration**: sometimes patron deities of poets, artists, writers, etc.

- **Mischief and misrule**: tricksters, thieves, and antiheroes. The theft of fire from higher powers (gods, spirits, ancestors, etc.) for the benefit of humanity is a common theme in classical mythology and in the mythologies of many different First Nations peoples around the world, including the Americas, Polynesia, and Australia.

- **The forge and creativity**: literal forges where metal is shaped and given new form, or the ability that humans possess to give creative ideas shapes of their own.

- **The hearth:** the home, the family, and the safety and warmth that they bring.
- **The sun:** the blazing star that keeps life on this planet alive. The information in this chapter is provided to give you an overview of some deities who are traditionally associated with the element of fire. There are many others in addition to those written about here: we would need another book or perhaps a series of books to go into sufficient detail about all of them.

Remember, the best way to learn about a deity or myth is directly from the culture they belong to, and in a way that gives more than you take away. Please, *please* do not treat the list of deities below as some kind of spiritual buffet or Pagan "pick-and-mix" selection. I've included some ideas at the end of this chapter about how to approach or explore a deity in a respectful, culturally sensitive manner.

Adranus *(Sicily)*: Adranus was worshipped by the Sicels and the Sicani, who inhabited the large island of Sicily long before it was colonised by Greek settlers in the eighth century BCE. A temple to Adranus was built at the foot of the volcano Mount Etna, under which he was believed to reside. The nearby town of Adrano was named after the god and still stands today.

Aed *(Ireland)*: Aed is a god in Irish mythology, often mentioned in sources as being a son of the Dagda. His name comes from the Old Irish word *áed* ("fire"), which in turn comes from Proto-Celtic *aidus*, which derives from a Proto-Indo-European *heyd* ("to burn, kindle"). Some sources refer to him as Aed Caem, or Aed the Fair. He often appears in a trio alongside his brothers Aengus (or Oengus) and Cermait in older sources. His father the Dagda is sometimes referred to as Aedh Alainn, which has been taken to mean "fiery, lustrous one," but could also be translated as "lovely/fine," which would be consistent with his son, the "fair."[64]

Both Aed and the Dagda can be related to fire and the fire of passion. Several sources tell of Aed being killed by a jealous husband after the god had an affair with his wife. He is also mentioned in the fifteenth-century Irish manuscript *Cath Muige Tuired Cunga* ("The Battle of Mag Tuired at Cong"), an early modern Irish saga about two battles fought by the Tuatha De Dannan for the sovereignty of Ireland.[65]

Agneyi *(India and Southeast Asia)*: In the Hindu religion, Agneyi or Agneya is the divine and powerful daughter of the fire god Agni and one of his consorts. Sanskrit texts such as the *Harivamsha* and the *Vishnu Purana* mention that she is the mother of many kings. The word *agneya* in Sanskrit is an adjective meaning "flammable, burning, fiery, of Agni" and so on. *Agneya* used as a proper noun is often given to the southeastern direction, which is associated with fire and the sun.

Agni *(India and Southeast Asia)*: Agni is a god of the sun, fire, and lightning in the Hindu religion, where he is regarded as a friend and protector of humanity, and a protector of the home. Types of fire associated with Agni include the sun, lightning, comets, sacrificial fire, domestic fires, the fire of the funeral pyre, and the digestive fire which is within all humans.[66]

Many Hindu texts explain Agni as existing on three planes at once: on the earth as fire, in the air as lightning, and in the sky as the sun itself.[67] Agni is sometimes associated with comfort;

---

64 Daimler, *The Dagda*, 29.
65 Trinity College, *Cath Muige Tuired Cunga*.
66 Cartwright, "Agni."
67 Lochtefeld, *The Illustrated Encyclopedia of Hinduism*, 14.

healing and vitality; knowledge; light, warmth, and power; protection, purification, and the removal of negativity; rebirth and renewal; sex and sexuality; lightning; and youth.[68]

Alaz *(Eastern Europe)*: Alaz is the god of fire in Turkic mythology. He is the son of the creator god Kayra. Also known as Alaz-Khan or Alas-Batra, he is usually depicted as an old man carrying a torch and dressed in a cloak of flames. Folklore about Alaz associates him with both the destructive and the purifying powers of fire, dealing dire punishments to anyone who disrespects or misuses fire.

Ama-Terasu *(Japan)*: Ama-terasu, sometimes called Amaterasu or Ama-terasu-ō-mikami is a Japanese sun goddess and one of the major *kami*—deities, sacred spirits, or energies—of the Shinto religion. She is the kami of the high plain of heaven, while her brother Susa-no-o-no-mikoto ruled the plain of earth and her sister, the moon goddess Tsuki-yomi-no-mikoto, ruled the realm of darkness.

According to myth cycles in the *Kojiki*, Ama-Terasu's brother behaved so poorly that the sun goddess became angry and hid herself in a cave, darkening the earth and the heavens. To coax her out of hiding and return light to the world, the other kami of the skies put on a show with singing and dancing.[69] In modern polytheism, Ama-terasu is sometimes associated with agriculture, life, growth, and fertility; beauty; compassion, gentleness, and empathy; energy (especially solar); peace, happiness, unity, and freedom; light and warmth; love and romance; wisdom; and wishes.[70]

---

68   Kynes, *Correspondences*, 337.
69   Ono, *Shinto*, 18–19.
70   Kynes, *Correspondences*, 310.

Apollo *(Greece)*: Apollo is among the best-known and widely worshipped of the Greco-Roman gods. He has been recognised as a god of the sun, prophecy, archery, music, dance, poetry, truth, healing, purification, protection, youth, and more. Twin brother of Artemis, goddess of the hunt, Apollo is the son of Zeus, king of the gods, and the goddess Leto, the daughter of Titans. He is often described as the most beautiful god in the Greek pantheon, and is usually depicted as a handsome, beardless young man. In Greek mythology he had many lovers of different genders.

In his role as god of music, song, poetry, and dance, Apollo is credited in Greek myth for creating string music and is sometimes depicted with a lyre, or leading the Muses in chorus. In this form he is often the patron god of poets, singers, and musicians. Some Pagan and witchy books that mention Apollo suggest that he may have had a connection to the Gaulish horned god Cernunnos, although there is insufficient evidence to say for sure whether this was the case. Common symbols of Apollo include the sun; a branch of laurel and a wreath; a bow and quiver of arrows; a raven; a lyre; a dolphin; a wolf; a swan; and a mouse.[71]

Auahitūroa *(New Zealand)*: Auahitūroa is the personification of comets in Maori mythology. He's also sometimes called Upoko-roa ("long-head"). In some versions of the myths, he carries with him the seed of fire, which he gives to his wife Mahuika, the personification of fire. From this union the pair produced five children: Konui, Koroa, Mapere, Manawa, and Koiti, who share their names with the names of the five fingers of the hand.[72]

---

71   Mierzwicki, *Hellenismos.*
72   Andersen, *Myths and Legends of the Polynesians*, 297.

Brigid *(Ireland)*: Brigit, Brede, Brighid, Brigid, Bride, Brigantia, and Bridget are just some of the names given to this goddess of pre-Christian Ireland, Scotland, Wales, England, and farther afield. In Irish mythology, she is a member of a specific tribe/group of gods called the Tuatha De Danann, and also daughter of the Dagda, the good god. Historically, Brigid has been associated with the spring season, fertility, poetry, healing, and smithing. Some accounts, such as the tenth-century *Cormac's Glossary*, describe Brigid the poetry goddess as having two sisters: Brigid the smith and Brigid the healer. Some have taken this to mean that she may be a triple or *triformis* goddess, but it's unclear if this is the case. Others treat Brigid the poet, Brigid the healer, and Brigid the smith as one single entity, but as author Morgan Daimler points out, this may be oversimplifying things.[73]

One thing we do know is that the goddess Brigid was connected in some way with the Celtic fire festival Imbolc (which inspired the modern Pagan holiday). It's also possible the festival was connected to *a* goddess Brigid: several figures called Brigid were honoured and venerated throughout the British Isles, and it's unclear whether they were all the same deity.[74] Many of the symbols and customs that we as modern Pagans associate with the goddess Brigid—like Brigid's crosses, or the custom of building a bed for her in ritual—actually come from Christian traditions and early celebrations for Saint Brigid.[75]

Caca and Cacus *(Rome)*: In Roman mythology, Caca and Cacus were two giants who were sister and brother and children of the

73 Daimler, *Brigid*.
74 Mankey, *Witch's Wheel of the Year*.
75 Mankey, *Witch's Wheel of the Year*.

god Vulcan. The pair were originally fire deities of Palatine Hill, which became the site of the city of Rome.[76]

Some stories describe Cacus as a monstrous fire-breathing beast who terrorized the countryside. He stole some of the giant Geryon's cattle from the hero Heracles (a.k.a. Hercules) and hid them in his lair, but a lowing cow betrayed Cacus's presence to Hercules, who burst in and killed him.[77] Other versions of the same tale have Caca be the one who betrays her brother, and is deified—elevated to the level of a goddess—for her service to Heracles/Hercules.

Cerridwen *(Wales)*: In mediaeval Welsh legend, Cerridwen was a witch, sorceress, and herbalist, and a key figure in the tale of the poet Taliesin. According to most versions of the legend, it was Cerridwen who prepared the cauldron of Awen (a Welsh, Cornish, and Breton word for poetic/artistic inspiration). She set out to do this for her hideously ugly son, Morfan. The mixture needed brewing for a year and a day, and Cerridwen put a blind man called Morda in charge of keeping the fire going beneath the cauldron while a young boy called Gwion Bach stirred. As he stirred, three drops of the liquid spattered onto Gwion Bach's thumb, scalding him. Instinctively, he sucked on the burn and in doing so consumed the liquid and inadvertently gained the knowledge and wisdom that Cerridwen had been brewing for her son. Gwion fled, and Cerridwen pursued him. The chase that followed saw both figures transform into different birds and animals as Gwion tried to escape and Cerridwen matched his pace. Finally, Gwion tried to hide by turning into a single grain of corn. Cerridwen changed into a black

---

76   Boardman et al., *The Oxford History of the Classical World*, 49.
77   Encyclopaedia Britannica, "Cacus and Caca."

hen, found him, and devoured him. But because of the potion, Gwion didn't die. Instead, Cerridwen soon realised she was pregnant, and that child was the famous bard Taliesin.

Some modern eclectic witches and Pagans use the name Cerridwen to represent the crone form of the triple goddess, representing knowledge and wisdom. To others she is associated with the element of fire because she is an initiatrix, presiding over transformations and monumental change.[78] Others still associate her with prophecy, fertility, and divination.

Chango *(West Africa)*: Chango (sometimes spelled Shango, Sango, or Xango) is an Orisha and lord of fire in many African Traditional Religions. He is usually seen as a deity of thunder, drumming, and fire, and appears in some stories throwing "thunderstones" to cause thunder, lightning, and destruction.[79]

The World Sango Festival is celebrated in Nigeria each August. In Santeria, he is honoured on December 4—the feast day for Santa Barbara in the Catholic Church—with feasting, prayers and offerings.[80]

Chantico *(Aztec Central America)*: Chantico is a deity of hearths and cooking fires in the Aztec religion. She is associated with warriors, stonecutters, and the town of Xochimilco. She is usually depicted as having bright yellow skin and two red lines on her face, and she is often portrayed with symbols or markings of warriorship.

The goddess is described in a number of pre-Columbian sources, some which use him/her pronouns interchangeably. This has led to some debate over Chantico's gender.

---

78   Hughes, *From the Cauldron Born.*
79   Murrell, *Afro-Caribbean Religions*, 32–33.
80   Dorsey, "12/4: Feast for Chango and Santa Barbara."

Dagda *(Ireland)*: Known by many names, the Dagda is the "good god" of Irish mythology. In this case, "good" doesn't necessarily relate to a simplistic good/evil binary. Rather, it means that the Dagda is a "great" or "excellent" god, possessing many skills and talents.

One name used in sources for the Dagda is Aedh Alainn, which has been taken to mean "fiery, lustrous one," but could also be translated as "lovely/fine": a quality he has in common with his son, Aed the Fair. Among other things, the Dagda is sometimes referred to as a god of "fire and earth." Manuscripts and other sources often describe him as being a very large man, and many more modern sources portray him with bright red hair.[81]

Dazhbog *(Slavic Europe)*: Dazhbog is the regenerating god of the solar fire who rides in the sky in Slavic mythology. As well as being a sun deity, he is also a god of the harvest, of springtime, and of physical strength, skill, and vitality. Slavic mythology tells of him leaving the house of the sun in the east each morning and riding his golden cart—drawn by four white horses with golden manes—across the sky each day to the west, where his sister, the sunset, would unharness the horses and lead them home.[82]

There is evidence and documentation of Dazhbog's worship throughout most Slavic tribes. His statue stood alongside those of six other gods outside the palace of Vladimir the Great in Kiev in the year 980 CE. In the modern world, he is the patron god of some modern Slavic Pagans: several sculptures and idols have been installed in Russia and in the Ukraine over recent

---

81 Daimler, *The Dagda*, 26.
82 Kryuchkova and Kryuchkova, *Encyclopedia of Slavic Gods and Spirits*, 48–49.

years, only to be either destroyed by vandals or taken down after outcry from churches.

En *(Albania)*: En or Enji is the reconstructed name of the fire god in Albanian pagan mythology. He is thought to have been worshipped by the Illyrians, a group of Indo-European tribes who inhabited part of the western Balkans in ancient times. During Roman times, he was one of the most prominent deities in the Albanian pantheon. In pre-Christian Albanian mythology, physical forces, elements, and objects were often attributed to deities or spirits. Deities were usually embodiments of a certain element, rather than a separate entity. En was the personification of divine fire. His cult was one of mystic fire and fire ceremonies.

En was demoted to the status of "demon" centuries ago with the coming of Christianity, but his name continues in the Albanian language today in the word for Thursday (*e enjte*).[83]

Fornax *(Rome)*: Fornax was the divine personification of ovens and forges in ancient Rome. She was associated with cooking, the hearth, and the home. Some Roman writers associated her with the goddess Vesta for this reason. There is also evidence that she was worshipped as a grain goddess, a deity of the harvest. Farmers made offerings to her in the hopes that she would regulate the grain's heat as it was cooked, bringing about well-cooked loaves.

Her festival, the *Fornacalia*, was celebrated on February 17. This was a day for ritually toasting the spelt (hulled wheat) for use in baking cakes and loaves. Each family in the district would come to their local meeting hall to celebrate and feast, and to sacrifice a handful of grain to Fornax by throwing it into the oven. This was thought to ensure the oven would not burn any

---

83   Lurker, *Dictionary of Gods and Goddesses,* 57.

loaves for the year to come. Symbols of Fornax could include clay or brick ovens, loaves of bread, and dried grains. Some modern witches and Pagans associate her with hearth and home, abundance and food security, or cooking and baking.

Gabija *(Lithuania)*: In Lithuanian mythology and folklore, Gabija is the spirit of fire and a protector of homes and families. Little is known about her origins or worship, but the sources and folktales that mention her often depict her as a woman dressed in red, or as a cat, stork, or rooster. As the personification of fire, she often punishes those who disrespect the element, bringing vengeance to those who stomp, spit, or urinate on fires.

Glöð and Logi *(Scandinavia)*: Glöð is a legendary queen from the Norse epic *Þorsteins saga Víkingssonar* ("The Saga of the Viking's Son, Thorstein"). She is the wife and consort of the Norse jotun (nature spirit) Logi, and the pair and their children are often described as fire gods and goddesses in some traditional texts.

Logi is the personification of wildfire. He appears in the *Prose Edda*, where he and the trickster god Loki compete in an eating contest. The two are pretty evenly matched in pace, but as well as eating the meat presented to him, the wildfire Logi also consumes the bones and even the crockery in which the meat was placed.

Gerra *(Ancient Mesopotamia)*: Gerra or Girra is the Babylonian and Akkadian god of fire and light, derived from the earlier Sumerian deity Gibil. As a refiner of metals, he is also a patron god of metallurgists. He was called upon for rituals of cleansing and consecration, especially when new houses or buildings were constructed, due to fire's role in baking bricks.[84]

---

84 Tudeau, "Girra (god)."

Almost no personified image of Gerra has been found or identified. Textual evidence suggests that his symbol was a flaming torch.

Grannus *(Gaulish Europe)*: Grannus—also spelled Grannos—is a Gaulish god of the sun, healing, and hot springs who was worshipped at the time of the Roman invasion. His name has been linked with a number of pro-Celtic words with meanings such as "sun," "burning," "shining," and "beard." Some scholars have taken this to be a reference to the sun's "beard," or the rays of the sun.

In many areas under Roman rule, Grannos was partially assimilated into their pantheon as Apollo-Grannos, despite the fact that the two gods don't have much else in common besides their association with healing.[85] In worship, he was sometimes paired with the Gaulish goddess Sirona (also spelled Dirona), a deity of healing springs and fertility. An inscription on a fountain in modern-day France that dates back to the first century CE mentions a ten-night annual festival held in the god's name.

Helios *(Greece)*: Helios is the personification of the sun in Greek myth. He is often depicted in art as wearing a radiant golden crown and riding in a beautiful chariot through the sky. One of the most well-known stories involving Helios is that of his son Phaethon, who lost control while trying to drive his father's chariot, setting the Earth on fire. If Zeus had not intervened by killing Phaethon with one of his thunderbolts, all mortals would have died.[86]

Helios is sometimes depicted in mythology as being all-seeing and all-hearing: it was only he and Hekate who heard Persephone's cries when she was carried off to the underworld,

---

85   MacCulloch, *The Celtic and Scandinavian Religions*, 29.
86   Boardman et al. *The Oxford History of the Classical World*, 192.

for example.[87] In modern witchcraft and Paganism, Helios is sometimes associated with agriculture, growth, and fertility; beauty; business and wealth; light and energy (especially solar energy); warmth; and wishes.[88]

Hephaestus *(Greece)*: Hephaestus is the Greek god of smithing, metalwork, artisans, fire, and (sometimes) volcanoes. He forged most of the mythical and magical weapons of the gods. His forge on Mount Olympus is where, according to some versions of the myth, the Titan Prometheus stole a burning coal to bring fire to humans.[89]

In ancient Greece, Hephaestus was worshipped in more industrial areas concerned with building and smithing, especially in Athens. Several of the myths and some of the Homeric poems (written by the ancient writer Homer) describe Hephaestus as being able to produce motion or energy. Using this, he created automatons and guardians for a number of temples and palaces.[90] Hephaestus' symbols are a smith's hammer, an anvil, and a pair of tongs. In modern witchcraft and Paganism, he is sometimes associated with binding, crafting, creativity, jealousy, revenge, skills, or wisdom.[91]

Ishum *(Ancient Mesopotamia)*: Ishum is a minor Akkadian god and herald who leads the gods into battle. Several sources describe him as a beacon or firebrand that lights the way. He is also the brother of the sun god, Shamash. While he was often seen as a harbinger of destruction, Ishum as a deity was generally thought of as benevolent.

---

87   Mierzwicki, *Hellenismos.*
88   Kynes, *Correspondences,* 347.
89   Boardman et al., *The Oxford History of the Classical World*, 260.
90   Boardman et al., *The Oxford History of the Classical World*, 260.
91   Kynes, *Correspondences*, 347.

Jowangshin *(Korea)*: In the ethnic Korean religion Shindo, Jowang-shin is a goddess of hearth fires, embodied as a bowl of water on a clay altar above the hearth. Rituals to her were usually carried out by housewives and servants, who would fill the bowl with fresh water every morning and kneel before it wishing for luck. The goddess was believed to write down the goings-on in a household and report them to heaven.

Jowangshin was worshipped for millennia in Korea. At festivals, she was honoured with *tteok* (a type of rice cake) and fresh fruit.

Kagu-Tsuchi *(Japan)*: Kagu-tsuchi (also known as Kagutsuchi, Hinokagatsuch, or Homusubi) is the kami of fire from Japanese mythology. He is the patron deity of blacksmiths, metalworkers, and potters. According to mythology, Kagu-tsuchi's birth burned his mother Isanami, who died. His father Izanagi was wracked by grief and beheaded Kagu-tsuchi, then chopped him up into eight pieces, each of which became a volcano.

Kagu-tsuchi is one of several gods venerated at the Agato Shrine, a Shinto shrine in the mountains northwest of Kyoto, thought to protect the city from fire. In modern popular culture, he has made appearances in various forms in video games, anime, and manga.

Kōjin *(Japan)*: Kōjin is a kami of fire, the hearth, and the kitchen in Japan's Shinto religion. He is sometimes written about as a *triformis* or three-form god, or is depicted as having three heads. Unlike Kagu-tsuchi, who often represents fire's destructive qualities, Kōjin represents the element when it is controlled and used for practical purposes.

Traditionally, a representation of him is put by the hearth fire, so that he might watch over the home. His spirit resides in *enoki* trees, under which it is customary to put old or broken dolls for him to care for.[92]

Kresnik *(Slavic Europe)*: Kresnik is an old Slavic god associated with fire, the sun, storms, and the summer solstice. It has been proposed that he is probably the same deity as Svarožič, the son of Slavic sun god Svarog, as both deities are portrayed as having golden hands and hair. In Slovenia, he has evolved into a culture hero who lives on a golden mountain, a farmer-king with strong magic power. When he is associated with the summer solstice, he often appears as a deer with golden antlers.

Loki *(Scandinavia)*: The Norse trickster god Loki is sometimes called a god of fire, but this is due in part to the confusion between him and the fire giant Logi or Loge. *Logi* in Norse literally translates to "flame," and while it has been suggested this might have something to do with the name *Loki*, linguists remain unconvinced. One of the rare Viking-age depictions of Loki is on the Snaptun stone, which was discovered on a beach in Denmark in 1950. This piece of soapstone was identified as being carved around 1000 BCE and depicts a moustachioed man with scarred lips, thought to be an interpretation of Loki after his lips were stitched closed by the dwarves in the *Prose Edda*. The stone has been identified as a hearth stone, made to hold the nozzle of a bellows. This suggests a possible connection between Loki and fire or smithing.[93]

In modern witchcraft and Paganism, Loki is often associated with acceptance and destiny; beauty; challenges and danger; changes, transformations, and unexpected obstacles; clairvoyance and communication; cleverness, cunning, and deceit;

---

92 Davis, *Myths and Legends of Japan*, 269.
93 Bloodofox, "The Snaptun Stone."

enmity; freedom and independence; knowledge and learning; magic and protection; moods; and support when needed.[94]

Mahuika *(New Zealand)*: In Maori mythology, Mahuika is the personification and guardian of fire, who produced five fire-children with Auahituroa, the personification of comets, when he brought the seed of fire to earth. It is from Mahuika that the culture-hero Maui got the secret of making fire, by tricking her into giving him five of her fingernails one by one.[95] She is also credited in some versions of the myths with playing a part in the creation of Rangitoto, a volcanic island in the Hauraki Gulf, near Auckland. Angry at a couple who had cursed her, Mahuika spoke to Ruaumoko, the god of earthquakes and eruptions, to destroy them.

In some parts of New Zealand and elsewhere in tropical Polynesia, Mahuika is a male deity. In other areas, there are similar deities named Mafui'e, Mafuike, Mahui'e, or Mahuike.[96]

Nëna e Vatrës *(Albania)*: In Albanian folklore and mythology, Nëna e Vatrës is a goddess, mother, and protector of the *väter*, the fire hearth. She is sometimes associated with ancestor worship or female-centred households. Offerings made to her are usually made by throwing some of a meal prepared into the fire or leaving it around the hearth. Nëna e Vatrës is said to become angry if the hearth isn't swept clean each night.

Nusku *(Ancient Mesopotamia)*: Nusku or Nuska was the scribe and messenger of the gods in Assyria and Babylonia, often called upon by kings. He is described as being an embodiment of sunlight, firelight, and sometimes moonlight, too. He is asso-

---

94   Kynes, *Correspondences*, 350.
95   Anderson, *Myths and Legends of the Polynesians*, 297.
96   Craig, *Dictionary of Polynesian Mythology*, 148.

ciated with the arts and with civilisation in general, because of the role fire has played in human progress. It's unclear in primary sources whether he was identical to or a brother of the Sumerian fire god Gibil.[97]

As messenger of the gods, Nusku travels freely between the sky, the land, and the depths of the sea. He is sometimes accompanied by the sun or moon on their journeys across the heavens each day and night.

Od Iyesi *(Eastern Europe)*: Od iyesi is the spirit or deity of fire in Turkic and Mongolian mythology. In Turkic languages, *Od* and its variations usually mean "fire." *Iye* usually refers to the protector or sovereign spirit of a natural force or object. Od iyesi is a protector of fires wherever they occur: as a protector-spirit of stoves, they are known as Soba iyesi. As hearth spirits, they are Ocak iyesi.

The female form of Od iyesi is Od Ena ("fire mother"). In Mongolian mythology, she was born at the beginning of the world, when the earth and the sky separated. Od iyesi's male form is Od Ede ("fire father"). Known as *Od Khan*, or the king of fire in Mongolian mythology and shamanistic traditions, he is often depicted as a reddish-orange humanoid who rides a brown goat.

Ognyena Maria *(Slavic Europe)*: Ognyena Maria, or "Fiery Mary," is a fire goddess in Slavic mythology. Considered by some to be a conflation of Margaret of Antioch and the Virgin Mary, she is a sibling and assistant to Perun, sky deity and the most powerful god of many Slavic pantheons.

Different cultures venerate or call on Ognyena Maria for different purposes: in Belarus, she is seen as a healing deity. In

---

97   Mackenzie, *Myths of Babylon and Assyria*, 478.

Bulgaria, she is known for providing protection from fires. In both Russia and the Ukraine, she is often associated with lightning and storms. Her feast in the Slavic folk calendar is towards the end of July.

Ogun *(West Africa)*: Ogun is an Orisha associated with blacksmiths, metalworking, war, and warriors in many of the African Traditional Religions. He plays a key role in the story of the creation of the universe, when he uses his machete to cut through the dense scrub that had blocked the path of the gods.[98]

Common symbols of Ogun are iron, dogs, and palm fronds. He has power over metal and also over forests, and is sometimes also associated with justice, crafting, skills, and technology. His shrines are often situated outdoors near trees, or indoors as smaller household shrines.[99]

Oya *(West Africa)*: Oya is an Orisha of wind and storms found in some African Traditional Religions. She is seen as the embodiment of change, and she is known for causing severe weather and lightning strikes. Sometimes she is known as Yansa or Oya-Iyansan, "the mother of nine," due to her nine children, represented by the nine colours in her skirt. She is often depicted with her whip, machete, or lightning bolts.

It is thought that Oya's Ashe (sacred essence or life force) is in the Niger river, which is also named *Oya* in the Yoruba language. Some devotees consider her to be the queen and guardian of the dead.[100]

Pele *(Hawaii)*: Pele is the goddess of fire and volcanoes in the indigenous Hawaiian religion. Out of respect, she is often

---

98 Dorsey, "Orisha Ogun: Lord of Iron, God of War."
99 Murrell, *Afro-Caribbean Religions*, 33–34.
100 Dorsey, "Oya." *Orishas, Goddesses and Voodoo Queens.*

referred to as *Tūtū Pele* or *Madam Pele*. She is credited with creating the Hawaiian volcanoes and islands, and is revered for her enduring presence and shaping of sacred lands.

Belief in and worship of Pele has endured despite it being "abolished" by white missionaries and colonisers in the early 1800s. One Hawaiian legend that has made its way into modernity holds that the goddess will sometimes appear as a woman in red walking the roads near the volcano Kīlauea as a warning of an impending eruption. It's also thought that the goddess curses those who dare take items from her island, though it's unclear whether this belief predates the twentieth century or was invented recently in order to deter tourists helping themselves to natural material. Regardless, the headquarters of the Hawaiian Volcanoes National Park receives hundreds of packages every year from all over the world—often addressed to Queen Pele—reporting misfortune and calamity, and begging for the items enclosed to be returned to the goddess to remove the curse.[101]

Prometheus *(Greece)*: Prometheus is a Titan known in Greek mythology for his intelligence and wit. In most versions of the tale, he brings (or restores) fire to humans by stealing it from the gods—from Hephaestus' forge in many versions—and smuggling it from Mount Olympus in a giant fennel stalk. For this and other crimes, Zeus punishes Prometheus by chaining him to a rock and having an eagle eat his immortal liver each day. Later myths have the hero Heracles (a.k.a. Hercules) kill the eagle and rescue the Titan.

Prometheus' dripping blood is said to have become a plant that numbed pain and produced feelings of euphoria, most

---

101 Cart, "Hawaii's Hot Rocks."

probably an opium poppy.[102] In modern witchcraft and Paganism, Prometheus is sometimes associated with communication/prophecy, strength, skills, grief, and wisdom.[103]

Ra *(Egypt)*: Ra or Re is the creator sun god and the ruler of the sky and the earth in ancient Egyptian religion. He is often associated with birth and rebirth, as he is reborn with the dawning of each new day. In Egyptian art, Ra is sometimes depicted as a falcon holding the disc of the sun. The centre for the worship of Ra was at Heliopolis, a major city in ancient Egypt, and he was considered to be the main deity in the Ennead, the cycle of nine key Egyptian gods. In one story, the sky goddess Nut carried Ra on her back to the heavens, where he became lord and creator of the world.[104]

In modern witchcraft and Paganism, Ra is sometimes associated with agriculture, fertility, life, and cycles; beginnings; change and changes; energy, power, and magic (especially solar); guardians; guidance, knowledge, truth, and insight; justice and revenge; light and warmth; the otherworld and the underworld; rebirth and renewal; the senses (especially sight); strength; travel; and wellbeing.[105]

Sekhmet *(Egypt)*: Sekhmet is a goddess associated with healing, warriors, the sun, fire, and the afterlife from the Kemetic pantheon. Usually portrayed with the head of a lioness, Sekhmet was considered a protector of the pharaohs of ancient Egypt. As a solar deity, she is the daughter of Ra and is often associated with the goddesses Hathor and Bastet. Priestesses of Sekhmet

---

102 Mierzwicki, *Hellenismos*.
103 Kynes, *Correspondences*, 356.
104 Drury, *Watkins*, 243.
105 Kynes, *Correspondences*, 357.

joined the general public at large annual festivals held in honour of the goddess.

Shapash *(Ancient Near East)*: Shapash is a Canaanite goddess of the sun, also known sometimes as Shapsh, Shapshu, and Shemesh. She plays an important role in the myth of Baal, where she acts as a judge among the gods. After Baal is killed, she helps bury and mourn him, then stops shining altogether. Her father, the supreme god El, eventually appeals to her to shine again. Shapash agrees, but vows to use her light to keep searching for Baal.

Svarog *(Slavic Europe)*: Svarog is a Slavic god of fire, smithing, and sunlight/the sun. He is usually referred to as a counterpart to—or interpretation of—Hephaestus. One of the only mentions of him in historical material comes from the Hypatian Codex, a fifteenth-century collection of several much older documents from the Ipatiev Monastery in Russia. The Codex contains the Slavic translation of a much older Greek document from the sixth century, which mentions Svarog as the Egyptian name for Haephestus. This Svarog is described as a smith in the sky who forged and provided early humans with the first ever metal weapons. The document also names the sun, Dazhbog, as Svarog's son and heir.

Similarly to Haephestus, symbols of Svarog could include smithing tools or bellows. In modern witchcraft and Paganism, he might be associated with crafting, creativity, skills, or wisdom.

Utu/Shamash *(Mesopotamia)*: Utu is an ancient Mesopotamian god of the sun, morality, justice, and truth. He is the twin brother of the goddess Inanna, and usually depicted as a kindly old man. He is mentioned in *The Epic of Gilgamesh*, where he helps Gilgamesh defeat the ogre Humbaba. In many versions of the myths, he rides a boat or chariot across the sky each day, using a jagged blade to cut through the mountains at dawn. As he rode each day, it was believed he saw everything that happened in the world.

To the Sumerians, Utu was known as Shamash, and was worshipped from very early on in ancient times. One of his main symbols is a gold disc with either wings or sunrays.

Verbt *(Albania)*: In Albanian folklore and mythology, Verbt is a weather and storm god whose winds and hailstorms cause lightning and fan the flames of fire. Invoking him or sending him away usually involves making a lot of noise. He's often portrayed as a god who hates untidiness and bad language, and as a deity who punishes anyone who speaks ill of him. He was venerated in northern Albania until relatively recently.[106]

Vesta *(Rome)*: Ancient Roman goddess Vesta (whose ancient Greek equivalent is Hestia) was the virgin goddess of hearth and home and among the *Dii Consentes*, the twelve major deities in the Roman pantheon. The temple of Vesta in Rome was maintained by virgin priestesses, known commonly today as Vestal Virgins, whose job it was to tend her sacred fire and performing other rituals connected to domestic life, including ritual sweeping of the temple on June 15, and the preparation of food for certain festivals. It was also thought that these priestesses tended the life and soul of the city and its people through the sacred fire of Vesta. As such, it was considered sacrilege and a gross forsaking of duty to let the fire go out, and the virgins were severely punished—usually with physical beatings—if this occurred. If the fire went out, it was relit with the rays of the

---

106 Elsie, *A Dictionary of Albanian Religion,* 259.

sun, concentrated onto kindling from an *arbor felix* ("auspicious tree," probably an oak) using a series of mirrors.[107]

The flame of Vesta was extinguished for the final time in 394 by order of the Christian emperor Theodosius I in his campaign to eliminate pagan practices in Rome.[108] In modern witchcraft and Paganism, Vesta is associated with community and family; fidelity; harmony and purification; the home; marriage; security and stability; warmth and heat; and witchcraft relating to the kitchen.[109]

Vulcan *(Rome)*: God of fire and crafting, Vulcan is Hephaestus's Roman counterpart. In Roman religion, he was the god of smithing, deserts, and volcanoes. The Roman festival of *Vulcanalia* was held every year on August 23, when the summer heat baked the land and made it prone to dangerous wildfires. Huge bonfires were built in Vulcan's honour on this night each year, and offerings of live fish were thrown into the flames in the hopes that the god would take them instead of the human lives with his flames. People would also hang out all their washing to dry in the sun on these days, and they would light a candle to work by before dawn.

Worship of and sacrifices to Vulcan grew even more popular after the great fire of Rome in 64 CE. In modern witchcraft and Paganism, he is sometimes associated with binding, community, creativity/skills, destruction, energy, or jealousy.[110]

Wayland the Smith *(Anglo-Saxon Europe)*: Wayland (or Weyland) the Smith is the Anglo-Saxon god of blacksmithing. Known

107 Boardman et al. *The Oxford History of the Classical World,* 72.
108 Boardman et al. *The Oxford History of the Classical World,* 72.
109 Kynes, *Correspondences,* 336.
110 Kynes, *Correspondences,* 360.

across Europe, he is first mentioned in text in the thirteenth-century *Poetic Edda*. Stories in folklore of the area hold that his smith was in the megalithic chamber tomb on the Ridgeway, not far from the Uffington White Horse in England.

In the Norse sagas, Wayland was Völundr, a smith with supernatural skills who was captured by a king and lamed so he could not escape. He was put to work by his captor, but took his revenge by killing the king's children.

Xiuhtecuhtli *(Aztec Central America)*: Xiuhtecuhtli is a deity of fire, warmth, and daylight in Aztec mythology. He is usually portrayed with his face painted with red and black pigment and his body adorned with turquoise stones (part of his name can be taken to mean "turquoise" and "year" as well as "fire").

Making offerings to Xiuhtecuhtli sometimes involved ritually burying statuettes of his likeness: usually a seated male with folded arms. Sources indicate that sacred fires were kept burning in his temples, and offerings of food were made before eating to thank him for the gift of fire.

Living Gods, Living Cultures

Some of the cultures and belief systems mentioned here have been/are being pieced together by reconstructionists, including historians. Others have continued as a culture throughout history in some form or another. As in all aspects of our practice, it is important to be respectful of the cultures from which these gods come from as we approach them. If you're planning on honouring or working with any deity, it's important to understand all you can about the cultural, spiritual, and physical landscape that shaped them; these deities form just one piece in rich, complex cultures and traditions.

It's also important to be mindful of cultural appropriation. If you are part of a dominant, privileged culture, you do not always have the right to work with deities that belong to cultures who have been (or who are currently being) oppressed, no matter how much these deities might "resonate" with you.

The Neopagan "pick-and-mix" approach to deity popular from the 1970s to the 2000s—in which most folks worked with deities from a range of pantheons without knowing much more than what those individual deities were "famous" for—seems to finally, thankfully, be on the decline now; people are starting—albeit slowly—to slow down, to think, and to not treat the gods as wish-granting genies or collectible statuettes (gotta catch 'em all!).

Put simply, people are starting to do their research. And while there are no hard and fast rules with this whole witchcraft and Paganism thing, doing your own research where you can will undoubtedly deepen your understanding and enrich your practice.

Connecting with Deity

If a myth, god, spirit, or mythical creature fascinates you, or if you're considering incorporating them into your practice, do a bit of research before you launch into anything. If you're not sure where to begin, even starting at a Wikipedia page will help deepen your understanding; look into the sources cited by the article to learn more. Jot down a few bullet points or get your nerd on and start a mini research journal. What was happening during the time these myths, beliefs, or stories originated? What was daily life like for the average person who lived during this time? What are the key changes that have occurred in this place/to these people between then and now?

Conclusion

Fire deities come in many forms, and stand for many things. Creators, healers, musicians, tricksters, solar gods, volcano deities, hearth spirits, lords and ladies of fire, and many more are all representative of this element in its many facets.

Chapter 4

SACRED SITES

Fire has been worshipped and venerated in different cultures and contexts around the world for millennia. This chapter will explore some well-known sites both old and new, and will examine what a sacred fire site might look like in your day-to-day world.

Sacred Fire Sites Around the World

The word *sacred* comes from a Latin root that means "holy." Today, the word is still used to describe something that is or has been made holy by religious ceremony, but its meaning has also been expanded to apply to something that is worthy of awe and respect.

Baba Gurgur *(Iraq)*: Baba Gurgur is an oil field and eternally burning gas flame near the city of Kirkuk in northern Iraq. Its name comes in part from the Turkish and Kurdish words for fire, and can be translated as "Father of Eternal Fire." In a tradition that is thought to date back to the earliest days of Zoroastrianism, women travel to Baba Gurgur to ask for a baby boy.

Fire of Kildare *(Ireland)*: Many sources describe fires being lit in honour of a goddess called Brigid at Kildare long before Christianity reached Ireland. By the twelfth century, the tradition had continued in a way: scholars and chroniclers wrote about the fire tended by nuns of Saint Brigid. The tradition died out with the suppression of monasteries in the sixteenth century, but a new flame was lit in 1993 at the Christian spirituality centre, *Solas Bhríde*. On Saint Brigid's Day in 2006, a perpetual flame was lit in its own special sculpture in the Kildare Town Square.[111]

Seafarers and Sea Bereaved Memorial *(Finland)*: Known locally as the Helsinki Eternal Flame, this monument was built in 1968 to honour and acknowledge those lost at sea. Designed and built by sculptor Oskari Jauhiainen and architect Eero Eerikäinen, it stands over twelve metres tall and is made of three bronze-plated columns that stand to make a lighthouse-like structure. An eternal flame burns on top, blown out by the occasional storm. Each year on All Saints' Day, the Church of Finland holds a ceremony to remember the dead.[112]

Jwalamukhi Devi Temple *(India)*: Jwalamukhi is a famous temple in Himachal Pradesh, northern India, dedicated to the goddess Jwalamukhi, the "deity of flaming face." In the foothills of the Dhauladhar mountain range in the sub-Himalayas, the goddess Sati's tongue is believed to have fallen at Jwalamukhi, and the goddess manifests as tiny blue flames that burn through fissures in the ancient rock. Offerings of food and drink are usually made to the sacred flames in the pit, which is in the centre of the temple.

Lalgambook/Mount Franklin *(Australia)*: Mount Franklin is a dormant volcano just north of Daylesford, here in Central Victoria. The crater and surrounding lands have been culturally significant to the Dja Dja Wurrung people for thousands

---

111 Solas Bhride Centre, "Lighting the Perpetual Flame: A Brief History."

112 Groundspeak, "Seafarers and Killed in the Sea Monument."

of years. The Mount Franklin Pagan Gathering has been held since 1981, and remains one of the longest-running modern Pagan gatherings in the world.

Olympic Flame: The Olympic flame is considered a symbol of continuity between ancient and modern games, and of the games themselves. Every four years, several months before the Olympic Games, the Olympic flame is lit at Olympia, Greece, kicking off the Olympic torch relay. The relay ends with the lighting of the Olympic cauldron during the opening ceremony of the Olympic Games that year. It continues to burn in the cauldron for the games' duration, then it is ritually extinguished during the closing ceremony.

Mauna Loa *(Hawaii)*: Located on Hawaii's big island, Mauna Loa is the largest volcano in the world. Some versions of Hawaiian myths state that is home to the volcano goddess Pele. Extensive trails and evidence of civilisation pre-contact point to Hawaiians perhaps making the journey up Mauna Loa make offerings to Pele before or during eruptions.

Mayon *(Philippines)*: With an almost completely symmetrical cone shape, Mayon is the third-largest volcano in the world and the most active in the Philippines. The name comes from the legendary princess-heroine Daragang Magayon (English: Beautiful Lady), upon whose burial grounds it's thought that the volcano grew. Many festivals and rituals are associated with the volcano and its landscape, which also appear on the one-hundred-pesos bill.

Mount Fuji *(Japan)*: Mount Fuji is an active volcano that last erupted in the 1700s. It is the second-largest volcano in the world, and the highest mountain in Japan. It is considered one of the country's three holy mountains, and it was declared a

UNESCO World Heritage Cultural Site in 2013. In Shinto mythology, Konohanasakuya-hime, wife of Ninigi, is the goddess of Mount Fuji, where the shrine *Fujisan Hongū Sengen Taisha* is dedicated to her.

Temple of Vesta *(Italy)*: The Temple of Vesta housed Vesta's holy fire, which was a symbol of Rome's prosperity and security. The surviving structure is still visible today and suggests twenty Corinthian columns built on a podium fifteen metres in diameter. The roof was probably vented to allow smoke to escape. During Roman times, the temple and its eternal flame were tended by the Vestal Virgins. You can read more about Vesta in the previous chapter.

United States Holocaust Memorial Museum *(United States of America)*: An eternal flame burns in the Hall of Remembrance of Washington, DC's United States Holocaust Memorial Museum, which sits adjacent to the Washington Monument. The flame was lit in 1993 by President Bill Clinton and Holocaust survivor Elie Wiesel. In the hall, visitors can light candles of remembrance, and reflect in the silence of the hexagonal hall.

Sacred Fire Near You

So far this chapter we've focused on famous sacred sites related to fire, and while these are fascinating, it's important to remember that sacred fire—just like sacred water, earth, and air—is all around us in the every day. You can work with, honour, and experience it in a number of ways and contexts:

The Sun: honour the sun in formal rituals such as dawn/dusk workings or celebrations for the solstices and equinoxes, or just spend some time soaking up some light. Just remember to slip/slop/slap (slip on a shirt, slop on some sunscreen, and slap on a hat).

Burned-Out Trees: Scorched stumps and trees that have been hit by lightning carry their own unique fire energy. Read Pat Rothfuss' novella *The Lightning Tree* for inspiration, then seek one out.

The Desert and Arid Landscapes: Biased? Probably. Australia is the driest inhabited continent on earth, after all. I'm not certain why the absence of water often equals big fire energy, but it does. Try holding a full moon ritual on a sand dune or in the vast stillness of a desert at least once in your life.

Volcanoes and Volcanic Country: If you live near an extinct or dormant volcano on public land, try going for a slow, meditative walk on or around it. Take your time and make a point of noticing the landscape as it was shaped by the volcano all those years ago. What sorts of rock are visible? Can you see the signs of lava cooling? Does the volcano have a crater? A vent? What other features can you find (caves/fertile soil/boulders/something else)? Get to know the land around you and the part fire played in making it that way.

Actual Fire: Weird, right? Being in the presence of a flame—even a fake or "safety" flame—is a simple way to connect with the element of fire. Meditate with candles, dance around a bonfire, or cook food on a bonfire or at an old-timey hearth. If you have access to an open fire, try sitting and feeling the heat on your face. As well as meditating about fire and its elemental qualities, think about how many people have sat just like you are now across the millennia, and the role that fire played in their lives.

Types of Sacred Fire

Fire has been respected and revered for many reasons and in its many aspects throughout history and across cultures. The welcoming hearth fire, the formidable forge fire, the spark of inspiration, the flame of passion, and fires of both purification and destruction are all powers unto themselves and are often respected as such.

Fire of the Hearth: A hearth is usually a stone or brick lined fireplace, sometimes with an oven for cooking. For centuries, the hearth was the centre of the home in many countries, which is why the term "hearth" can also be used to refer to someone's home or household. This is an idea kept in some forms of modern Asatru, where "hearth" or "kindred" is sometimes used to refer to a local group of worshippers. In some ancient European and Asian cultures, there were hearth deities and spirits.

Because of its importance in the lives of so many—in cold, pre-industrial times they kept people warm and fed—many superstitions and folk beliefs exist around hearths. Kindling a fire in the fireplace of a new house has long been considered a good omen in many parts of the world; likewise was lighting a fire at the beginning of a new year.

My favourite account of this comes out of Shropshire in the 1800s, where one man had a tradition of entering farmhouses in his district without knocking or speaking, silently stirring and maintaining the fire before he greeted any of the family who lived there.[113] In parts of England, it was considered very bad luck for a visitor to stir or tend the fire unless they had known their hosts for at least seven years, or in some cases had been drunk with them three times.[114]

In many areas before the advent of modern heating and cooking, fires burned in hearths all day and into the night. This is probably the origin of the idea that hearth fires (and some-

---

113 Opie and Tatem, *A Dictionary of Superstitions*, 152.
114 Opie and Tatem, *A Dictionary of Superstitions*, 154.

times campfires too) are associated with comfort, the warmth of home, companionship, and rest.

Fire of the Forge: A forge is another kind of hearth, used for heating and shaping metal. Blacksmiths use forges to heat metal to a temperature hot enough that it becomes workable and easier to shape on an anvil with a hammer.

Forging and blacksmithing formed a crucial part in the growth and development of civilisation for thousands of years, and as such blacksmiths were revered and sometimes even deified in mythologies and folklore from around the world. The Bible's book of Genesis immortalises the blacksmith Tubal Cain as a "forger of all instruments of bronze and steel," and in ancient cultures gods such as Hephaestus, Wayland the Smith, and Vulcan played key roles in the lives of gods and mortals alike.

But when we talk about fires of the forge, we also are talking about the fire of will: to shape something to our liking as a blacksmith shapes a sword.

The forge has the ability to shape things with its terrible heat, and the element of fire is often associated with transformation, initiation, even rebirth. One of the most obvious examples of this is the motif of the phoenix, which appears in the mythologies of many different cultures.

Another common trope in literature, mythology, and pop culture is the idea of "fire-forged" friendships: when a group of people who are initially hostile or indifferent to each other become firm friends or even lovers because of shared challenging experiences: fighting side-by-side in the heat of battle, completing a quest, going on a journey, etc.

What with modern society and all, many of us may have only seen forges in movies or in video games. But they are still around: fairs featuring "lost" trades seem to be coming back in vogue, and there seems to be a renewed interest in smithing in the form of the hobby—maybe an entire subculture?—of backyard forging and smithing on the internet.

Fire of Passion and Inspiration: The idea of "fire in the head" as mentioned by Irish poet W. B. Yeats in his poem "The Song of Wandering Aengus" has since been combined by some modern bards and Druids with the idea of Awen, a Welsh, Cornish, and Breton word for poetic/artistic inspiration that forms a key part of some modern Druid practices.

Fire is also related to inspiration and passion in a number of witchcraft and magical traditions. The element of fire is often one worked with to bring new ideas to fruition, to bring success in creative ventures, or to "ignite" someone's feelings of lust.

These associations with fire are not necessarily ones we make consciously or because we are occultists, either. Just look at some of the language that most people use to describe feelings of being creative or inspired: *a spark of inspiration, a lightbulb moment, a burning passion.* When we talk about passionate or volatile people, we use phrases like *hot-headed, burning with fury, a fiery rage, hot tempered,* and so on. Discussing romance and sex, you often hear desirable people described as hot or as making somebody (feel) hot. Some consider chillies and other spicy foods to be reliable aphrodisiacs, too, although personally I usually just go for a cider and a nap after a good hot curry.

Fire as Purification: Fire as a means of purifying/removing evil is a common theme in many literary and mythological works. It seems to be one of the Christian god's favoured solutions in the Bible: it's used for the total destruction of "wickedness," as with the razing of the city of Sodom, or to rid people of sins, as in the Catholic concept of purgatory, in which the dead's sins are burned away before they may enter heaven.

In many mythologies around the world, it is the only way that true evil (or sometimes the undead) can be destroyed; this is surely a concept that inspired parts of contemporary works such as *Harry Potter and the Deathly Hallows,* in which "fiend-fire" is one of the only ways to destroy horcruxes.

The idea that fire cleanses is an old one. Long before the existence of any scientific germ theory to explain disease, humans had learned that fire made rotting corpses and things that had been in contact with sick people and animals harmless. If washing or purifying things with water didn't work, most knew that fire would do the job as a last resort, which makes fire the ultimate means of cleansing and purification in cultures all over the world.

Many superstitions exist around fire and the dead, too. A centuries-old folk belief from parts of Scotland is that all fires should be extinguished where a corpse is kept.[115] This possibly has something to do with the fact that a warmer room decomposes a body much more quickly and noticeably than a cold one.

• • • •

How to Incorporate Fire into Your Own Sacred Sites

Dean Forest has been a practicing Pagan for around twenty years. His personal practice is grounded in devotional polytheism, animism, and a dash of reconstructionism. He has a background in Heathenry, Druidry, and Hellenism and never stops exploring the vast diversity of modern Paganism. Dean studies archaeology, volunteers in environmental conservation, and lives in a forest on the fringes of Melbourne, Australia.

---

115 Opie and Tatem, *A Dictionary of Superstitions,* 152.

YOU CAN INCORPORATE fire into your own sacred site today. If you don't have a space where you do Pagan and/or witchcraft practices, you can set one up somewhere that is a little bit quiet; choose an appropriate receptacle for the kind of fire you will be using and think about what ritual use you have in mind for that fire. In an indoor space, this can be as simple as lighting some candles, burning a small amount of incense or herbs on a charcoal disk, burning oil in a clay oil lamp (olive oil is a good choice as it is smokeless and fairly cheap and accessible), or you can burn small amounts of solids or liquids in a heat proof container, such as a little cast iron bowl or cauldron. Place your fire receptacle on a heat proof tile to avoid scorching the surfaces underneath.

If you have an outdoor ritual space, then you can use a portable fire pit or a chimenea, or build a permanent fire pit out of bricks or concrete blocks. Line the bottom with a brick hearth if you are building from scratch, and keep a fine layer of clean, dry, sieved sand at the bottom. Cure the fire receptacle by lighting a few small fires the first few times, gradually building the size of the fire up to what you will be using for rituals. Doing this helps prevent cracking or warping your brand-new fire pit. Terracotta pits often come with a warranty of between six months and two years, but they will last a lot longer if well cared for. Treated steel, which has a special kind of black paint on it, is a bit sturdier, and cast iron should last a lifetime. You'll need to make sure there is plenty of room for the smoke to clear out if your space is partially under cover. Torches can be incorporated into your space at key points as well. Once established, you might even like to hold a small ritual to bless your sacred space and incorporate carrying fire around the boundaries and kindling a sacred flame.

From tealight candles to a bonfire, you can use your fire to focus your mind in meditation; for scrying into the smoke or flames;

for prayer or magic; and for giving offerings to the gods, such as grain, incense, herbs, bay leaf, eucalyptus, pine, and small amounts of olive oil or wine. Or you can use an oil burner for essential oils. Having a regular practice—whether that is monthly, fortnightly, weekly, or even daily—will help you better deepen your magical practice and build closer relationships to your gods and spirits. After all, we all learn and grow through the regular practice of any other art, skill, or activity in our lives. One way to incorporate the properties of fire at your altar or shrine is by lighting a candle as you pray, work, or make offerings. Light one candle for each deity or spirit you are working with, or for each part of a short household ritual or devotional. Focus your thoughts as you light each one. When you have finished the ritual, blow out all the candles. Another simple way of doing this is to leave a candle going in a safe container such as a lantern for a vigil for a particular purpose, like strengthening the sun over the twelve nights of Yule. Having a small hearth shrine in your kitchen to a deity of the hearth and home, such as Brigid, Frigga, Hestia, or Vesta, and lighting a candle there while you cook is another good way to make sacred fire a central part of a modern home.

Dean Forest

• • • •

Conclusion

From sleeping volcanoes and world heritage sites that have been active for centuries right up to your very own sacred fire, we can experience and venerate this element in countless ways. While it may not always be as obvious as the impact of earth, air, or water, fire makes its own mark on the landscapes around us, just as it did on the landscapes of our ancestors.

PART
2

WORKING WITH THE
ELEMENT OF FIRE

*Fingers-Mazda, the first thief in the
world, stole fire from the gods. But he
was unable to fence it. It was too hot.*

—TERRY PRATCHETT, *MEN AT ARMS*

Chapter 5

THE ELEMENT OF FIRE IN MAGIC

When it comes to magic(k), Aleister Crowley might have said it best when he defined it as "the science and art of causing change to occur in conformity with will." Fire and the four elements play a part in many different types and traditions of magic, in a range of different ways.

Magical Intentions of Fire

Many of the issues, intentions, and powers of fire as an element can be categorised in the following ways.[116] These are just some of the common magical associations with the element of fire—there are plenty more to discover.

Fire as Destroyer

Discord, causing: conflict; influence; revenge; lightning and bad weather

Fear, dispelling: taking action; authority; courage; defence; energy; faith or lights in darkness

Fire as Destroyer is called on in spells and rituals to banish, to cause strife, to defend or to ruin, and more.

---

116 D'Este and Rankine, *Practical Elemental Magick*, 14–15.

Fire as Inspiration

Creativity, increasing: awakenings; ambitions; passion and inspiration

Energy, increasing: activating or awakening; light; life and vitality

Strength, increasing: defence; energy and magic; leadership and power

Willpower, strengthening: concentration and focus; divination and psychic ability; intelligence and intuition

Fire as inspiration is called on in spells and rituals to bring about new ideas or undertakings, for courage or clear-headedness in leading or making decisions, and more.

Fire as Passion

Anger, controlling: calm; freedom; protection; release; transformation

Courage, enhancing: ambitions; confidence and purpose; honour; truth

Leadership, developing: taking action; ambitions and ambitiousness; authority; communication

Passion, increasing: creativity; desire and lust; love; motivation; warmth

Sex-drive, increasing: awakening passions; desire and lust; sex and sexuality

Fire as passion is called on in spells and rituals to inspire love or lust, to enrage someone or inflame a situation, to take action towards ambitions, and more.

Fire as Purification

Healing, giving: consecrating and blessing; protection, healing; life; purification and purity

Vigour, increasing: agriculture, life, growth, and fertility

Fire as purification is called on in spells and rituals to heal the sick, to protect the weak or sickly, to purify space or people, and more.

Fire of the Forge

Career success: taking action or getting movement on plans; passion; purpose and decisiveness

Patronage, obtaining: communication; confidence; creativity; honour

Promotion, gaining: ambitions, ambitiousness, purpose, and motivation

Fire of the forge is called on in spells and rituals to transform or change, to remain strong or steadfast, to encourage motivation, and so on.

Fire of the Hearth

Harmony, developing: freedom; inspiration and motivation; life; love; protection; weather

Money, acquiring: ambition; influence; justice

Peace, establishing: war and battles; protection, defence, and defensive magic

Wealth, improving: life, fertility, and growth; energy and motivation; power

Fire of the hearth is called on in spells and rituals to protect the home/family, to encourage abundance and prosperity, and more.

The Element of Fire in Alchemy

Originating in Greco-Roman Egypt in the first few centuries CE, alchemy is a school of thought and a proto-scientific tradition that was practiced across Europe, Asia, and Africa for centuries.

Its practitioners sought to condense, purify, transform, and perfect certain materials. Some practitioners saw alchemy as fundamentally spiritual and philosophical. Much of the work attributed to the ancient Greek figure Hermes Trismegistus forms not only one of the primary sources for alchemical theory, but are also sacred texts of Hermeticism, an esoteric tradition that influenced some ceremonial magic orders, fraternal orders such as Rosicrucianism and Freemasonry, traditional Wicca, and in turn some of the eclectic witchcrafts and paganisms that are practiced today.

Alchemists distinguished between the four elements based on their "qualities": the hot, the cold, the moist/fluid, and the dry. Each element was identified with a different combination of two qualities. As opposites, hot/cold and fluid/dry could not be coupled together. The four combinations of qualities that are possible were applied to the four elements: water with cold and fluid, earth with cold and dry, air with hot and fluid, and fire with hot and dry. In each element, one quality dominates the other: dryness in earth, coldness in water, fluidity in air, and heat in fire.[117]

In their notes and writing, many alchemists used different symbols to represent different elements, ingredients, and processes. This was less about being mysterious and confounding outsiders than some people think: in most cases it was merely a form of shorthand.[118] A common symbol used to indicate the element of fire is an equilateral triangle with its point at the top. This is still widely used in many traditions of witchcraft today, having made its way into our material via traditional Wicca, ceremonial magic, and so on. In modern witchcraft, some practitioners use or create an image of this symbol in rituals for manifestation or transformation.

---

117 Holmyard, *Alchemy*, 27–28.
118 Holmyard, *Alchemy*, 247.

Fire and Astrology

The use of astrology—whose practitioners assert that the movement and relative positions of celestial bodies have an influence in human and earthly affairs—can be dated back as far as around the second millennium BCE. Different cultures have had many different methods and traditions involving using the stars, the planets, and the sky itself to divine the future or get clarity on issues in the present. The first books on astrology that look similar to that which is practiced by many witches, Pagans, and New Age folks today were produced in the late mediaeval period in Europe.

Astrology was a common practice among scholars during the Renaissance, though intellectual interest in the practice had begun to wane by the Enlightenment. It wasn't until the rise of spiritualism in the nineteenth century that the public's curiosity was once again piqued. By the early twentieth century, a few of psychiatrist Carl Jung's theories and concepts relating to astrology led to the development of psychological astrology. The intersection of the New Age and early Neopagan movements in America and elsewhere during the 1960s and 1970s helped cement its presence in the core material and practice of many eclectic witches and occultists today.

Western astrology and planet lore also form key areas of study in many Western mystery traditions. Of the twelve zodiac signs, three can be attributed to each of the four classical elements. Grouped together, these three signs are sometimes known as triplicities and are always located 120 degrees away from each other in the earth's plane of orbit. The triplicity of zodiac signs most commonly associated with fire are Aries, Leo, and Sagittarius.

Aries

Latin for "ram," Aries is the first sign in the zodiac. In Western astrology, the Sun enters Aries when it reaches the March equinox, which takes place on or around the 21st of that month. The name originates from the constellation of the same name, and while the ram that represents Aries is often thought of as Chrysomallus—the mythical flying ram from Greek mythology that provides the golden fleece—modern Western astrology often also uses more generic imagery of rams to represent this sign.

Aries people are thought to be bold, courageous, and resourceful, but lacking in persistence and tact.

Leo

Leo is the fifth sign in the zodiac, named for the Greek word for "lion." The Sun enters Leo in towards the end of July and leaves at around August 22 each year in Western astrology. The constellation that Leo was named after is associated with the Nemean lion, a mythical beast that was slain by Heracles/Hercules.

Modern astrology holds that those born under this sign tend to be strong-willed and natural leaders, but they can be unwilling to compromise.

Sagittarius

The ninth astrological sign Sagittarius is traversed by the Sun between approximately November 23 and December 21 in Western astrology. It is named after the constellation with the same name, which in ancient Greece was associated with Chiron, the centaur and archer who mentored the hero Achilles. Today's iconography of Sagittarius often personifies the sign as a centaur or human archer, or sometimes just as a bow and arrows.

Those born under the sign of Sagittarius are thought to be logical and forthright, "telling it like they see it."

Tools of Fire

Swords, Daggers, and Athames

As they usually are forged in fire and heat, blades of all kinds are one of the witches' working tools most commonly associated with fire. Some grimoires and other ceremonial magic texts call for the creation of some blades to be done on the day and during the hour of Mars, the fiery planet.[119] Some traditions forbid the use of metal in ritual, and use daggers and athames carved from wood instead.[120]

The word *athame*—and no, I am not wading into the long-standing debate over how it should be pronounced—is a relatively new one, first used around 1949. It is the name given to a knife—usually (but not exclusively) double-edged with a crossguard, handle, and pommel—used for magical purposes.[121]

Daggers and athames are usually used for enforcing the will of the wielder in ritual, including directing energy and marking out the borders of the magic circle or other sacred space. They are not generally used for cutting physical things (or people!).

In ritual, swords are used for similar purposes and others, depending on the flavour of witchcraft or magic being practiced. Many modern eclectic witches don't tend to bother with one or make do with a handmade staff instead. Some traditions of witchcraft consider the sword to be the symbol of the High Priest, able to be worn by the High Priestess if he is absent.[122]

Always check out local laws about owning and possessing edged weapons before you try to procure a sword, and avoid carrying athames or other blades in public or using them in rituals held in public places. Even this far into the twenty-first century, non-Pagan

---

119   D'Este and Rankine, *Practical Elemental Magick*, 88.
120   Philips and Philips, *The Witches of Oz*, 8.
121   Mankey, *The Witch's Athame*.
122   Tuan, "The Working Tools of the Witch: The Sword," 42–44.

folks aren't always accepting or accommodating to things that are unusual or unexpected for them, not to mention that the sight of anyone wielding a blade in public can be cause for alarm in those not expecting it. Local laws in many places leave you open to a hefty fine if you're caught with a weapon, ceremonial or otherwise. If you're buying an athame, always be comfortable with the price: it's considered bad luck to haggle over the price of working tools.[123]

To consecrate a dagger or athame, some traditions like to use a lodestone or magnet to magnetise the blade,[124] while others decorate the blade or handle with certain symbols, or use certain blends of herbal essences to oil the blade.

Some traditions of witchcraft also associate the athame with air, because of the way it moves through the air when wielded. It's been pointed out—by Janet and Stewart Farrar and others—that this alternative association seems to have its roots in some Golden Dawn material, possibly as a deliberate "blind" or misdirection,[125] but as with most of what I've written about, there is no hard and fast way to elemental associations; whatever makes sense to you is perfectly fine.

Wands

Wands have been associated with magic and ceremony since ancient times. Some practitioners prefer to associate the wand with the element of air and the creative abilities of the human mind. Others associate them with the element of fire because of the relationship between fire and wood, or to the fragments we know about tree worship in ancient Europe.[126]

---

123 Mankey, *The Witch's Athame.*
124 Grimassi, *Encyclopedia*, 28.
125 Farrar and Farrar, *A Witches' Bible*, 251.
126 Grimassi, *Encyclopedia*, 383.

While the dagger is commonly used for commanding and directing, the wand is often associated with creating. This is often why it is a wand and not a blade that is used to consecrate a new working tool, and also why a blade rather than a wand would be used for banishing. Wands are also sometimes used to evoke gods and goddesses, bestow blessings, charge objects, and so on. They are also the key tool featured in some witches' sabbat rituals.

There are many different types of wands, and some witches have more than one for this reason: plain wooden wands, phallic wands, staves, walking sticks, solar wands, lunar wands, seasonal wands, and more.

Wands are one of the easiest of the working tools to create yourself. Many traditional instructions on wand making give the old measurement of one cubit: the length from the fingertips to the elbow. The wood from a hazel or other nut-bearing tree is often suggested as suitable material.[127]

Again, there are no unbreakable rules about which wood you choose: if there is a tree that is special to you and it's consented to you cutting a wand from it, go for it. Once you've cut wood from a tree, strip the bark from it, oil it with linseed or olive oil and leave it for a few days before you try to shape it further or carve any symbols or details into it. In the last few decades, it's become more and more trendy to have crystals and other bits and pieces glued onto one's wand. These are completely optional: your wand/s can be as simple or as intricate as you like.

---

127 D'Este and Rankine, *Practical Elemental Magick,* 89.

Other Tools of Fire

Candlestick

There's no reason that the thing holding your fire can't be related to fire too. Candlesticks are all fire-related of course, but go for brass, terracotta, wood, or a bright, fiery colour if you really want to get the point across. (Yeah, yeah, I know there is a line here about Alexandrians and our fetish for brass candlesticks. I just think they're nifty.)

Charcoal Discs

These are used in some incense burners called censers or thuribles (which in witchy circles are usually associated with air), and are different to the charcoal left over from fires or used in barbeques. You can buy rolls of these from New Age/witchy shops or smoke supply shops. You can also get them from some Middle Eastern grocery stores, as they are what is used in hookah pipes. In Melbourne, we sometimes buy them from shops that supply the Catholic and Greek Orthodox churches. The easiest way to light a charcoal disc is with a continuous/jet lighter, as you sometimes need to hold the flame to it for a few seconds to get it lit. Before you start, make sure the disc is clean, dry, and sitting in a fireproof container. If you're using a thurible, it sometimes helps to line it with scrunched tinfoil so that the outer casing doesn't heat up too much. The disc will sparkle slightly when it is burning. Then it's ready for you to sprinkle some loose incense on top: most charcoal discs have a divot in the top to keep the incense from just rolling off. Never handle a burning charcoal disc with your bare hands—use a spoon or a small pair of metal tongs.

Ferrocerium Rods

These are rods made of ferrocerium: a synthetic pyrophoric alloy that produces hot sparks when struck. These are usually sold as "fire steel" to campers, bushcrafters, and survivalists as a no-fuss fire starter, but I've seen the occasional one at Pagan festivals lately too. Olde-Worlde? Absolutely not. Untraditional? You bet. But I doubt you'd get much resistance from anyone who's had trouble getting a fire to light on a frigid night while their fellow ritualists stood around shivering with their hands stuffed in their armpits. People who try to tell you otherwise tend to be the same people who try to tell you Gerald Gardner wouldn't have used the internet, even if he'd had access to it in his lifetime.

Fireproof Cauldrons and Dishes

Some folks like to use cauldrons and deep dishes to drop things that are burning or have burned. Make sure they are made out of metal if you do this. If you don't have the whole cast-iron-pot-on-little-legs setup, use a big coffee or milo tin—the caterer's sized ones are great for this. Have water or dirt handy to chuck over fires that get out of control, and for the good of your lungs, your brain, your landlord, or just your paintwork, don't burn stuff inside!

Matches and Lighters

Fire is the only element of the four that can be created, and matches/lighters are probably the cheapest and easiest way to create it. They're also often the most forgotten, so always triple or quadruple check that you have them before you leave the house for a ritual away from home. I'm old and daggy and a non-smoker, so I usually just go for matches when I need to light a candle or bonfire. I am definitely coming around to lighting charcoal discs with a jet lighter though.

Fire and the Tarot

Tarot cards are probably the most popular divinatory tool used by witches and others to get a looky-loo at the future—or the present.

If the tarot is new or newish to you and you want to learn, look for tarot books by authors like Rachel Pollack, Eden Gray, etc., then go on to explore other authors that interest you. This will provide a fantastic framework for starting out using tarot without the bells, whistles, or faery dust. There are also some cracking tarot websites and stuff on social media, too, but try to access a range of resources to help you build your understanding.

I've used the Rider-Waite deck and its fire imagery in my descriptions and explanations below.

IV: The Emperor

Dressed in shades of red, the Emperor sits proudly on a stately throne decorated with rams' heads (a symbol of Aries and of Mars[128]). In his right hand he holds a sceptre topped with an Egyptian ankh, a symbol of life. His left hand holds a globe, a symbol of authority and dominion. In his positive aspects, the Emperor stands for order and stability over chaos or uncertainty. In negative aspects, he signifies unjust laws and rules or corrupt rulers.[129] In these aspects the card can be associated with the fire of the forge: the fire of bending something to your will.

Divinatory Meaning: Authority, kingship, government, and leadership. Control of the masses. Mental prowess; the domination of logic and intelligence over creativity and passion, head over heart.

Reversed: Emotional immaturity or bondage to parents/the family home. Sometimes a physical injury or an injury in the household or home. In this position, this card can also sometimes denote issues with an inheritance.

---

128 Gray, *The Tarot Revealed*, 158.
129 Gray, *The Tarot Revealed*, 158.

The Emperor card in Magical Workings: ambition and confidence; authority, strength, and control; battles and war; energy and power.[130]

VIII: Strength

The Strength card depicts a woman in white robes closing—or prising open—a lion's jaws. Above her head is the lemniscate, a symbol of eternal life and one we also saw in card I, the Magician. She wears a garland of red flowers in her hair and a chain of them around her waist. This card does not usually indicate strength in a physical sense;[131] rather, it is often symbolic of the "victory" of the higher aspects of the soul, or of the preparation and steeling of spirit sometimes needed to make inner journeys.[132] Here we see the fire of spirit, of courage, and of ambition. That's not to say that this card is only representative of arduous or harrowing journeys of spirit. Instead, with a sense of peace, it encourages the querant to "tame" the lion and unfold their personality.[133] Journeys aren't just made up of challenges, and self-discovery shouldn't always be a total headfuck.

Divinatory meaning: The triumph of spiritual power over the material, love over hate, or the rational nature over carnal desires.

Reversed: The abuse of power. Discord and the domination of the material. This card can also sometimes point to a need to look inwards.

The Strength card in Magical Workings: action; control and power; courage and overcoming obstacles; energy.[134]

---

130 Kynes, *Correspondences*, 446.
131 Waite, *The Pictorial Key to the Tarot*, 103.
132 Drury, *Watkins*, 274.
133 Pollack, *Seventy-Eight Degrees of Wisdom*, 68.
134 Kynes, *Correspondences*, 449.

XV: The Devil

The Devil is the antithesis of the archangel in Temperance, the previous card. The figure sits on a half-block, with bat-like wings and goat-like horns. Its right hand is upraised and extended in a sign that is the reverse of that made by the Hierophant in card V. Its left hand holds a flaming torch, pointed at the ground, and there is a reversed pentagram on its forehead. The two figures chained to the block look human except for their tails, which signify what Waite calls "the animal nature" present in all humans.[135] The chains around their necks represents the dangers and trappings of the material, and there are obvious references here to Adam and Eve and what befell them once they had consumed the forbidden fruit. Many look at these aspects and declare this is a card of violent sexual energy, but the fire here represents more than that: this is the vigour, creativity, and life energy that we keep locked away in our darker, "shadow" selves, behind all the black curtains and heavy roller doors of our subconscious.[136] Sometimes we need to examine what we've repressed and hidden from ourselves before we can go any further.

Divinatory meaning: Discontent, illness, bondage to the material. Sensation without understanding or reflection.

Reversed: A spiritual understanding, albeit a difficult one. Disentangling from material trappings. Indecision or fear.

The Devil card in Magical Workings: anger; the subconscious; endurance; influence; limitations and boundaries.[137]

---

135 Waite, *The Pictorial Key to the Tarot*, 128.
136 Pollack, *Seventy-Eight Degrees of Wisdom*, 104.
137 Kynes, *Correspondences*, 445.

XVI: The Tower

The Tower card depicts mortals' arrogant attempts to scale the heights of heaven or deity. It is often compared to the biblical Tower of Babel.[138] This is where we see fire in its destructive aspect. The card depicts a tall tower struck by lightning, a crown toppling from its highest point. It suggests the breaking down (or total destruction) of existing forms, structures, schools of thought, or what Waite himself called houses of "doctrine" or "falsehood"[139] to make room for new ones.[140] The falling drops of light we see here are also present on the ace cards in the suits of wands, cups, and swords, as well as on card XVIII, the Moon. These are seriffed versions of the Hebrew letter *yodh*, and here signify life force descending from the spiritual realms above to the material plane of existence.[141]

Divinatory Meaning: The overthrow of existing lifestyles or ways of thinking. Unforeseen catastrophe, conflict, or destruction. New concepts upsetting or upending the old. The fall of materialism or of selfish ambition. Ruin, carnage, or financial collapse.

Reversed: Struggle, oppression, or imprisonment. Sometimes the same ruin and destruction as above but to a lesser extent.

The Tower card in Magical Workings: ambition; enmity, battles, and war; change and changes (especially unexpected changes); courage; danger and destruction.[142]

XIX: The Sun

The Sun card depicts a naked child sitting on the back of a white horse, bearing a red banner or standard as they ride away from a

---

138 Drury, *Watkins*, 289.
139 Waite, *The Pictorial Key to the Tarot*, 132.
140 Gray, *The Tarot Revealed*, 182.
141 Gray, *The Tarot Revealed*, 182.
142 Kynes, *Correspondences*, 450.

walled garden. A glorious sun blazes overhead. The sun in this illustration sometimes represents consciousness in the spirit: the knowing of oneself that is required for many undertakings.[143] As the sun travels across the entire world every day, it is often associated with knowledge and omniscience.[144] In the Waite version of these images, the child riding away from grey walls of the garden often represents a breaking free or a bursting forth of energy: a creative liberation into the world of art and nature, away from the drudgery of the rational world.[145] It is in The Sun card we find the fire of creativity, the fire of the forge.

Divinatory Meanings: The beauty of life. Joy and happiness. Optimism, energy, and wonder. Seeing the world in a new way. Unity, knowledge, widening one's perspective.[146]

Reversed: Less clarity of thought. Simple happiness. The same qualities as before are there but might be a little harder to find.[147]

The Sun card in Magical Workings: accomplishment, enlightenment, and success; happiness, pleasure, and optimism; healing; truth.[148]

Conclusion

The element of fire is a versatile one in magic. Practitioners of many traditions and systems call upon fire in its different aspects to transform, to change, to destroy, to create, to heal, to inspire, and for many other reasons besides. Many call on this element just to light the way when the path seems unclear, or to bring a spark of warmth when our inner or outer world turns cold.

---

143 Waite, *The Pictorial Key to the Tarot*, 144.
144 Pollack, *Seventy-Eight Degrees of Wisdom*, 118.
145 Pollack, *Seventy-Eight Degrees of Wisdom*, 119.
146 Pollack, *Seventy-Eight Degrees of Wisdom*, 120.
147 Pollack, *Seventy-Eight Degrees of Wisdom*, 120.
148 Kynes, *Correspondences*, 449.

Chapter 6

HERBS AND BOTANICALS

Quite a few plants are magically associated with fire for their colour, flavour, or even how they look. In researching the histories and magical associations of the plants in this chapter, I discovered some more unique associations, too: many were used in the fire-lighting process back in the day. Some have ages-old folkloric associations with this element, which are my favourite kind of associations.

In folklore, herbalism has gone hand in hand with witchcraft for centuries. But you don't need a zillion little jars and a sprawling garden of exotic and sometimes poisonous plants to get started.

Working with Herbs

Things to remember when working with herbs and other plant matter,

- **Always research and exercise caution** with an herb or plant before you burn it, ingest it in food/drink, rub it on your skin, etc., for the first time. Many herbs become toxic when burned. Some will irritate the skin or eyes or cause side effects like sickness or even brain damage or death if consumed. If you're planning on consuming

CHAPTER 6

wildcrafted (foraged) herbs or plants or using them on
your body in any way, always bring a qualified, experienced herbalist or horticulturalist with you when you go
foraging. Some poisonous and edible plants look almost
identical. People have fallen seriously ill or literally died
because they mistook one for the other.

- **Make sure you're picking what you think you're picking.** Have a printout or a good book on herbs that you
can bring along with you. Be sure to wash foraged leaves
and fruit well before you use them. Be respectful of local
laws around foraging for food, and respect the plants and
other creatures (humans and otherwise) who might rely
on these plants and trees later. Never take more than you
need, and use everything you take.

- **Seek consent** before exposing another person to any herb
or plant for magical purposes.

- **Keep dangerous herbs away from children and pets.**
Store them safely and out of reach. If you're growing
herbs, keep poisonous or dangerous herbs in a separate
part of the garden to your edibles, and do not allow children or pets to play in that spot. The smoke from burning many herbs is dangerous to pets. Put down the lighter
and check first.

A Few Words on "Smudging"

It's become very trendy over the last couple of decades for some
people to cleanse their homes and other spaces of "bad energy" by
burning white sage or other herbs and calling it "smudging." This
is a term that originates in North America. Smudging is a practice

sacred to some (not all) indigenous tribes from that region. Traditionally, the leaves of four sacred plants are burned in a special container, with the smoke being wafted by hand or with an eagle feather/s to cleanse, protect, or heal a person or place.

In some parts of the United States it was illegal for Native American people to practice their religion until the late 1970s—even later in some areas. Many were incarcerated or even killed just for working to keep traditions alive by performing traditional ceremonies, and smudging was often a practice included in these.

As such, smudging is not really something to be taken lightly. Nor is it a trendy and "witchy" thing you can do to rid your home of bad energy. When non-native people burn sage or palo santo to "smudge" their homes, they are potentially minimising cultural and ceremonial significance of this ritual, and also having a disastrous effect on how these herbs are grown, harvested, and supplied.

If you love cleansing spaces, etc., with smoke, that's fine. Just please practise ethical witchcraft and consider these alternatives to white sage or palo santo:

- Mugwort (use sparingly!)
- Wormwood*
- Juniper
- Pine
- Mint
- Rosemary

Instead of saying "smudging," try using the old Anglo-Saxon word *recaning*, the old Scottish word *saining*, or just the word *censing*.

Chapter 6

Herbs, Flowers, and Plants Associated with Fire

For each entry, I've tried to look into why many of these plants may have been associated with the element of fire in the first place. Some are obvious: colours, appearances, scents, or flavours give the associations away. Others are more surprising. I've also tried to include notes on what these herbs look like in plant form; these are much more than plastic sachets of dried plant matter you can buy, after all.

Angelica
(Angelica spp. Usually Angelica archangelica)
healing; stability; protection; purification

WARNING: Angelica is more or less identical to several very poisonous plants. NEVER try to wildcraft angelica; instead go for some that you have grown yourself, or buy some from a reputable seller.

Also known as: Holy Ghost root, lungwort, garden angelica (*A. archangelica*); masterwort, arch-angel, angelic herb, purple stem angelica, high angelica (*A. atropurpurea*)

A fairly common garden plant, *A. archangelica* is a tall biennial with glossy green leaves. When its yellowy-white flowers are finished, the plant will produce seed-heads a bit like a sunflower's. Its aromatic root has been used widely in herbal medicine to treat cramps, urinary tract infections, and stomach disorders, and the seeds are used to flavour liqueurs. You can buy dried angelica root (usually *Angelica archangelica*) from witchy suppliers and some health food shops. Because there are so many poisonous angelica lookalikes easily mistaken for angelica, be sure to only buy it from a trusted seller who knows what they're doing. In a garden, angelica will usually be okay to grow and even self-seed if there is a bit of shade in a temperate climate. As a biennial, it will die after flowering and seeding in its second year. Removing the flowering heads to stop the plant from seeding can make it last another couple of years.

Magical Uses: Angelica is associated with the element of fire because of its mythology involving the Archangel Michael, the archangel of fire who features in the material of some ceremonial magicians and in contemporary Paganism and witchcraft. Legends of how it got its name involve an angel (usually Michael) appearing to a monk in a dream and showing him a herbal remedy to treat symptoms of the plague and heal the sick.[149] Because of this, it was sometimes worn as a means to avoid catching the plague during the Middle Ages.[150] The plant also blooms around Saint Michael's Day in parts of Europe.

Basil
(Ocimum basilicum)
attraction; love; relationships; sex and sexuality

Also known as: sweet basil, common basil, St. Joseph's wort, witches' herb (*O. basilicum*); bush basil (*O. minimum*); Tulsi basil, holy basil, sacred basil (*O. sanctum*); Amazonian basil (*O. campechianum*)

Native to India, the Middle East and some Pacific Islands, basil's leaves are pleasantly spicy and strongly flavoured. Basil leaves are used commonly in Mediterranean cooking, and the smell of basil leaves helps to keep pest insects at bay. Placing a pot of basil on the window sill will deter flies, and growing basil in your garden

149 Illes, *The Element Encyclopedia*, 535.
150 Dunwich, *The Wicca Garden*, 23.

can help keep aphids and fruit-flies at bay without driving off the bees. Basil plants grow to around forty to fifty centimetres high and will grow spikes of purply-white flowers before going to seed. Common basil (*O. basilicum*) can be purchased dried or in fresh bunches from supermarkets or fruit and veg shops. In hot climates, basil will grow as a perennial. If you live in a cooler climate, you're better off treating it as an annual as it will not tolerate wintry weather or temperatures; you're also better off starting basil seeds in pots indoors then transplanting the seedling to the garden later, when the weather has warmed up. Ancient Roman writers claimed that basil and rue would only grow well if the person planting them cursed and swore as they sowed the seeds.[151] Maybe make sure you have a good relationship with your neighbours if you want to give this a go.

Magical Uses: Basil has several different associations to fire and sacred fire across different cultures: in Hindu culture, holy basil (*O. sanctum*) is sometimes associated with women, women's mysteries, and marriage. It is sometimes burned as part of sacred fire during wedding ceremonies.[152] In modern witchcraft books, basil is sometimes associated with love spells and divination relating to love and romance. In some parts of Sicily, a centuries old tradition sees young couples still sometimes giving each other courting gifts of potted basil and cucumbers on St. John's Day (around midsummer).[153]

---

151 Frazer, *The Golden Bough*, Part I, vol. II, 42.
152 Frazer, *The Golden Bough*, Part I, vol. II, 25–27.
153 Frazer, *The Golden Bough*, Part IV, vol. I, 245.

Black Pepper
(Piper nigrum)

banishing; binding; justice; security

Native to India, pepper is very well travelled. It's been traded along spice routes for centuries. *Piper nigrum* is a climbing perennial vine. Its green flowers develop into dark red fruit, which in its various stages and colours are sold as commercial pepper. Green peppercorns are picked when the fruit is unripe. Soaked for a week, the pulp will leave these corns so that only the seeds remain. Dried out, these seeds are what we know as black pepper, the pulp is white pepper. Black pepper is a staple ingredient in pantries the world over. You can buy whole peppercorns (which you can put in a mortar and pestle or a fancy grinder if need be) or their powdered form at grocery stores. Pepper vine prefers warm and tropical climates. Outside, it needs a frost-free position. It will grow in an indoor pot with a bit of TLC, but be aware that this vine is quite prolific and will grow as long as eight metres if you let it!

Magical Uses: Black pepper is often associated with fire because of its flavour, and also because of its associations with banishing and purification. In the past, black pepper has been used for banishing, binding, and even exorcisms.[154] In some American witchcraft traditions, sprinkling black pepper with cayenne pepper in your shoes or rubbing it into the soles of your feet is thought to give protection from hexes and curses.[155]

154 Frazer, *The Golden Bough*, Part II, vol. I, 106.
155 Illes, *The Element Encyclopedia*, 580.

Chamomile
(Matricaria chamomilla and Anthemis nobilis)
calm; sleep; dreams; protection

WARNING: Roman chamomile (*Anthemis nobilis*) should not be consumed by people who are pregnant or breastfeeding.

Also known as: camomile, German chamomile, true chamomile, wild chamomile (*Matricaria chamomilla*); Roman chamomile (*Anthemis nobilis*)

The chamomile plant has feathery divided leaves and small white flowers with a yellow centre that resembles that of a daisy. These flowers have a pungent scent. It is a very common garden plant and a gardener or nursery near you will likely have some. German chamomile is a tall annual and a very vigorous grower and seeder. Be prepared to find it in every nook and cranny if you plant it in your garden. Roman chamomile is low-growing and spreads to form a mat. You can also buy dried chamomile flowers from witchy retailers and some health food shops. Look for food/tea grade, irradiation-free.

Magical Uses: Chamomile has long been thought of as connected with calm and sleep. Chamomile tea has long been associated with calming and soothing effects. In modern witchcraft, it is often associated with the element of fire, presumably fire of the hearth because of its common magical attribution to qualities such as peace, protection, breaking hexes/curses, and returning harmony to the home.

Cinnamon
(Cinnamomum verum and Cinnamomum
Cassia/Cinnamomum zeylanicum)
attraction; desire; sex magic, stimulation

WARNING: Cinnamon oil, which is sometimes used to anoint candles, is a skin irritant. It can also cause kidney problems if ingested.

Also known as: true cinnamon, bakers' cinnamon, Ceylon cinnamon, soft-stick cinnamon (*C. verum*); Chinese cinnamon (*C. Cassia*)

Cinnamon was one of the spices carried and traded by the caravans and merchants in ancient times, when the spice trade was a cornerstone of whole empires. Most of the culinary cinnamon sticks sold in the United States, the United Kingdom, and India are actually cassia, also known as Chinese cinnamon (*C. Cassia*, also sometimes known as *C. zelanicum*). This comes from an evergreen tree native to southern China. It is used in similar ways to cinnamon, and it is sold as cinnamon in many countries. Pretty much all ground cinnamon available for sale anywhere is also cassia. True cinnamon comes from the inner layer of bark of the cinnamon tree (*C. verum*), a tall evergreen tree that is native to Sri Lanka. The bark is hand-peeled and then dried into small sticks called quills, which are ground or left to be bought whole. This cinnamon is not usually found in grocery stores or even health food stores in most countries; in North America and many other places in the world, food packaging laws don't dictate that "cinnamon" has to be labelled as cassia. Cinnamon and cassia have slightly different flavours. Quills of cassia are fairly thick, while true cinnamon quills are a darker shade of brown and are thinner, more fragile, and flaky. You can buy dried sticks of true cinnamon online and from some health food stores. If you're buying online always go for food grade cinnamon, as the sticks used for incense and aromatherapy, etc., are often treated with a lot more chemicals and pesticides.

Magical Uses: Cinnamon is most likely associated with the element of fire because of its common use as an ingredient in aphrodisiacs and workings for love. It is sometimes included in soaps, candles, or charms to attract or increase sexual attraction. Cinnamon oil is often used to anoint candles for love and sex spells.

Clove
(Eugenia caryophyllata, Syzygium aromaticum, and Eugenia aromatica)
courage; healing; protection; purification

WARNING: Cloves can irritate the skin, especially when cut or crushed. Commercially bought clove oil is also a skin irritant.

The name "clove" comes from the Latin word *clavus* ("nail").[156] Clove trees (*Syzygium aromaticum*) are native to a group of islands in eastern Indonesia, and were grown there almost exclusively until modern times. They are a close relative of lilly pilly trees (*Syzygium* sp.). Cloves we buy for cooking and other purposes are the dried unopened flower heads from the trees' bright red blooms. The clove came to Europe during the very early days of the spice trade, but had been widely used in Asia for a long time before that. Dried whole cloves can be purchased in the spice aisle of supermarkets and grocery stores. If you live somewhere where you have

---

156 Kirton, *Harvest*, 417.

access to a clove tree, lucky you! Harvest and dry the unopened flower buds when they turn bright red.

Magical Uses: Cloves are associated with the element of fire because of their protective and banishing magical properties, and also because they are often burned when used magically. The smoke from a burning clove is used by some modern witches to steel themselves before an anticipated conflict. Burning dried cloves one by one over a candle is also thought to be useful in helping to determine whether the cause of an illness is something mundane, or magical interference such as the Evil Eye. Sprinkling powdered cloves onto lit charcoals and using it to fumigate your body, clothing, and home is thought to stop malicious gossip about you.[157] Some Conjure practitioners have also shared that clove oil and infusions are sometimes used to drive away negative situations and people.

Dill
(Anethum graveolens)
hexes (setting, breaking); protection; purification; witches and witchcraft (ward off, protect from)

Also known as: dillseed, dillweed, dilly[158]

Dill is an annual plant with blue-green feathery foliage, umbels of flat yellow flowers, and a smooth, speckled stem. Its leaves and seeds are used in cooking. Growing dill is a great way to attract bees to your garden and repel pests like cabbage moths. It can be grown easily from seed in around eight weeks, and self-seeds pretty well. Dill leaves can be picked any time of the year. Pick leaves from the centre of the plant to delay flowering (as annuals

---

157 Illes, *The Element Encyclopedia*, 502.
158 Kynes, *Correspondences*, 173.

die after they flower), and trim back flowers as they form. Dill leaves can be purchased fresh or dried in some supermarkets and health food stores. Because of its similar leaves, dill is sometimes confused with fennel. If in doubt, check the stems: dill's stem will be slender, while fennel has a bulbous stem.

Magical Uses: Dill is associated with fire because of its protective and banishing qualities. It is often used to maintain psychic and physical protection and safety around the hearth and home. Some modern witches place dill above a door to prevent anyone harbouring hostile or envious feelings from entering. It is also thought that scattering salt and powdered dill around your home/office/property will counteract any magic worked against you.[159]

Fennel
(Foeniculum spp.)

purifying and protection; fertility; healing (or prevent evil from entering) the home; strength and vitality

Also known as: sweet fennel, wild fennel

Fennel appears in folklore from all around the world, including Asia, Egypt, and Europe. Its long, feathery foliage looks very similar to that of dill but it has a strong aniseed taste. In ancient Greece, woody stalks of giant fennel (*Ferula communis*) were used as wands or staves in mystery rites. The wand or staff, called a *thyrsus*, was often decorated with ribbons, vines, and/or leaves, and topped with a pinecone, grapes, or berries. It was often associated with Dionysus (or the Roman Bacchus) and his followers,[160] and is mentioned in ancient texts such as the *Iliad*. The stalks of this

---

159 Illes, *The Element Encyclopedia*, 890.
160 Frazer, *The Golden Bough*, Part I, vol. II, 42.

giant form of fennel grow to about five feet long by three inches thick, and they are encased in tough bark. When dried, the stalk's white, pithy core burns like a wick without damaging the bark. This would have made these stalks a popular option for torches for people from all walks of life, and is probably why, in Greek mythology, it was fennel that was used by Prometheus to carry fire from the gods to humankind.[161] You can buy fennel bulbs and leaves fresh in some grocery stores. Keep an eye on it if you're growing it in a garden. It can easily get out of control and take over, and is considered a weed in some parts of the world.

Magical Uses: Fennel is also considered one of the sacred herbs in many traditions of southern European witchcraft. As well as for its use in torch making, it is also often associated with the element of fire because of its protective or healing/strengthening associations. In mediaeval England, bunches of fennel were hung in kitchens to ward off evil spirits and witches. Ancient Greek athletes ate fennel when competing in early Olympic games, believing it strengthened their muscles, while in ancient Rome the scholar Pliny believed that fennel enhanced the eye's ability to see the beauty of nature with enhanced clarity, and because of this it held a reputation across many centuries for being able to improve eyesight.[162]

Flax
(Linum usitatissimum)
the sun and solar magic; prosperity; protection; psychic ability

Also known as: linseed

---

161 Frazer, *The Golden Bough*, Part I, vol. II, 42.
162 Drury, *Watkins*, 101.

Flax is an annual with small, grey-green leaves and deep blue flowers. It will grow and self-seed happily anywhere if the soil is rich enough, but should be confined to pots and watched carefully to prevent it becoming a problem weed in your garden. It is from flax seeds that we get linseed oil, which is sometimes used to darken or polish wood. The fibres from flax stems are used to make linen. The pre-Christian Germanic goddess Hulda—also known as Holda, Holla, and later Frau Holle in the Grimms' fairy tale of the same name—is credited with teaching humans how to spin linen from flax.[163] Flax was also once associated with women's primal power. In many parts of northern Germany, flax and corn were often personified into a maternal figure who looked over the crops. If "Mother Flax" had been seen, a good harvest could be predicted. The Bavarian Flax-Mother and Corn-Mother have often been compared to the Corn and Barley Mothers of ancient Greece.[164] Dried flax seeds, flax flour, and linseed oil are all available commercially. Try the organics aisle of the supermarket or health food store, or a hardware store for linseed oil.

Magical Uses: Flax is most likely related to fire because of its use in bonfire customs. In some European countries, people sometimes danced around bonfires around the time of Candlemas or Beltane (see chapter 12) to promote healthy, abundant flax crops,[165] the direction of the flames sometimes dictating the direction in which the seeds were sown.[166] In many countries it was also customary for young couples to leap over bonfires to encourage flax to grow tall, and people took burned pieces

163 Illes, *The Element Encyclopedia*, 949.
164 Frazer, *The Golden Bough,* Part V, vol. I, 132–33.
165 Frazer, *The Golden Bough,* Part I, vol. I, 138–39.
166 Frazer, *The Golden Bough,* Part VII, vol. I, 140.

of wood from spent bonfires to bury in their flax fields.[167] In some contemporary traditions of witchcraft, sprinkling flax seeds over a home's threshold is thought to end disruptions and promote harmony.[168] A traditional Bavarian custom also used flax seeds as a divinatory tool. Sown in a pot on the last three days of *Fastnacht* (the Christian *Carnival* season before Lent begins), the healthiest seedling from three seeds planted acts as an omen as to whether to sow crops early, mid- or later in the year.[169] This association of flax seeds with omens and fortune telling has also made its way into some traditions of modern witchcraft, where drinking flax seed tea is thought to enhance divination skills.

Frankincense
(Boswellia spp.)
blessing; consecrating; purification; divination; psychic ability

Also known as: olibanum; Coptic frankincense, luban, yigaar (*B. frereana*); Indian frankincense, Sallaki (*B. serrata*); Sudanese frankincense (*B. papyrifera*)

The name frankincense comes from the Old French *franc ensens* ("pure/high quality incense"). This fragrant gum resin has been used in sacred ritual for millennia, and has been traded for over six thousand years. The frankincense we and many other faiths use in ritual is the dried, resinous sap of different species in the *Burseraceae* family. Among these are *B. sacra* (also known as *Boswellia carterii*), which is native to the Arabian peninsula and Somalia (in northeastern Africa); *B. fereana*, which also originates from Soma-

---

167 Frazer, *The Golden Bough,* Part VII, vol. I, 119.
168 Illes, *The Element Encyclopedia,* 483.
169 Frazer, *The Golden Bough,* Part IV, vol. I, 244.

lia; *B. serrata* from India; and *B. papyrifera*, which is native to Ethiopia and Sudan. Frankincense is farmed by slashing the bark of the trees and allowing the sap that bleeds out to dry naturally. The resin is sorted by hand, and it is sold according to its quality. Generally, the more opaque frankincense resin is, the higher the quality.

Ethical considerations: In many parts of the world, Boswellia trees are in decline because of high demand and habitat loss due to human-generated climate change. The increased price (due to higher demand), along with increased populations in these growing areas, has kicked off a scramble for resin which is more or less completely unregulated.[170] Overharvesting of the sap is causing the trees to die as they simply aren't given the time they need to recover like they used to.[171] This is leading to the early harvesting and decline of immature trees, and improper and unsustainable harvesting techniques altogether, such as completely stripping the bark and killing the trees in one fell swoop. Despite what some suspect labelling would have you think, there is not currently a way to determine whether frankincense has been sourced sustainably or using some of the methods mentioned above.[172] It is not possible to purchase frankincense and be sure that you aren't adding to an ecological disaster. Because there are entire communities that rely on the frankincense trade, this poses an ethical dilemma, to say the least. Before you purchase frankincense again, read about the challenges faced by those living and working in the frankincense trade, and keep them in mind when you purchase and use this resin.

170 Save Frankincense, "Frankincense Decline."
171 Patinkin, "World's Last Wild Frankincense Forests Are Under Threat."
172 Save Frankincense, "Certifiable Resin Supply Chain."

Magical Uses: Burning frankincense is thought to be very good protection for anyone undertaking magical or ritual workings, and it is commonly used in places of worship the world over. The Catholic Church purchase most of their quality frankincense by the tonne from Somalia, where in some places the sap still is tapped from the trees using methods dating back to biblical times.[173] In some witchcrafts, frankincense is thought to be able to break addictions, bad habits, and unhealthy relationships. Adding a few drops of essential oil of frankincense to a bath is thought to enhance psychic powers.

Garlic
(Allium sativum)
cleansing; purification; healing and vitality; sex magic

Thought to be native to Siberia, garlic has been widely known and used in food and medicine throughout Asia and the Middle East for thousands of years. The ancient Greek historian Herodotus wrote that the builders of the Great Pyramid in Egypt had been given a clove of garlic each day to boost their health, and it's also mentioned in the work of other ancient scholars such as Homer, Virgil, and Horace as a remedy by people during their times.[174] The useable part of the garlic plant is its bulb, which is really an orb of smaller bulbs (cloves) enclosed in a papery white skin. It is an annual and will grow fairly easily in gardens and pots if it's given enough sun, moisture, and quality soil kept free from weeds; buy some organic (or pesticide free) garlic from the supermarket and plant single cloves straight into the soil in spring. You can also buy fresh garlic at most grocery stores. Try to aim for

---

173 Patinkin, "World's Last Wild Frankincense Forests Are Under Threat."
174 Drury, *Watkins*, 112.

locally grown, organic garlic if you are using it in something you plan to ingest or use on your body, as garlic imported from a long way away is treated with some pretty full-on chemicals just so it lasts the trip. It's never particularly fresh, either. If you're buying pre-crushed or dried garlic, make sure you check the list of ingredients to ensure you aren't buying lots of extra filler.

Magical Uses: Garlic is related to the element of fire because of its associations with purification and passion. Some American witchcraft traditions burn garlic peel with sulphur, cloves, or incense resins as a means of spiritually cleansing a space. In some traditions this is performed as a regular maintenance ritual, taking place whenever enough garlic peel has been saved to create sufficient smoke.[175] In modern witchcraft, garlic is also often associated with cleansing or banishing negative energies. It is thought that a braid of twelve garlic heads hung over a door will banish jealous people,[176] or even protect the home from burglars.[177] In both modern and traditional charms, garlic cloves are often paired for workings involving sex or lust. For example, two garlic cloves held together with a steel nail and wrapped in red thread is thought by some to inflame another's heart with passion.[178] Ancient Greek magicians would sometimes seek favour from the goddess Hekate by visiting crossroads at midnight to place garlic bulbs as offerings, too.[179]

---

175 Illes, *The Element Encyclopedia*, 196.
176 Illes, *The Element Encyclopedia*, 133.
177 Illes, *The Element Encyclopedia*, 995.
178 Illes, *The Element Encyclopedia*, 679.
179 Drury, *Watkins*, 112.

Ginger
(Zingiber officinale)
prosperity; love; luck; lust; money; pregnancy and childbirth

Ginger is a perennial plant native to southeast Asia and grown widely in tropical climates all over the world. The plant grows from large, creeping roots that put up reed-like leaves of a very bright green colour. Ginger flowers are yellow or white with purple lips. It is the thick, fragrant ginger rhizome (root) that is valued and used. These can be bought fresh from grocery and produce stores. It's also commonly available dried, ground, candied, or preserved in syrup. If you want to try growing ginger, just keep in mind it needs a warm, humid environment to thrive. I've had pieces take root in my pantry in the warmer months, but never had much luck keeping them alive beyond this as it gets too cold here in winter. To grow ginger from a root piece, bury it just below the surface of some rich, well-drained soil in a large pot and water it regularly without giving it "wet feet." When the leaves start to appear, make sure it stays well-watered and in a frost-free spot. As the leaves get bigger, keep them slightly sprayed to encourage a humid environment. The plant will go dormant in winter but can be kept alive in a greenhouse. If you live in Australia, native ginger (*Alpinea coerulea*) is local to some rainforest areas in the eastern states and grows happily in similar conditions in backyard gardens. The centres of this plant's new shoots have a mild gingery flavour and are often used as a ginger substitute.

Magical Uses: Ginger is most likely associated with fire because of its correspondences with energy, sex, birth, and rebirth. Quite a few contemporary witchcraft books associate ginger with sex, childbirth, and maternal or "feminine" energy, possibly because in many cultures most of the work done to cultivate and harvest ginger was usually done by women.[180] Several modern texts also suggest using ginger in magical workings to bring joy and fun into one's life.[181] Sometimes it's associated with money: sprinkling its powdered form into a pocket or purse is thought to increase your finances, while planting ginger roots in the ground is believed by some to draw money towards you. Jamaican ginger is considered the strongest of all by cooks. I have no idea if this is also true of its esoteric qualities, but it could be worth a try if you can get your hands on it.

Ginseng
(Panax spp.)

beauty; hexes (breaking); longevity; protection; wishes

Also known as: wonder of the world root[182]

Ginseng is used for medicinal purposes and as an aphrodisiac in different cultures. It is also added to some energy drinks. *P. schinseng* is the variety of ginseng which grows in China, while *P. quinqufolium* grows in North America. Ginseng plants grow umbels of greenish-white flowers, red berries, and a thick taproot, which is the part of the plant that is used. Ginseng is sometimes called "mandrake,"[183] as its intact root will sometimes resemble a human, just like that of the mandragora. Unlike true mandrakes, however, ginseng is not toxic and is used widely in Chinese medicine. Some Asian grocery stores sell cut fresh ginseng root. Witchy retailers, tea shops, and health food stores sometimes stock a dried version, which is usually imported from China. Always look for food/tea

---

180 Frazer, *The Golden Bough*, Part V, vol. I, 123.
181 Illes, *The Element Encyclopedia*, 751.
182 Illes, *The Element Encyclopedia*, 527.
183 Valiente, *An ABC of Witchcraft*, 228.

grade, irradiation-free, when purchasing dried herbs. With regular water and fertiliser, ginseng will grow to about thirty centimetres by thirty centimetres in a garden or pot in a shady, frost-free location.

Magical uses: Magical associations with ginseng and fire most likely originate in Chinese medicine, which relates several varieties of ginseng to the body's fire, heat, and dryness. Some contemporary witches burn ginseng to break a hex, while a ginseng root wrapped in red thread and carried on one's person is thought to encourage beauty and grace. Wrapped in red and green thread along with the first dollar earned in a new business, it is thought to generate more income. In Hoodoo, ginseng is sometimes nicknamed "wonder of the world root." Carving a wish into a ginseng root and tossing it into a waterway is thought to bring about success in even hard-to-fulfil wishes.[184]

Hibiscus
(Hibiscus spp.)
Divination and psychic ability; love, lust, sex, and sexuality; warmth

Also known as: Queensland jam plant, rosella (*H. sabdariffa*); Hawaiian hibiscus (*H. rosa-sinensis*).[185]

Hibiscus are native to China and are very popular in Australia. Flower breeders here have produced more hybrid species than anywhere else in the world.[186] The various species of hibiscus are in the Malvaceae family, which includes other flowering plants such as ablutions (Chinese lanterns), mallow, hollyhocks, lavatera, and

---

184 Illes, *The Element Encyclopedia*, 763.
185 Kirton, *Harvest*, 414.
186 Kirton, *Dig Deeper*, 208.

alyogyne. Many varieties have edible flowers which are used in tea and cooking. You can purchase dried hibiscus flowers from some witchy retailers, tea-makers, and health food stores. Make sure they're food/tea grade and irradiation free before you buy. Annual forms of hibiscus such as rosella (*Hibiscus sabdariffa*) are best suited to tropical climates. They should be grown in a sunny spot, in well-drained soil with added mulch and organic matter. Calyxes should be picked when they turn dark red, and stored fresh, dried, or frozen. If you're growing perennial hibiscus for its flowers, it will need a hard pruning every year in late spring.

Magical Uses: Hibiscus' associations to the element of fire likely come to us from traditional Chinese medicine, where various parts of the plant and flower are sometimes used to remove heat from certain parts of the body. Interestingly, there are parts of some hibiscus plants that are fire resistant. In modern witchcraft, sprinkling crushed hibiscus flowers in a lover's pockets is thought by some to encourage fidelity. Wearing a particularly perfect hibiscus flower on your person then offering it to the object of your affection is thought to encourage them to reciprocate. Hibiscuses are sometimes associated with divination, too. One common method is to designate each flower as a person or possible situation and float them in a bowl of water to watch things play out.

Marigold
(Calendula officinalis, Tagetes spp. and others)
energy (general, solar); protection; purification; the sun; love; life and rebirth

Also known as: "marigold" is a word used around the world to identify a number of different plants, including:

- *Calendula officinalis:* bride of the sun, drunkard, pot marigold, ruddles, or Scotch marigold. These are thought to be native to southern Europe. These are annuals with round, bright flowers in yellow and orange. Flowers have edible petals which are sometimes used in salads.

- *Tagetes erecta:* **Aztec marigold, African marigold, or Mexican marigold.** Native to Mexico, these tall (up to around 90 cm), bright flowers have been used in medicine and ritual for centuries. They also feature in Day of the Dead decorations.

- *Tagetes patula:* **French marigold.** This is a spreading annual with bright, velvety flowers used in ritual, medicine, and dyes. It too is native to Mexico.

- *Tagetes lucida:* **Mexican marigold, Mexican mint marigold, sweet mace, or Texas tarragon.** This is a perennial flowering plant native to Mexico and central America. It was valued by the Aztecs as a key component in a ritual incense called Yauhtli.

- *Tagetes tenuifolia:* **signet marigold or golden marigold.** This wildflower is native to Mexico, Colombia, and Peru. Its bright yellow florets are often used as decoration or garnish.

- *Baileya multiradiata:* **desert marigold.** Even though it shares the same name, this North American wildflower is only a distant relative to other plants we know as marigolds.

- *Caltha palustris:* **marsh-marigold or king's cup (poisonous).** This relative of the buttercup is native to marshes and woodlands in the Northern Hemisphere. It is highly toxic and is considered an invasive weed in some areas.

- *Glebionis segetum:* **corn marigold or corn daisy.** Originally native to the eastern Mediterranean, this perennial plant is now found all over Europe and even farther afield. Its leaves are sometimes used in salads in Greece.

Dried marigold petals are available from some tea makers and health food stores. You can also buy seedlings quite cheaply from nurseries. Annual marigolds will grow quickly, finishing and self-seeding in almost any type of soil in temperate areas.

Magical Uses: Their bright colours and sunlike shapes have given many cause to associate marigolds with sun and with the element of fire throughout history and across the world. Because they are considered fadeless, planting pot marigolds in the earth will encourage unfading love and passion. According to an old Slavic tradition, it is possible to attract and keep the object of your affections by digging up the earth from one of their footprints and putting it in a flower pot with a marigold.[187] In Bavaria and other parts of Europe, garlands of pot marigolds were used to decorate tombstones on All Souls' Day, as they continued to bloom late into the summer.[188] Marsh marigolds (a.k.a. kings' cup, *Caltha palustris*) are mentioned in many traditional methods for protection from witches, and in some American traditional witchcrafts marigolds threaded together on red thread and hung as garlands over the door are thought to keep evil from entering your home.

---

187 Frazer, *The Golden Bough*, Part I, vol. I, 211.
188 Frazer, *The Golden Bough*, Part IV, vol. II, 71.

Nettle
(Urtica dioica, Urtica urens,
Urtica pilulifera and others)
banishing; calming; hexes (breaking); protection; thunderstorms (protection from)

WARNING: All varieties of nettles sting, and being stung by them is the *worst*. Wear gloves when picking or handling them. They lose their sting when cooked (Google a recipe for nettle pie and thank me later) or dried/brewed in a tea, though.

Also known as: stinging nettle (*U. dioica*); Roman nettle (*U. pilulifera*)

Nettles have been used by humans as food and medicine for thousands of years. Most varieties have square stems and dark green serrated leaves covered with fine hair. They have tiny seeds that are spread on the wind, and tough roots that creep a long way underground. You can buy dried nettle leaves and roots from tea makers, health food stores, and some witchy retailers. Look for tea/food grade, irradiation free. Nettles are considered a weed in most parts of the world, but they only grow in healthy soil. If they pop up in your garden, you're probably doing something right.

Magical Uses: Nettles could have originally been associated with fire because of their sting, which caused mediaeval Europeans to associate them with the devil. The associations could also have come about because nettles are often burned when used magically or ritually. In parts of pre-Christian Scandinavia, nettles were associated with the god Thor, and throwing them into a fire was a folk tradition for warding off thunderstorms in many parts of Europe.[189] Even today, many American witch-craft books assert that throwing nettles onto a fire is thought to minimise or prevent damage being done by wildfires, or to ward off evil. Others call for nettles to be burned while focusing your intent to add power to a banishing, or to stuff poppets with them in workings with the same intent. Modern spell books often cite nettles as being a good protector, too. They feature in spells for safety from harm, physical and otherwise. Another traditional association with nettles is that they disperse dark-ness. In modern witchcraft, they have often found their way into some magical workings relating to mental health (which, like any other healing working, should always be done along-side professional medical treatment or advice).

Peony
(Paeonia spp.)
protection; mental health; healing and healers; dreams

Also known as: peony rose

Peonies are among the earliest recorded medicinal plants. They have been grown in their native China for over 2,500 years.[190] Many varieties of peony have very long lifespans. There are some over a century old growing in temple gardens in some Asian coun-tries. In the Middle Ages it was believed that peonies, like man-drakes, would shriek so horribly that they would kill anyone who heard them.[191] Peonies prefer cooler climates. If you're planting one in your garden choose an open spot with good light and shel-ter from strong winds. You can buy dried peony root from witchy

---

189 Watts, *Elsevier's Dictionary of Plant Lore*, 264.
190 Kirton, *Dig Deeper*, 40.
191 Readers' Digest Association, *Folklore*, 85.

retailers and places that sell dried herbs for tea making. Always check that it is food/tea grade before you purchase, as cheaper forms are sometimes treated with synthetic perfumes which can be toxic if burned or ingested.

Magical Uses: The peony could have originally been associated with fire because of its long-held associations with the healing arts. In ancient Greece, the peony was associated with Asklepios, the healer son of Apollo, and it was considered a healing plant. Peonies are named after Paeon, a student of Asklepios who was saved by Zeus when Asklepios became jealous of his student's skill in healing and medicine. Many versions of the myth have Zeus turning Paeon into a flower so that he can escape Asklepios' wrath. The association of peonies with healing continued for centuries. A fourteenth-century image of a herbalist depicts him holding a peony poised like a magic wand. An infusion of peony roots added to a bath is supposed to provide spiritual healing/cleansing for someone who has suffered abuse, violence, or profound humiliation. A peony root infusion is also sometimes used to cleanse modern witchcraft ritual spaces. Dried peony roots carved into auspicious shapes can also be carried for protection. Historically, peonies were also associated with mental health and as a remedy for "lunacy." Peony roots knotted into a necklace allegedly prevents nightmares or lessens their impact. People once believed that they had the power to keep away evil spirits and disastrous storms.[192]

---

192 Readers' Digest Association, *Folklore*, 85.

Peppermint
(Mentha piperita)

cleansing, clearing, and purification; luck; healing; love and lust

WARNING: While peppermint oil is often mentioned in witchy texts and "prescribed" in New Age remedies, there is no uniform standard for quality, safety, or suggested amounts. Think twice before you ingest it or let it come into contact with your skin.

Also known as: brandy mint[193]

Peppermint is an edible type of more than forty species of mint (*Mentha* sp.). Black peppermint has purplish stems and leaves, while white has a green stem and leaves. Both are valued for their oil, which contains menthol. In the garden, most members of the mint family will grow prolifically if given the chance. Keep them confined to pots if you don't fancy pulling up mint for the next decade or so. Witchy and tea retailers sometimes carry dried peppermint leaves. Peppermint plants are fairly common in nurseries, too.

Magical Uses: Peppermint may have originally been associated with the element of fire because of its supposed healing properties. Teas containing peppermint have been used across several cultures for their supposed healing properties. One of many folk remedies out there claims that peppermint leaves placed over a photograph of an ill person will encourage the healing process. Peppermint branches are sometimes used for asperging ritual spaces in modern witchcraft, and offerings of peppermint leaves will allegedly encourage friendly spirits. When carried with chervil, peppermint is thought to bring luck and protec-

---

193 Kynes, *Correspondences*, 230.

tion. Practitioners in some traditional witchcrafts have shared that adding an infusion of peppermint to floorwash rinse water is considered to be beneficial for romance or seduction.[194]

Poppy
(Papaver spp.)

death and the afterlife; dreams and sleep; fertility and child-birth; money, luck, and prosperity

WARNING: Do not attempt to use opium poppies (*P. somniferum*) for medicinal purposes. They have the potential to be toxic in their raw form, and should only be prepared and prescribed under strict medical supervision.

Also known as: corn poppy, Flanders poppy (*P. rhoeas*); opium poppy (*P. somniferum*)

Poppies are tall annuals with coarse, almost ragged-looking leaves and large flower heads in a range of colours that can be single or double (ruffled). When these flowers die, the seed heads dry out into ready-made dispensers that sprinkle poppyseed on the wind. These flowers are often associated with opium and illicit drugs in this day and age. It is illegal to grow opium poppies (*P. somniferum*) in most parts of Australia as it is in many parts of the world, but in springtime they sometimes crop up after a soaking rain in old gold-mining areas near where I live, where they were grown by Chinese miners and their families in the 1800s. Poppies will grow from seed in most temperate parts of the world, as long as the soil is moist and there is plenty of sunshine. Dried, toasted poppyseeds can be purchased in the baking or health food sections of most grocery stores.

---

194 Illes, *The Element Encyclopedia*, 714.

Magical Uses: Poppies may have initially been associated with fire because of their striking red colour, and because of their use in healing the world over for thousands of years. As the source of opium, poppies were also often associated with sleep or a state of oblivion by the nineteenth century. This was built on during World War One, where soldiers' folklore told that red poppies were among the first plants to spring up on the battlefields because they grew from the spilled blood of their comrades. Seeing these poppies blooming on the battlefield of Ypres in Belgium in 1915 led Canadian Lieutenant Colonel John McCrae to write the poem *In Flanders Fields*. The poem was picked up by a YMCA branch in America, and the red "Flanders" poppy was soon known throughout the allied countries as a flower of remembrance to be worn on Armistice Day (November 11).[195] In recent years it has also become a common addition to the wreaths laid on ANZAC Day in Australia and New Zealand (April 25). Because this day is so close to Samhain here in the Southern Hemisphere, it also occasionally finds its way onto contemporary Pagan and witch seasonal and ancestral altars at this time of year. Other uses for poppies in modern witchcraft include placing dried poppy seedpods in a window to draw money towards you.[196] Their use in modern workings for fertility and healthy childbirth can be traced back to ancient Greece, where they were a symbol of the goddess Demeter, and have been long associated with her in ancient and classical art and writing.[197]

195 Australian War Memorial, "Red Poppies."
196 Illes, *The Element Encyclopedia*, 824.
197 Frazer, *The Golden Bough*. Part V, vol. I, 43.

Rosemary
(Rosmarinus officinalis)

healing; hexes (breaking, protection from); memory and memories; the mind; purification; youth

Native to the Mediterranean, rosemary is versatile and popular in kitchen gardens. From spring to autumn, rosemary bushes are covered in small blue flowers. The rosemary plant has thin, needle-like leaves that hold fragrant oil. There are prostrate (creeping along the ground) and bush forms, and varieties with pink, blue, or white flowers. These plants prefer a well-drained, warm location but will tolerate frosts once they're established. It will grow from a cutting with a bit of TLC; make sure the pieces are not too woody and have solid "heels" or points of growth. You can buy dried rosemary in the spice aisle of most supermarkets. Some even sell fresh sprigs.

Magical Uses: Rosemary has centuries-old mythic and magical associations, and has long been thought to protect against plague and sickness, and to enhance memory.[198] It is probably because of these associations with healing, as well as its folkloric uses in protective workings, that rosemary is associated with fire. Rosemary was thought to keep sickness and old age at bay in several European traditions. One legend tells the story of Queen Isabel of Hungary (possibly a nickname for Queen Elizabeth of Hungary), who supposedly suffered terribly from the effects of old age until a herbalist gave her an alcohol rub known as Hungary water, containing rosemary and several other essential oils.[199] On the topic of promoting youthfulness and good health, a jolly Easter tradition dating back to

198 Kirton, *Harvest*, 377.
199 Illes, *The Element Encyclopedia*, 1034–35.

the twelfth century in parts of Germany is called *schmeckostern* ("Easter smacks"). This practice sees couples beating each other with rosemary, birch, willow, or fir to keep them young and healthy and to bring good luck.[200] Just make sure you always keep your smacks safe and consensual if you try this at home. In mediaeval Europe, rosemary was believed to ward off evil spirits, witches, and faeries, as well as provide protection against storms (*Rosmarinus* = "dew of the sea").[201] Burned on May Day, it was believed to protect from witchcraft on the day that witches were supposedly at their most powerful.[202] In modern witchcraft and Paganism, rosemary is still sometimes burned to cleanse ritual space. It is also still associated with remembrance in modern times. Sprigs are sometimes worn in buttonholes or distributed at funerals.

Rue

(Ruta graveolens)

banishing; consecrating/blessing; grace; hexes (breaking, protection from); protection; purification; witches and witchcraft (overcoming, protection from)

WARNING: Rue is unsafe for people who are pregnant or for those actively trying to conceive. It can also irritate the skin.

Also known as: herb of grace; herb of repentance[203]

Considered native from the Mediterranean to eastern Siberia, rue grows as a shrubby, squat plant with greenish-yellow flowers and dusty green-coloured foliage. Rue leaves have a strong flavour

---

200 Frazer, *The Golden Bough*, Part VI, 270.

201 Drury, *Watkins*, 165.

202 Frazer, *The Golden Bough*, Part VI, 158.

203 Little, *The Complete Book of Herbs and Spices*, 152.

and smell, and are used in foods and beverages, herbal vinegars, cosmetics, and perfumes. Grown in the garden, rue can act as a great natural repellent to pest insects such as cabbage moths. Do not plant it near basil or sage as it will poison them. You can buy dried rue from witchy retailers, tea makers, and health food stores. Always buy tea/food grade, irradiation free.

Magical Uses: Rue could be associated with fire as it has been traditionally thrown onto midsummer fires in many European cultures for centuries.[204] It is often associated with grace, repentance, and memory. Shakespeare calls it the "sour herb of grace" in *Richard II*. In the Middle Ages, people burned rue or hung it around their houses—especially near doors or windows—to protect against witchcraft. Some modern witches use rue in protection spells and baths. It is also often listed as a component for breaking hexes. In Roman times, the herb was associated with the goddess Diana and her daughter Aradia. Followers of Diana revered rue plants and flowers, using it to make love charms.[205] A modern iteration of this calls for you to place rue in a shoe belonging to someone you desire and hang it above your bed to draw that person to you ... possibly because they want their shoe back?

Saffron
(*Crocus sativus*)
fertility; abundance and the harvest; good fortune; desire, lust, and sex magic; sex and sexuality

WARNING: Saffron is not safe to consume in significant amounts while pregnant.

---

204 Frazer, *The Golden Bough*, Part VII, vol. I, 213.
205 Drury, *Watkins*, 249.

Also known as: Alicante crocus, Valencia crocus[206]

Saffron originates from the eastern Mediterranean. After being introduced into Spain it became—and remained—the most expensive spice on the planet, used to colour and flavour dishes in many cuisines. Saffron comes from saffron stigmas, the tiny stalks in the centre of the saffron crocus. It takes thousands of stigmas to make just a few grams of saffron, and each saffron flower only grows three. This means a very labour-intensive harvesting and processing method, which is why this spice is so expensive. For as long as saffron has been sold in the spice trade, there have been people out there adulterating it, "cutting" it with cheaper product to stretch profits further.[207] Cheaper versions available online and elsewhere are often adulterated with gardenia, dyed red cotton, horse hairs, or sticks in the case of dried stamens. Powdered saffron is even more commonly adulterated, with fillers like turmeric, paprika, or others often added. The saffron crocus no longer grows as a wild plant anywhere in the world, so wildcrafting is out. What this means for you as a consumer is that you'll need to use discernment. Research alternatives to saffron. There are plenty. If it's what you have your heart set on, try to go for a higher grade saffron if you can afford it, or organic as it's less likely to have been cut with something synthetic. Buying dried whole stamens rather than powdered saffron is also one way to narrow the chances of fillers being added.

Magical Uses: Saffron's associations with the element of fire likely originate in India, where it has been burned for centuries as one of the seven traditional tantric perfumes, along with sandalwood, jasmine, patchouli, amber, nardin, and musk. There are

206 Little, *The Complete Book of Herbs and Spices*, 152.
207 Willard, *Secrets of Saffron*, 102.

accounts of saffron being used in Persia (now mostly modern-day Iran) for charms to make the wind blow to winnow corn fields, removing the chaff without destroying the stalks.[208] It's also considered sacred to Pan by some Hellenic Pagans. Saffron is said to have grown wild at the entrance to the Corycian cave on the slopes of Mount Parnassus,[209] an area considered sacred to Pan and the Corycian Nymphs.

St. John's Wort
(Hypericum perforatum)
banishing; beginnings, transformation, and rebirth; healing, health, and vitality; protection from lighting and storms; the sun and the summer solstice

WARNING: This plant is a noxious, invasive weed in more than twenty countries around the world. Growing it in these areas would be at the height of inconsideration and disrespect of the land you live on. Please do not.

Also known as: *fuga daemonum*,[210] Klamath weed[211]

St. John's wort is a medium-sized perennial that grows in the grasslands and woods of Britain, Europe, and Asia. In many parts of the world (including Australia, New Zealand, India, North and South America, and South Africa), it is considered a noxious weed and wreaks havoc upon pastures, crops, and native bushland. While it has been considered a healer's plant for centuries, there is not yet scientific evidence that this is the case. Two key ingredients

---

208 Frazer, *The Golden Bough*, Part I, vol. I, 320.
209 Frazer, *The Golden Bough*, Part IV, vol. I, 154.
210 Frazer, *The Golden Bough*, Part VII, vol. II, 55.
211 Little, *The Complete Book of Herbs and Spices*, 15.

in the oil produced by St. John's wort—hypericin and hyperforin—are being studied for their potential antibiotic qualities, but there has been nothing conclusive as yet. St. John's wort is dried and prepared as a tea ingredient in parts of Asia and the Middle East. You can buy it from some tea shops, herbal shops, witchy shops, and health food shops. Look for food/tea grade, irradiation free.

Magical Uses: St. John's wort is probably associated with fire because of its long history of association with midsummer and midsummer bonfires. It blooms around Midsummer's Day in many regions, and in the past its yellow petals and stamens made it a popular choice for magic and divination around that time. In some parts of Germany, it was customary to put a sprig of St. John's wort in your shoe before sunrise on Midsummer's Day in order to walk as far as you liked without getting tired.[212] In the Middle Ages, St. John's wort was hung in doors and windows to keep away witches, the Devil, and evil spirits. This custom lasted in Germany as late as the nineteenth century.[213] In England during the fifteenth century, it was thought that carrying sprigs of St. John's wort on your person meant that the Devil could not come closer than nine paces from you.[214] St. John's wort was also used in talismans and charms. In the mountains between what are now Belgium and Germany, the flowers were woven into garlands and thrown onto roofs or hung above doorways to protect against fire and lightning.[215]

---

212 Frazer, *The Golden Bough*, Part VII, vol. II, 54.
213 Frazer, *The Golden Bough*, Part VI, 160.
214 Opie and Tatem, *A Dictionary of Superstitions*, 336.
215 Frazer, *The Golden Bough*, Part VII, vol. I, 169.

Thistle
(Cirsium vulgare, Onopordum
acanthium and others)
banishing; confidence; hexes (breaking); magic (defensive);
protection; purification; strength.

Also known as: common thistle, field thistle (*Cirsium* sp); Scotch/
Scottish thistle, cotton thistle (*Onopordum acanthium*); blessed
thistle, Lady's thistle,[216] musk thistle (*Carduus* sp.); carline
thistle (*Carlina* sp.); distaff thistle (*Carthamus* sp.); star thistle (*Centaurea* sp.); sow thistle (*Cicerbita* sp. and *Sonchus* sp.);
blessed thistle (*Cnicus* sp.); globe thistle (*Echinops* sp.); Syrian
thistle (*Notobasis* sp.); golden thistle, oyster thistle (*Scolymus*
sp.); milk thistle (*Silybum* sp); Russian thistle, tartar thistle,
tumbleweed (*Kali* sp.); flowering thistle, purple prickly poppy
(*Argemone Mexicana*). "Thistle" is a common name given to
many prickly and spiny plants. Most thistles have sharp prickles on the edges of their leaves. Some also have prickles on the
flat surfaces of their leaves and on their stalks, too. Many grow
flowers that attract birds and insects. Most varieties of thistles
are invasive weeds. Do not encourage them by planting them in
your garden! If you live in the countryside, you might be able
to wildcraft some from parks, forests, or roadsides, but make
sure you bring some gardening gloves. Several different types
of thistle are available dried. Seek them out in tea shops, health
food stores, or witchy shops. Always buy food/tea grade, irradiation free.

Magical Uses: Thistles could have originally been associated with
the element of fire because of their use as fire-starting material.
Because they are annuals, they die each year. The seeds spread

---

216 Cunningham, *Encyclopedia of Magical Herbs*, 208–209.

on the wind, floating in soft white down—there is lots of lore in the thistledown itself, some associating it with faeries—and leaving behind the desiccated husk of the plant. These husks make an excellent fire starter and have been used for this purpose for thousands of years. In some southern Slavic countries, cut thistles were placed above doorways and on farm gates to ward off witchcraft. Some even wore them as garlands or fashioned wreaths to protect cattle.[217] In folklore, a shirt made from thistles spun and woven into "fabric" will break any hexes that have been cast upon the wearer. Believing it brought strength and good luck, the Romans carried "blessed" thistle (*Carduus benedictus*) with them as they set out to conquer the British Isles.

Vervain
(*Verbena officinalis*)

strength and courage; the military; protection; purification; health and vitality; love and lost lovers

Also known as: Britannica,[218] Druid's weed,[219] enchanter's plant,[220] magic herb,[221] verbena

Not to be confused with its lemon-scented relative *Lippia citriodora,* this variety of *Verbena* grows wild by roadsides and in dry grasslands in many countries. It is a medium-sized plant with rough, notched leaves and spikes of pale mauve flowers. Several American witchcraft books I consulted while researching for this book claimed the name *vervain* is "Celtic" (though they don't stip-

---

217 Frazer, *The Golden Bough*, Part I, vol. II, 339–40.
218 Cunningham, *Encyclopedia of Magical Herbs*, 216–218.
219 Drury, *Watkins*, 298.
220 Kynes, *Correspondences*, 192.
221 Little, *The Complete Book of Herbs and Spices*, 187.

ulate which Celtic language) and means *to break/drive away stones*, in reference to the plant's supposed ability to remove kidney stones, which has not been proven by science. The name is actually derived from Latin, which used the word *verbena* to describe any twigs, sprigs, or sticks with leaves used in religious ceremonies. Vervain plants are fairly drought tolerant but need adequate space between them. Dried vervain can be found at witchy retailers, tea shops, and health food stores. Look for food/tea grade, irradiation free.

Magical Uses: Vervain has a long history of magical associations. It's possible that it was originally associated with the element of fire as it was one of the herbs traditionally thrown onto midsummer bonfires in many cultures across Europe.[222] The ancient Romans considered vervain sacred, believing it was able to repel enemies at war. As such, vervain was associated with the god Mars and was worn by Roman messengers and ambassadors visiting other nations.[223] For centuries, vervain was gathered in parts of Belgium and placed about the house to protect from thunder, lightning, sorcery, and thieves.[224] Up until well into the eighteenth century, people in areas of England and Wales also used to hang sprigs of vervain outside their doors to drive off evil spirits.[225] There are records of vervain being used much earlier than this for a similar purpose, too. In 77 CE, the scholar Pliny recorded instances of Romans using it to purify houses and living spaces. There is also evidence of vervain being used to protect the body as well as the home. An 1878 English book of folklore claimed that vervain leaves carried in a black

---

222 Frazer, *The Golden Bough*, Part VII, vol. I, 195.
223 Drury, *Watkins*, 298.
224 Frazer, *The Golden Bough*, Part VII, vol. II, 62.
225 Little, *The Complete Book of Herbs and Spices*, 187.

silk bag would strengthen sickly children. In the Middle Ages, it was a main ingredient in love philtres, including those that some claimed would return happiness to an abandoned lover. This was still a common practice in some rural areas by the end of the 1800s.[226]

Trees and Sacred Woods

Because most people don't have the garden space to grow full trees, I've left out growing instructions for the trees listed below, but I'm sure you could Google them if you're super keen and lucky enough to have the space to plant trees.

Where I could, I've included instructions and information on how different woods burn. These are woods that have common magical correspondences relating to the element of fire. If you're planning on burning any wood on a ritual fire, make sure it is dry, seasoned, and not green in any way. See chapter 10 for more tips on preparing firewood and building and maintaining a safe, effective ritual fire.

Acacia/Wattle
(Acacia spp.)
dream work; protection; psychic ability; purification; spirituality; the sun and sunlight; visions

Also known as: acacia (all varieties); Babul (*A. arabica*)[227]; Cootamundra wattle (*A. baileyana*); mimosa bush (*A. dealbata*); American gum arabic, cat's claw (*A. greggii*)[228]; Mount Morgan wattle, Queensland silver wattle (*A. podalyriifolia*); golden wattle (*A. pycnantha*); cape gum, Egyptian thorn, gum arabic

---

226 Opie and Tatem, *A Dictionary of Superstitions*, 420.
227 Kynes, *Correspondences*, 148.
228 Kynes, *Correspondences*, 148.

tree (*A. americana*);[229] sami wood (*A. Suma*); prickly Moses (*A. ulicifolia*)

There are more than 1,200 species of wattle in Australia alone, all vastly different and flowering at different times of year. Wattles—also known as acacias—are medium-sized trees common across most of the southern continents, but they can be found in Europe and North America, too. Some thorny varieties known as mimosa bushes are unique to Africa. Many of the Australian wattle trees burst into radiant golden blossoms in winter and spring, and the golden wattle (*A. pycnantha*) has been Australia's national floral emblem since the 1980s. Dry, seasoned acacia wood burns hot. It makes excellent firewood for outdoor rituals on cold nights. Acacia gum or gum arabic is resin from *A. senegal*. When properly prepared, it can be used as a binder or base in incense blends. Find it at witchy retailers or wherever you buy raw incense ingredients.

Magical Uses: Acacia is most likely associated with fire because of its widespread use in sacred fires since ancient times. In parts of India, *A. catechu* was a key component of fire rituals sacred to the fire god Agni, tended by fire priests known as *Agnihotris*. *A. suma* is one of several plants known as *sami wood* in Sanskrit and Hindi. It is also associated with Agni, who completely concealed himself in sami wood and caused light to leave the world.[230] The Egyptian god Osiris is sometimes referred to in inscriptions as "the solitary one in the acacia" and "the one in the tree."[231] Acacia flowers and berries appear as key motifs in the ancient Egyptian story "The Two Brothers," which was written down during the reign of Rameses II, about 1300 BCE. In the ancient deserts of

---

229 Cunningham, *Encyclopedia of Magical Herbs*, 27.
230 Gupta, *Plant Myths*, 18.
231 Frazer, *The Golden Bough*, Part IV, vol. II, 111.

Arabia, the nomadic Bedouins told stories of an ancient and solitary acacia tree which they believed to be possessed by a djinn (a fire spirit—see chapter 2). In some countries in East Africa, *A. albida* has been used to kindle fires in temples and for other ceremonies for centuries.[232] In India, *A. Senegal* is still sometimes used in ritual fires or as a material in temple building. Modern witches might use a leafy acacia branch to asperge a space to cleanse and protect it before a magical working. Acacia is also associated with protection at night. Placing acacia twigs above your bed is thought to ward off nocturnal spiritual nasties.

Ash
(Fraxinus spp.)

creativity and the arts; protection and hex-breaking; divination, dreams, and intuition; healing, health, and vitality

WARNING: If you live in Europe or North America, check your supplies of ash firewood regularly for emerald ash borers. These metallic green beetles are an invasive species and have had a devastating effect on the entire *Fraxus* genus on both continents. If you spot these beetles, contact your local government environmental management agency without delay.

Also known as: nion, white ash (*F. americana*);[233] claret ash (*F. angustifolia* "Raywood");[234] common ash, European ash, golden ash (*F. excelsior*); black ash (*F. nigra*);[235] red ash (*F. pennsylvanica*)[236]

These large deciduous trees belong to the same family as olives and are native to northern Europe. The ash tree has had strong

---

232 Frazer, *The Golden Bough*, 210.

233 Cunningham, *Encyclopedia of Magical Herbs*, 38–41.

234 Kirton, *Dig Deeper*, 326.

235 Kynes, *Correspondences*, 149.

236 Mitchell, *A Field Guide*, 379.

mythological and magical associations for centuries. In British mythology, they are considered to be one of many sacred trees.[237] In Norse mythology, Yggdrasil the World Tree is an ash. The foliage of many ash trees turns brilliant fiery colours in autumn—look for the bright yellow (*F. excelsior*) or red (*F. angustifolia*) leaves to decorate your equinox altar. In dryer years when fire restrictions are still in place here, I've seen a bowl of these bright leaves used to represent fire in the place of a candle or lantern in outdoor rituals at the height of fire season. When dried and seasoned, ash burns reasonably hot and is easy to split. Some witchy retailers sell ash bark as a spell component.

Magical Uses: Ash could have originally been associated with the element of fire because of its long-held associations with lightning and storms. Fifteenth-century text *Les Evangiles des Quenouilles* (*The Distaff Gospels*) was a collection of popular beliefs and folk wisdom from late mediaeval women. It includes a charm for driving off storms; the charm uses four staves cut from an ash tree, each one marked with a cross. The ash tree sometimes appears in folkloric remedies for warts, and in parts of England, passing a child through the cleft of an ash tree was thought to be a cure for any number of illnesses, too, including rickets.[238] In contemporary witchcraft, dried ash seed pods—sometimes called ash keys—are used in protection magic. There is record of a similar practice in northern England around 1895, when a bunch of ash keys carried on the person would protect the bearer from witchcraft.[239]

---

237 Gardner, "The Nine Sacred Trees" in *Llewellyn's Magical Sampler*, 70–75.
238 Frazer, *The Golden Bough*, Part VII, vol. II, 168.
239 Opie and Tatem, *A Dictionary of Superstitions*, 8.

In modern witchcraft, ash is a popular choice for wand-making. It's also sometimes used to make staves and besom (ritual broom) handles.

Bay Laurel
(Laurus nobilis)

divination, dreams, and psychic ability; banishing; protection; love

Also known as: bay tree, poet's laurel,[240] sweet bay

With their dark, slightly wrinkled bark and glossy green leaves, bay trees grow up to around ten metres tall in open country, but they're commonly grown as shrubs in pots and tubs in many countries around the world. Wood from bay trees takes longer to season than most others—it will need to be left to dry for at least eighteen months if split, or two years for unsplit or larger logs. Bay wood can sometimes be smokier and more pungent than other wood when it burns. Always burn wood that is properly seasoned, and burn bay wood outdoors only. Bay leaves are used to flavour a range of dishes both savoury and sweet, and they are commonplace in supermarket spice aisles. These are just right for Daphnomancy (see below). If you know someone with a bay tree, you can also propagate your own bay shrub from cutting in a large tub.

Magical Uses: In Greek mythology, the Naiad nymph Daphne turned into a laurel tree to evade the god Apollo after he was struck by one of the love-inducing arrows of Eros. The laurel became sacred to Apollo; winners of competitions held in his honour were awarded crowns of bay leaves, and priestesses of Apollo are thought to have burned bay leaves as part of their

---

240 Mitchell, *A Field Guide*, 268.

divination and trance work. Daphnomancy, the practice of burning bay leaves as a form of pyromancy or divination, is mentioned in several modern witchcraft books and seems to be a contemporary tribute to the ancient Greek practices. Different authors have different opinions on the symbols, but in general a crackling, bright flame is seen as a good omen. A sputtering, sullen, or dying/dead flame is seen as bad news.[241] There are also numerous accounts of bay trees being a deterrent to thunder, lightning, and storms. An 1846 collection of seasonal proverbs counsels readers that "he who carrieth a bay-leaf shall never take harm from thunder."[242] Throughout folklore and history there are many traditions involving bay leaves and St. Valentine's Day, including putting bay leaves sprinkled with rose water under your pillow to encourage dreams of your future spouse.[243]

Hawthorn
(Crataegus spp.)

healing; protection (home, self); faeries; luck; prosperity

Also known as: may; may tree; may bush; bread-and-cheese tree; ladies' meat; hagthorn; thornapple; black hawthorn, Douglas' thornapple (*C. douglasii*); cockspur thorn (*C. crus-galli*); English hawthorn, Paul's scarlet, smooth hawthorn (*C. laevigata*); Midlands hawthorn (*C. oxyacanthoides*); quickthorn, whitethorn (*C. monogyna*); Washington thorn (*C. phaenopyrum*). The thorn family is a vast and varied one, with more than a thousand different species native to North America, Europe,

---

241 Illes, *The Element Encyclopedia*, 311.
242 Opie and Tatem, *A Dictionary of Superstitions*, 14.
243 Opie and Tatem, *A Dictionary of Superstitions*, 14.

and Asia.[244] Most of these species are thick, spiky shrubs, but some will grow into full trees in the right conditions. Hawthorns usually grow green or purplish-red foliage and long, sharp thorns. Most species bloom white in the springtime, and produce red or yellow fruit (called haws) in the autumn. Hawthorn is considered one of the sacred trees of Britain. Here in the Central Victorian countryside in southeast Australia, European settlers planted hawthorn hedgerows to shelter their farms from the wind. Many of these hedges are still intact today, and hawthorn lines country laneways and dots roadsides and paddocks for miles around. We know that Beltane season is upon us around here when the hawthorns start to bloom, and the season is over when the last bloom has fallen. We use the white hawthorn (*C. monogyna* and *C. Oxyacanthoides*) blossoms to decorate the top of the maypole at the Mount Franklin Pagan Gathering, along with some rare red hawthorn blooms (*C. laevigata*). Centuries-old folklore in many countries warns against cutting down or harming hawthorn. The 1792 *Statistical Account of Scotland* reported this "superstitious veneration" of hawthorn trees and bushes, and described their "mortal dread" about cutting off or harming any part of the plant. The account also suggested that those who dared to do so would be punished severely. Some poetry and stories suggest that this punishment comes from the fair folk. Whatever the origin of this bad luck, it seems some people were punished. Numerous accounts from Ireland, England, and Scotland tell of the misfortunes that befell those who ignored these warnings: people who lost otherwise healthy children, those who died from blood poisoning after pricking themselves on the thorns while

---

244 Mitchell, *A Field Guide*, 274.

removing the plant ... even an entire village made barren until a new tree was planted.[245]

Magical Uses: One thing that may have contributed to hawthorn originally being associated with the element of fire is its connections with the heart and with heart health, and with the goddess Brigid. Folkloric accounts dating back to the 1500s claim hawthorn as a protection against lightning. One account from Shropshire in the 1800s details that a hawthorn stick gathered (not cut) on Holy Thursday (the Thursday before Easter) and placed in the home would ensure the home from ever being struck.[246] Hawthorn was among a number of woods grown in some areas of Germany to ward off witches. The ancient Romans had similar reasons for hanging sprigs of hawthorn above doorways. In some parts of Germany, hawthorn was placed outside stables and cowsheds on May Day to keep the cows healthy and increase milk production. In Ireland, some cattle farmers brought branches inside for the same reason. According to Arthurian legend, the wizard Merlin sleeps still beneath the hawthorns at the fountain of Barenton in France. Breton peasants used to visit the fountain to pray for rain, and the fountain and the plants around it are still believed to have healing properties.[247] In many parts of England it was common to make and wear garlands of hawthorn flowers for luck and prosperity on May Day.

245 Opie and Tatem, *A Dictionary of Superstitions*, 400.
246 Opie and Tatem, *A Dictionary of Superstitions*, 400.
247 Frazer, *The Golden Bough*, Part VI, 153.

Juniper
(Juniperus spp.)

divination; dream work; protection; psychic ability; purification (general, spiritual)

Also known as: gin berry, hackmatack, horse savin; common juniper (*J. communis*); Chinese juniper (*J. chinensis*); shore juniper (*J. conferta*); Syrian juniper (*J. drupacea*); temple juniper (*J. rigida*); Rocky Mountain juniper (*J. scopulorum*); pencil juniper, red cedar (*J. virginiana*)

Most species of juniper are native to the Northern Hemisphere. It grows wild in many parts of the world. Junipers have sharp, needle-like leaves or small, overlapping triangular leaves. Their flowers are usually cone-shaped, and the entire plant's scent is a giveaway that it is part of the conifer (pine) family. It grows in many sizes depending on species, from a small bush no bigger than a metre or so high to tall trees of twenty metres or more. Some junipers such as *J. virginiana* are given the common name "cedar." This is the "red cedar" that is commonly used in cabinetmaking, but it is not related to true cedar (*Cedrus* sp.). Juniper produces a lot of smoke when burned. Always burn dry, seasoned juniper wood outdoors or somewhere with good ventilation. Like all conifers, burning juniper causes creosote (flammable coal-tar) to build up in chimneys. Avoid burning it in indoor fireplaces and wood heaters.

Magical Uses: One reason juniper may be related to fire is because of its early use in incenses and fragrant fires, especially those used in embalming. Juniper berries are sometimes included in contemporary cleansing rituals for altars and ritual space, too. These berries are also sometimes strung on thread to be worn on the person or hung in homes for protection. Sprigs of juniper hung above a door are thought to prevent evil from entering.[248] The wood is also thought to enhance psychic powers when burned or carried and, used sparingly, it makes a good addition to incenses blended for this purpose.

Oak
(Quercus spp.)
deity, spirits, and spirituality; strength and courage; the sun and the summer solstice; protection from fire and lightning

Also known as: English oak (*Q. alba*); red oak (*Q. borealis*); turkey oak (*Q. cerris*); scarlet oak (*Q. coccinea*); Holm oak (*Q. ilex*); white oak (*Q. velutina*); etc.

Oak wood is renowned for its strength, and has been used in tools, weapons, and shipbuilding for centuries. There are almost one thousand species native to different regions of the Northern Hemisphere. Different species produce different shapes, sizes, and colours of acorns. Here in the Victorian goldfields, many areas were completely stripped of topsoil during the gold rush of the mid-1800s. This reduced native forests and marshlands to barren moonscapes in some places. Around the area where I live, a pioneering forester called John La Gerche planted oak trees in the scarred clay as part of a movement to reforest the area. These trees still stand today, and Central Victoria is dotted with oak forests and secret oak groves tucked amidst forests of beautiful native eucalypts. I'm lucky enough to live in a little house in the shade of an enormous La Gerche oak, and as I write this, I can see its green leaves and new acorns nodding in the late summer sun outside my window. Remember how I said oak is renowned for its strength? This means oak logs are difficult to split. If you're buying

---

248 Cunningham, *Encyclopedia of Magical Herbs*, 133.

oak wood for firewood, spending the extra bit to have it delivered pre-split will save you grief in the long run. When properly seasoned, oak logs burn fairly hot. Gathered fallen oak kindling, not so much. You can buy oak incense blends, miniature cords of oak wood, and acorns from some witchy suppliers. Oaks are common in many countries, too, which means (responsibly) wildcrafting your own acorns or leaves could be an option.

Magical Uses: Considered to be one of the sacred trees of the British Isles, oaks have mythical and magical associations stretching back thousands of years. Its association with the element of fire could have something to do with its supposed protective qualities against fire and lightning, or with the centuries-old associations with the summer solstice and the lighter half of the year, which later formed part of the drama of the Oak and Holly Kings. While we know very little about the ancient Druids, we do know that both oak and mistletoe were a key component of most of their rites.[249] In biblical times, the oak tree was considered sacred to the Jews because it is thought that Abraham encountered an angel of god beneath its branches. The Bible also tells the story of devotees of the Phoenician god Baal making sacrificial offerings "under every leafy oak" in Ezekiel 6:13. Carrying a small piece of oak on the person is thought to protect the wearer. Hung in the home, it is thought to bring good luck and protect from fire, theft, lightning, and illness. Doreen Valiente speculates that this is why old houses in England often have oak leaves or acorns included somewhere in their detailing.[250] The ancient Romans considered the oak sacred to the sky and thunder god Jupiter. Interestingly, in ancient Norse

---

249 Drury, *Watkins*, 213.
250 Valiente, *An ABC of Witchcraft*, 321.

culture, oaks ("thunder trees") were dedicated to the god Thor. In pre-Christian Ireland, they were (and still are) considered the sacred tree of the god Dagda.[251] In Prussia, it was believed that the gods inhabited tall trees, including oaks, and that the deities would give sometimes audible answers if worshippers asked questions of the trees. As such, oaks were venerated and worshipped.[252]

Olive
(Olea europea and others)

deity, worship, and spirituality; power; triumph; hope; peace; destruction and rebirth

Also known as: cultivated olive, European olive (*Olea europae*); American olive (*Osmanthus americanus*)

Belonging to the same family as lilac, jasmine, and privet (yes, the hedging plant), olive trees are native to Asia, Africa, and the Mediterranean. Olives are of major agricultural importance and are one of the key ingredients in Mediterranean cuisine. Olives as a foodstuff can't be eaten raw; they need to be pickled. In Egypt, evidence of olives as a food source go back as early as 2000 BCE.[253] Olive wood is prized for its durability and colour. When properly seasoned it is very dense and burns slowly, releasing a great scent as it does. If you live in Europe or in warmer areas of Australia or North America, you might be able to source olive firewood from olive farms, either directly or through a sustainable firewood business. As olive trees are heavily pruned, wood is a by-product of the olive farming industry and is often just left to rot on the ground.

251 Drury, *Watkins*, 213.
252 Frazer, *The Golden Bough*, Part I, vol. II, 43.
253 Kirton, *Dig Deeper*, 93.

This makes olive wood an attractive option for those looking for a renewable firewood option that is less harsh on the environment.

Magical Uses: Olive trees may have initially been related to fire partly because of Greek mythology, in which they were considered sacred to the Greek goddess Athena and a fire-related miracle. It's Athena who is credited in Greek mythology for first causing the trees to fruit, and she is depicted with olive trees in many of her representations in ancient art. Legend has it that Athena's original olive tree on the Acropolis (an ancient citadel overlooking Athens) was burned by the Persian king Xerxes I during his invasion of Athens in 480 BCE, but the tree reappeared as if by magic.[254] Olive leaf crowns were also a symbol of power in ancient Greece. Many depictions of the gods include wreathed crowns of olive branches, and winners of important races and early Olympic competitions were often crowned in the same way. It's thought that these crowns were sometimes cut from a sacred tree near the temple of Zeus using a golden sickle.[255] In Christian mythology, olives are often a symbol of peace and divine blessing because a dove brought a sprig of olive to Noah to let him know that dry land had appeared and the flood was subsiding.

Pine
(Pinus spp.)

activating and awakening; beginnings; cycles; fertility; rebirth and renewal; transformation

WARNING: Never burn treated pine, which is used to make pine furniture, floorboards, fence posts, etc. This pine is soaked in

---

254 Drury, *Watkins*, 216.
255 Frazer, *The Golden Bough*, Part IV, vol. II, 238–240.

chemicals to stave off rot and boring insects, and releases highly toxic fumes when burned.

Also known as: Christmas tree; Austrian pine (*P. nigra* "Arnold"); Bhutan pine (*P. wallichiana*); maritime pine (*P. pinaster*); Monterey pine, radiata pine (*P. radiata*); Scots pine, Scotch pine (*P. sylvestris*)

The pine family includes more than one hundred species in the Northern and Southern Hemispheres. Some of these varieties are among the most ancient on the planet, with lineage dating back more than 290 million years.[256] Most pine trees grow needles in bundles of two, three, or five, and grow either round or conical pinecones. The cones of some trees, such as *P. pinea*, produce edible pine nuts. Many species are very resinous; they produce a large amount of sap which is often secreted through the bark. Pine isn't the hottest-burning wood. It burns quite quickly and releases a lot of mess and smoke. Dry pine sticks and seasoned, open pinecones make good kindling for this reason, but watch out for the dripping molten sap. When burned, pine produces high levels of creosote, or flammable coal tar, that sticks to the inside of chimneys causing serious fire hazards. Avoid burning pine in indoor fireplaces, wood heaters, or other chimneyed fire drums.

Magical Uses: Unlike many resins, dried pine resin goes sticky and smoky when burned, and as such isn't much good for incense. This quick-burning resin may have been one of the reasons pine wood and trees were originally associated with the element of fire. Another reason could be its associations with the winter solstice and with rebirth/fertility in general. In ancient Egypt, many versions of the myth of Osiris have an image of him being

---

256 Kirton, *Dig Deeper*, 416.

buried within a pine tree after his murder to assist him to come back to life through divine resurrection.[257] Dionysus, too, is often associated with the pine tree, with either he or his followers depicted holding wands topped with pine cones. The Oracle at Delphi once commanded people to worship a particular pine tree "equally with the god."[258] Pinecones were also sometimes thrown into the sacred vaults of Demeter as a means to quicken the ground and encourage fruitfulness.[259] Many modern witchcraft texts assert that pinecones are considered beneficial for happy marriages and fertility for all genders. Some traditions of witchcraft use priapic wands and staves, which are often topped with a pinecone, acorn, or carved phallus.

Rowan
(Sorbus spp.)

blessings; defence; destruction; divination; enchantment; hexes (protection from); magic (general, faery); protection; psychic ability

Also known as: whitebeam, witch tree, quickbeam, whitty tree, service tree,[260] common rowan, mountain ash (*S. aucuparia*); red rowan, Chinese scarlet rowan (*S.* "Embley"); Hupeh rowan (*S. hupehensis*); Sargent's rowan (*S. sargentiana*); whitebeam (*S. aria*)

There are around one hundred species of rowan trees around the world. In Europe, Asia, and some parts of North America, they are commonplace in parks and nature reserves. With smooth, silvery-grey bark and neat leaves, rowans are known to grow at high altitudes, and are sometimes seen in mountainous areas. Rowan

---

257 Frazer, *The Golden Bough*, Part IV, vol. II, 110.
258 Frazer, *The Golden Bough*, Part V, vol. I, 4.
259 Frazer, *The Golden Bough*, Part IV, vol. I, 278.
260 Gardner, "The Nine Sacred Trees."

makes good firewood when properly seasoned. It puts out a decent amount of heat and burns slowly. The trees are protected as significant trees in some parts of the world. Always source your firewood from someone who uses sustainable (and legal) firewood collection practices. Some witchy retailers sell dried rowan berries or twigs.

Magical Uses: Rowans were considered sacred among some ancient British peoples. Of all trees, these probably have the most widespread reputation as having protective properties; tales about rowan wood exist in English, Irish, Scandinavian, and even Icelandic folklore. This widespread association could have something to do with why the tree was first associated with the element of fire. In Norway during the Middle Ages, sailors and fishermen carried a piece of rowan with them on voyages for good luck.[261] In parts of Sweden, shepherd boys would sometimes cut a rowan "wand," which was stuck in the ground to protect the sheep and cattle from witchcraft and animal attacks throughout the summer.[262] Rowan seeds can sometimes be spread by birds. In some Scandinavian countries, a *floegroenn*, ("flying rowan") was a rowan found growing out of the top of another tree. These were considered to be "exceedingly effective against witchcraft." The logic behind this was that, as the tree didn't touch the ground, witches would have no power over it. In Sweden, *floegroenn* was also used to make rods used in divination.[263] In areas of Ireland and Britain, rowan would often be hung about doors to protect against witchcraft on May Day.[264]

261 Frazer, *The Golden Bough*, Part VI, 267.
262 Frazer, *The Golden Bough*, Part I, vol. II, 341–42.
263 Frazer, *The Golden Bough*, Part VII, vol. II, 282.
264 Frazer, *The Golden Bough*, Part I, vol. II, 53.

• • • •

Incense for the Element of Fire

Ryan McLeod is an Alexandrian witch based in Victoria, Australia, and has walked the Pagan path for two decades. During this time he has mastered the art of creating ritual incense, oils, and salves. Mcleod's incense workshops have been a resounding success at the Australian Wiccan Conference and the Mount Franklin Pagan Gathering. He can be reached at www.ryanmcleod.com.au

Incense Cones

Incense cones are a great way to use your own incense for ritual if you do not want to deal with a hot charcoal. All ingredients should be powdered, by using either a mortar and pestle or a spice grinder. The cedar must be purchased powdered.

INGREDIENTS:
> cedar: 3 parts
> bay: 1 part
> black pepper: ½ part
> Xanthan gum (to bind the ingredients together): ⅛ part
> water as needed

To make your cones, mix all dried ingredients together. Add a small amount of water and mix thoroughly. Keep adding water and mixing until you form a dough. Pull off a small sized amount and form into a cone shape with the base being no thicker that a pencil. The taller and thinner your incense cone is the better it will burn.

Allow at least one week to dry before using.

Incense Pellets

Incense pellets are burnt on a hot charcoal disc. The scent is slowly released.

INGREDIENTS:
> dried figs: ground in a paste as needed
>
> copal resin: 2 parts
>
> allspice: ½ part
>
> cinnamon: 1 part
>
> juniper berries: 1 part

In a food processor, blend figs into a paste and put aside. Use a mortar and pestle to powder the copal; add in juniper berries and crush. Add in cinnamon and allspice and mix together thoroughly. then add small amounts of your fig paste as needed to make a dough. Form the dough into pea-sized balls and allow to dry for a week on baking paper in a warm part of the house. Transfer your pellets into a jar and store for at least three months before using.

Loose Incense Blend

This recipe is for incense that can be burned in a censer/thurible.

INGREDIENTS:
> dragons blood: 2 parts
>
> dried ginger: 1 part
>
> nutmeg: ½ part
>
> clove: ¼ part

Combine and sprinkle over hot coals to use.

Censing Bundle/Stick

INGREDIENTS:
> rosemary sprigs
>
> juniper sprigs
>
> patchouli sprigs*

Use new growth branches of rosemary, juniper, and Patchouli. Tie together by wrapping in a piece of orange thread.

* Note: if you can only source dried patchouli, sprinkle it between the fresh branches of the rosemary and juniper before you tie them.

Ryan McLeod

• • • •

Conclusion

Herbs and plants associated with fire might be red or yellow, spicy or peppery, or might have just been a good fire-starter for our ancestors. The correspondences listed here are some of the most common ones, but that's not to say that they are set in stone. You might have your own reasons for associating other plants with fire, and those are no more or less valid than the ones we've looked at in this chapter.

As well as providing lists of correspondences for herbs, it was my aim to explore why those correspondences might exists in the case of individual herbs and plant species. Just as with everything else we do in our lives, knowing *why* we're doing it in the first place can give us a greater understanding and appreciation of what it is we're setting out to do, and help us examine why it attracts us in the first place.

Chapter 7

STONES AND CRYSTALS

Most crystals are formed over thousands of years, as molten rock far beneath the earth's surface cools and hardens. Little wonder, then, that so many of them are associated with the element of fire for magical workings.

There are a few things to consider when working with crystals and other stones:

- **Some crystals and stones are very expensive, but have many cheaper alternatives with the same correspondences.** Investigate correspondences (I highly recommend *Llewellyn's Complete Book of Correspondences* by Sandra Kynes) and you'll be pleasantly surprised just how many alternatives there are. You'll also save yourself shelling out more than you need to.

- **Having lots of crystals doesn't make you a better witch.** Consider having a few "go to" stones with correspondences that suit the work you do. Amassing loads of expensive shiny things makes you a consumer, not more magic or mystical. They might as well be ornamental plates or Pokémon cards or pop vinyl figures. If you're looking to improve your witchcraft, look further than the aesthetically pleasing filters on social media and get on with the work.

- **Working with crystals is not mandatory to being a witch.** I've been doing the witch thing for well over two decades now. Crystals are not the centre of my practice. You won't find piles of pretty stones on my altar, windowsills, or even in my bra (I seriously didn't know that was a thing until a year ago). I do not take luxurious, Instagrammable bubble baths with flower petals and neat arrangements of crystals and stones around the rim. When I *do* use crystals, it is for a specific ritual purpose, often as part of a talisman or other working. Learning some of their key correspondences formed a part of my training, as I built up a "toolbox" of useful skills.

- **The mining, processing, and sale of many crystals are deeply problematic.** Crystals are a non-renewable resource, and those who mine them are low-paid, often underage workers working in unsafe conditions. The industry is not officially regulated, which means these exploitations go unchecked. Furthermore, mineral extraction in some countries is linked to severe human rights violations, environmental harm or even to helping fund extremist organisations. Most crystal retailers will not be able to tell you where their stock comes from, so there is often no way of knowing just how ethical your crystals are.[265]

In the last few decades, collecting and working with crystals has gone from being a niche New Age interest to a valid mainstream hobby, and the sale of crystals makes up a hefty slice of the

---

265 Wiseman, "Are Crystals the New Blood Diamonds?"

multi-trillion dollar "wellness" industry. Not all witches feel drawn to contributing to that, or to using crystals in their regular work. Does that make them less witchy than those who do? Nah, mate.

Crystals, Metals, Minerals, and More

Like the herbal correspondences in the chapter before this one, some of these stones' and metals' association with the element of fire come to us from ceremonial magic and the grimoire tradition. Some are newer than that. Sometimes a stone or metal's colour or origins are a clear giveaway as to why it is associated with this element. Sometimes it's less clear than that until you go deeper into the history of its use in magic.

Amber

activating; energy (general, solar); healing; love (attracting); the sun and solar magic

Amber is fossilised tree resin, and it has been valued and traded for its beautiful yellowy-brown colour since Neolithic times. Because it begins as runny, sticky tree sap, some pieces of amber contain plant matter or insects—think of the mosquito from the first *Jurassic Park* film. Most of the amber bought and sold in the world today is Baltic amber, also known as "true" amber. It mostly comes from the Kaliningrad region of Russia.

Ethical Considerations: Baltic amber is mined from huge open-cut mines in Russia. This involves the clearing of large swathes of land, then drilling, digging, and blasting large pits. The process of disrupting the ground causes a number of pollutants that affect the air quality, flora, and fauna in areas around the mine itself. Caribbean amber is usually mined using a process called bell-pitting, which is considered quite primitive and dangerous.

These shafts and caverns are rarely shored with proper supports, and are not tested for safety.

Magical Uses: Amber is associated with the element of fire because it was for centuries connected with both gold and the sun by alchemists.[266] Today, some consider wearing amber to be beneficial to heal and strengthen muscles, the respiratory system, and more. Wearing amber beads is thought to promote healing and general good health, especially when worn as jewellery on the wrist or throat.[267] It's also commonly used in spells for love and sex.

Brass

energy; healing; magic (defensive, solar); prosperity; money and wealth (attracting)

Brass is an alloy of copper and zinc. Because of its gold colour and malleability it has been used for centuries for decorative purposes, machinery and electrical components, musical instruments, jewellery, and more, often as a substitute for real gold or to represent the sun. You can buy brass strips, sheets, rods, and more from hardware shops and hobby stores.

Magical Uses: Brass has been associated with the sun and (to a lesser extent) healing since ancient times, which is probably how it came to be associated with the element of fire. An old superstition holds that wearing a brass ring may help ease stomach cramps. In folklore, a brass key dropped down the back of your shirt was thought to help relieve a nosebleed. Brass has also been associated with money and money-attracting magic for some time. Charging a brass bell with your intentions and ring-

266 Drury, *Watkins*, 15.
267 Hall, *The Crystal Bible*, 51.

ing it in direct sunlight is one method that some use. During prosperity rituals, placing money-attracting items or talismans on a brass dish is thought to imbue them with extra power. Another simple money-attracting charm involves inscribing a pentagram on a small piece of brass using an engraving tool and then carrying the token on your person.[268]

Carnelian

harmony; healing; power (general, personal); protection (general, psychic); rebirth and renewal

Carnelian is a brownish-red semi-precious stone. It is often confused with another semi-precious stone called sard, which is often indistinguishable from a carnelian. The name *carnelian* comes from Latin *cornum*, a type of cherry. It has been found in Indonesia, Brazil, India, Russia, and Germany.

Ethical Considerations: Most of the carnelian bought and sold today comes from Peru and Sri Lanka, where the mining industries are not well-regulated. Peru, especially, has come under fire in recent years for a long list of human rights violations in many of its gold and mineral mines.[269]

Magical Uses: Its orange-red colours and its ancient associations with protection are likely why we relate carnelian to the element of fire today. A protection charm that has its origins in part in the *Egyptian Book of the Dead* calls for a carnelian to be attached to a cord and worn about the waist at navel level.

---

268 Cunningham, *Crystal, Gem & Metal Magic*, 236.
269 Human Rights Watch, "The Hidden Cost of Jewellery: Human Rights in Supply Chains and the Responsibility of Jewellery Companies."

This is thought to prevent psychic attack.[270] Try placing a carnelian by the front door to bring protection and abundance to the home, or carry one on your person for courage, or to ease a restless mind.

Cat's Eye (Cymophane)

animals; beauty; creativity; generosity; happiness; insight; luck; magic (animal); optimism; protection; rebirth and renewal; wealth[271]

Cat's eye or cymophane is a yellowish variation of the gemstone chrysoberyl. The name *cymophane* comes from ancient Greek words meaning "wave" and "appearance." It is found in Brazil, India, China, Sri Lanka, and Zimbabwe.

Ethical Considerations: Most commercially available cymophane is mined in Brazil, where workers are often grossly underpaid and work in cramped, unsafe conditions. The mines are owned by multinational companies and no profits go back to local communities, many who are struggling with poverty after years of drought.[272]

Magical Uses: Cat's eye could have been originally associated with the element of fire because of its connections to creativity and creative forces. Carrying a cat's eye stone on your person is also believed by some to stimulate the intellect and promote creativity. Charging a cat's eye stone with your intent and then carrying it on your person is believed by some to promote "invisibility," or your actions/movements going unnoticed. Worn on the right side of the body, cat's eye stones are thought by some to bring confidence, serenity, happiness, and good luck.

---

270 Illes, *The Element Encyclopedia*, 922.
271 Kynes, *Correspondences*, 224.
272 Brasileiro, "Brazilian mines produce world's priciest gems under fire."

Flint

protection; healing; divination; balance; nature spirits[273]

Flint has been used to make stone tools and create fire since prehistoric times. It is a sedimentary form of quartz, formed over millennia by the silt and sediment in the bottom of lakes, rivers, and oceans. It's dark grey, brown, or sometimes greenish in colour, and sometimes appears waxy. Flint nodules and masses are found in banks of sedimentary rock all over the world, often along streams or on beaches.

Magical Uses: Flint's magical associations with fire are rooted in its use as a firestarter since prehistoric times. When struck against steel, flint produces enough sparks to ignite dry tinder or gunpowder. In Armenia, folktales tell of lightning being created with flint much the same way as it creates fire. In some parts of the British Isles, flint knives were sometimes set in silver and carried as a protection against faeries or other spirits. In some parts of Scandinavia, flint knives sometimes acted as an idol or representation of house or local spirits, and were revered as such. During the Middle Ages, a holed piece of flint was supposed to be useful for many sorts of magic, including as a talisman for keeping witches away.[274]

Garnet

attraction; balance; calm; confidence and courage; darkness and dark places; lust, sex, and sexuality

Garnet is a semi-precious stone that has been valued by humans since the Bronze Age. They come in many colours but dark red is

---

273 Dunwich, *Guide to Gemstone Sorcery*, 102.
274 Frazer, *The Golden Bough*, Part VI, 162.

the best known. The name *garnet* probably comes from the Middle English *gernet* ("dark red"), although there are other theories too (see below). Different types of garnet can be found all over the world.

Ethical Considerations: The four largest garnet producers and exporters are India, China, Australia, and the United States. Garnets are sometimes mined alongside coal or diamonds in large-scale mines owned by multinational companies.[275]

Magical Uses: It is likely because of its deep red colour that garnet was initially related to the element of fire. One theory about the etymology of the word *garnet* relates it to the Latin *granatum*, a word for "pomegranate," because of the stone's resemblance to the fruit in colour and sometimes shape. With this in mind, garnets could be endowed with similar magical or ritual correspondences to pomegranates, including strength and courage for journeys into dark places. Wearing or carrying a garnet is thought to enhance your perceptions of yourself and improve your self-confidence. Some believe that wearing garnet jewellery will attract the love of your life, or inspire feelings of love and serenity.

Gold

energy; healing; magic (general, defensive, solar); money; prosperity; protection; vitality

Gold is a soft, yellow precious metal that has been used for coins, jewellery, and decoration for thousands of years. It is mined all around the world. As far as we can tell, it was among the first metals used by humans. It is thought to have been present when the solar system formed. It can be found in ores formed from the

---

275 Critchfield, "What is Garnet?"

Precambrian period onwards. The name *gold* derives from a proto-Indo-European word meaning "to shine or gleam."

Ethical Considerations: Modern industrial gold mining destroys landscape and produces a high amount of toxic waste—much of which finds its way straight into waterways. Practices like cyanide leaching and open-cut mining mean that the gold mining industry produces around twenty tonnes of toxic waste per 0.333-ounce gold ring.[276] Where I live in Central Victoria, the gold rush ended more than a century ago. There is still no topsoil here, and there are waterholes in the nearby forests that are still poisoned with cyanide after all that time. It's a similar story in most places around the world where they have been "lucky" enough to have a gold rush.

Magical Uses: Gold is most likely associated with fire because of its use in alchemy and its associations with the sun. It's also been associated with healing for centuries. It is even mentioned as part of a "health tonic" in Geoffrey Chaucer's *Canterbury Tales,* which were written towards the end of the 1300s. Several folkloric accounts from the 1700s and 1800s tell of cunning men and women rubbing a gold coin on the chest of sickly children to heal and settle them.[277] In parts of Germany, plants considered magic, such as hawkweed (*Hieracium pilosella*), were dug up using a gold coin on Midsummer's Day. An account from ancient Roman author Pliny describes white-robed Gaulish Druids cutting mistletoe with a golden scythe as part of a ceremony to bring fruitfulness to animals and crops.[278]

---

276 Earthworks, "How the 20 Tons of Mine Waste Per Gold Ring Figure was Calculated."

277 Opie and Tatem, *A Dictionary of Superstitions*, 175.

278 Frazer, *The Golden Bough*, Part VII, vol. II, 57.

Obsidian

clairvoyance, divination, and psychic ability; grounding and calm; peace; spirituality

Obsidian is a volcanic glass, formed as an extrusive (forced out while still molten) igneous rock. It is hard but brittle, and forms when lava cools very rapidly. Obsidian is known to have very sharp edges, and it is used for scalpel blades in some parts of the world. It is usually a deep black or blackish green. The name *obsidian* is actually an ancient misprint of *obsianus* (lapis), which was the name of the Roman first credited with finding a lapis. It is found on the surface of volcanic soil all over the world.

Magical Uses: Obsidian is associated with the element of fire because of its volcanic origins. It has been used in rituals and ceremonies in many different cultures for thousands of years. In several different ancient cultures, it was used for divinatory purposes, in the manner of a scrying mirror.[279] The reflective faces of obsidian also make it a popular choice for many for protection magic, especially to direct energy away from oneself. Some traditions of witchcraft associate obsidian with the sabbat of Yule, the winter solstice. Others consider it a grounding stone, and hold or stand on it when they are feeling flighty or out of sorts. Try placing a piece of obsidian at your desk or workstation if you find workplace stress getting the better of you.

Pyrite

divination and the mind; money; prosperity; psychic ability; success; wealth

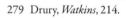

279 Drury, *Watkins*, 214.

Also known as fool's gold, pyrite is a semi-precious stone and an iron sulphide—a compound of iron and sulphur. Its shine and hue make it look very similar to gold, which is why it is known as fool's gold. It is the most widespread and common sulphide in the world. As a sedimentary rock, it can be found underground and in bodies of water all over the globe.

Magical Uses: When struck to iron, pyrite makes sparks. The name *pyrite* comes from *pyr*, an ancient Greek word for fire. Larger pieces of pyrite are sometimes used as divinatory tools or in workings to improve psychic awareness. Placing a piece of pyrite on a desk or workspace is considered by some to bring luck and success in business, and it is used by some modern witches in money or abundance workings. Try placing pyrite on your altar alongside a gold or silver candle to bring money your way.

Ruby

healing, health, and vitality; life; peace; power (general, magical); prosperity; strength; wealth

Rubies are precious gemstones coloured pink to dark blood-red. They are a variety of the mineral corundum, or aluminium oxide. The name *ruby* comes from the Latin word for red, *ruber*. They are mined around the world, in Afghanistan, Myanmar, Pakistan, Vietnam, Australia, India, Sri Lanka, Russia, and the United States.

Ethical Considerations: Many rubies available commercially today are mined in places like Myanmar, where the gemstone industry is rife with extreme human rights violations, environmental corruption, and the exploitation and subjugation of minorities.[280]

---

280 Atkin, "Do You Know Where Your Healing Crystals Come From?"

Magical Uses: It is the ruby's colour that associates it with the element of fire. In some traditions of witchcraft, the stone is associated with the sabbats of Samhain and the Spring Equinox. On the Kabbalistic Tree of Life, rubies are associated with the sephirah Geburah (power). Wearing ruby jewellery is considered by some to maintain a visual commentary on the health of your blood. Some claim that a ruby regularly worn against the skin will dull in the presence of a blood disorder, infection, or circulatory problems. A ruby set in gold and worn on the index or ring finger is thought by some to attract wealth and good luck to the wearer—although if you own a gold ring with a ruby set in it, you're probably doing okay for yourself already?

Spinel

energy and vitality; love and kindness; success; wealth

Spinel is a semi-precious crystal containing magnesium and aluminium, among other things. The name *spinel* comes from the Latin *spinella*, meaning spine. This is in reference to the pointed shape of these crystals. Spinels are often octahedral in shape, and come in shades of pink, blue, black, brown, or yellow. They have been found for many years in the gemstone-bearing gravel of Sri Lanka and in the limestone of the Badakshan Province in modern-day Afghanistan and Tajikistan, and of Mogok in Myanmar.

Ethical Considerations: Spinel from Myanmar and some other areas comes from mines known for extreme human rights violations, environmental corruption, and worse.[281]

Magical Uses: It's not clear when or why spinel was first associated with the element of fire in magic. Possibly it's because

---

281 Atkin, "Do You Know Where Your Healing Crystals Come From?"

of its associations with energy and vitality over the last few decades. Wearing spinel is considered by some to boost energy levels throughout the day, especially during times of physical exertion. Blue spinel is sometimes associated with communication, especially opening up lines of communication that may have become closed to you. Green spinel placed in the home or carried about the person is considered by some to promote love, compassion, and kindness. Spinel is also sometimes used in workings for attracting money, wealth, or good luck.

Sunstone

energy (general, sexual, solar); healing; introspection; luck (attracting); magic (solar); protection

Sunstone is a semi-precious stone that is translucent and appears spangled. It has been found in Norway, Sweden, the United States, and even on beaches in southern Australia.

Magical Uses: The sunstone's fiery namesake is presumably why it is associated with this element. The use of sunstones in magical workings has only cropped up in the last couple of decades. When researching them for his *Encyclopedia of Crystal, Gem and Metal Magic* during the 1980s, iconic witchy author Scott Cunningham had trouble finding many references to them at all in this context.[282] Almost forty years on, sunstones seem to have a few different associations. Worn about the person they are thought to energise the body during times of stress or ill health. Some wear sunstone, or place it about the home, to reinvigorate themselves if they're feeling flat or in an energetic rut. The stone is also sometimes worn to improve self-confidence and self-worth, and to promote assertiveness/the ability to say no. Try placing a

---

282 Cunningham, *Crystal, Gem & Metal Magic*, 216.

sunstone in your home in front of a white candle to encourage protective energies into the house.

Iron

battle and war; defence (psychic, magical); grounding; magic (defensive); protection; psychic ability; reversal; security; strength

Iron has been used by humans for thousands of years, and it has had associations with magic and superstition for almost as long. In the fires of the forge, it can be worked into any number of tools, weapons, or artefacts. In the Middle Ages, it was considered to be one of the best protections against witches, witchcraft, evil spirits, and more.[283]

IRON AS PROTECTOR

Iron's ancient associations with protection from otherworldly creatures have reached as far as modern pop culture. Horseshoes have long been considered lucky or protective, partly because they contain iron.[284] An old folkloric belief from parts of England holds that witches cannot harm you as long as you have an iron poker in your hearth fire.[285] In many folktales and modern traditions of magic, iron is a protection against faeries and faerie magic, too.

IRON AS HEALER

Iron, often combined with water, has been associated with healing and vitality for thousands of years. Around 77 CE, Pliny the Elder wrote about a health tonic made from water that had had white-hot iron plunged into it. An interesting English superstition recorded in the late 1700s held that a rusty sword stood on its end beside the bed would relieve cramps. Multiple folkloric accounts

---

283 Drury, *Watkins*, 150.
284 Drury, *Watkins*, 150.
285 Opie and Tatem, *A Dictionary of Superstitions*, 154.

dating back as far as the 1500s call for iron to be used in the treatment of warts.[286]

IRON AS TABOO

Iron was and is also considered a taboo in some circumstances. For example, it was generally forbidden from Greek sanctuaries. In some traditions of witchcraft, iron is forbidden in circles and sacred space, and magical tools such as athames are made of wood.

If an iron engraving tool needed to be brought in to inscribe stones in the sacred grove of the Arval brethren in ancient Rome, they would sacrifice a lamb or pig as the tool entered and left the sacred space.[287] In parts of Russia, plants and herbs harvested on Midsummer's Day—such as loosestrife (*Lythrum salicaria*)—were never dug up or cut with iron tools.[288] Similarly, the Roman author Pliny reported that the Druids considered iron tools to limit the efficacy of some medicinal plants.[289]

Volcanic Rocks

The three main classes or types of rock are sedimentary (formed by the silt and sediment such as sand and shells from rivers and bodies of water), metamorphic (formed by changes such as heat or pressure under the earth's surface), and igneous (formed by cooled molten rock called magma).

Igneous rocks (from the Latin word for fire, *ignis*) are another creative alternative to a fire signifier when you can't have real flames on your altar or in your circle, especially when they are painted or decorated with appropriate colours or grouped with

---

286 Opie and Tatem, *A Dictionary of Superstitions*, 209.
287 Frazer, *The Golden Bough*, Part II, 226.
288 Frazer, *The Golden Bough*, Part VII, vol. II, 65.
289 Frazer, *The Golden Bough*, 78–81.

other fire symbols. They also have magical correspondences associated with fire, and are often easier to source than some of the more expensive stones listed earlier in this chapter.

There are two types of igneous rock: intrusive igneous rocks, which crystallise below the earth's surface, where the slower cooling rate means larger crystals form; and extrusive igneous rocks, which erupt onto the earth's surface and cool much more quickly. When this cooling is especially quick, the magma forms volcanic glasses such as obsidian.[290]

Some common igneous rocks include:

Basalt: An extrusive igneous rock formed by cooling magma that is rich in magnesium and iron. Around 90 percent of all volcanic rock on earth is basalt.[291] It also can be found on celestial bodies: those dark patches visible on the moon are basalt plains. Basalt is usually dark grey or black.

Dacite: Named after the Roman province Dacia where it was first described, dacite is bluish-grey and forms in lava flows and the eruptions of undersea volcanoes.

Granite: Granite is another very common igneous rock. Granite has a coarse, grainy texture (the name "granite" comes from the Latin *granum*, a word for grain). It is usually light coloured and comes in various shades of grey-blue, pink, and cream.

Pumice: Pumice is a highly porous volcanic rock with a rough texture that makes it popular as a natural foot scrubber. Pumice is formed from the bubbly foam that occurs when magma is violently ejected from a volcano. It is usually (but not always) a lighter colour.

---

290 King, "Igneous Rocks."
291 The University of Auckland, "Basalt."

Scoria: Like pumice, scoria is also highly porous and has cavities of air all the way through. These cavities give scoria a lower density than many other rocks; it is quite light, and smaller rocks will often float in water. Scoria is formed by gases escaping cooling magma, causing it to bubble and simmer. It is usually dark brown, black, or purplish red.

To cleanse or consecrate stones for ritual use

Many folks like to consecrate their stones before they use them, as they might do with other witchy tools. Others like to cleanse and "recharge" their stones often. Whether you do this or not is up to you, but some ways you might go about cleansing and consecrating your stones might include:

- **Letting them sit exposed to the light of the full moon.** Set them on your altar during your full moon rite, or leave them on your windowsill where they can be touched by the moonlight.

- **Place them out in a rainstorm**. I've known witches who do this with a range of their magical tools. This probably isn't great for metals, though.

- **Bury them.** No, really. If you're using the power of something that's been pulled out of the earth and you feel as though it needs recalibrating, putting it back underground for a while is just as likely to do the trick as anything else.

- **Anoint them.** This is a concept borrowed from a few of my mates with ceremonial leanings. Make up an anointing oil, cast a circle if you need to, and anoint each stone, verbally "initiating" it into magical work and giving it a specific purpose.

Conclusion

It's unsurprising that so many rocks, stones, and metals are associated with the element of fire—after all, most of them are formed in the hottest, gooiest parts of the earth's mantle and deeper down besides. With a bit of research and care, you can incorporate fire stones into your workings in ways that minimise harm to our planet or the creatures who call it home.

Chapter 8

ANIMALS

The concept of using animals and animal correspondences in magical and devotional workings is truly ancient in many cultures across the world. As modern witches and Pagans, most of what we understand and use about correspondences comes from the Western magical traditions, and more emphasis on correspondences in recent decades has caused more and more people to ask ...

"What does this animal mean?"

It's a question my fellow mods and I get regularly in the online groups and forums we're in charge of. This is a complicated question with no single answer; no type of animal has an overarching "meaning" or symbolism. These symbolisms vary wildly between cultures, regions, magical traditions, and personal experiences, and usually tell us more about the people doing the viewing than the animals being viewed. Animals also live on this planet in their own right, not as a divinatory tool for you whenever you happen to see them. Seeing a raven doesn't necessarily mean anything other than the raven happened to be passing by, minding its own business as it went to find lunch. It's not there to tell you to leave your awful spouse/take that trip/get a tattoo/whatever.

There are also so many species, subsets, and subspecies of every category of animal, and these vary around the world. The correspondences for each of these—if there even are correspondences for all of them—are going to vary greatly too. Lumping all animals of one type together is completely missing the point. A close friend of mine and a fellow witchy teacher uses the example of spiders. There are more than thirty-five thousand different species of spider the world over, with more being discovered every year. Some live in trees, some spin webs, some dig burrows, some live on water, and so on. Would all of these really "represent" the exact same thing?

As I mentioned in chapter 3, it's also important to be mindful of other cultures when considering animal symbols and mythology. No story should be taken on its own, out of context of its culture, and not all stories and mythological figures are ours for the taking. Remember: the best way to learn about a culture is from the people within that culture, and in a way that gives more than you take away.

Animals and the Element of Fire

All this might have scared you off seeing animals as symbols at all. I hope it didn't. I encourage you to be mindful and not to use broad brushes when thinking about animals in magic, or treat them like furry, breathing oracle cards with no minds or lives of their own.

Below are some animals that are commonly associated with fire, written about in general terms and with some examples of how these correspondences came to be.

Bee

As far back as the Bronze Age, there is evidence of bees being venerated as culturally and mythologically significant. In Egyptian mythology, bees grew from the tears of the sun god Ra when they landed on the desert sand.[292] In ancient Greece, a priestess of goddesses such as Artemis or Demeter was usually called a *Melissa* (bee/honey bee).

In modern witchcraft and Paganism, bees are also sometimes associated with abundance and prosperity; the afterlife, spirits, and communication with the dead; agriculture and fertility; family, relationships, and community; concentration, motivation, and focus; energy, power, and vitality; knowledge, hidden wisdom, and the mind; the otherworld and the underworld; purification; rebirth and renewal; and spirituality.[293]

Cicada

Cicadas are a superfamily of insects with more than three thousand species worldwide and more still being discovered. Some species date back to the late Triassic period. Cicadas can be associated with both the fire of creativity and that of rebirth and transformation. In ancient Greece, they were eaten as a delicacy and were also associated with music and the Muses. Their song was seen as one of pure ecstasy. It is possible that their associations with rebirth, transformation, and immortality stems from their long life cycles and the long stretches of time they spend deep underground.

In modern witchcraft and Paganism, cicadas are often associated with happiness; the home; honesty; innocence; longevity; patience; success; and transformation.[294]

---

292 Norton, "Honey, I Love You."
293 Kynes, *Correspondences*, 303.
294 Kynes, *Correspondences*, 304.

Crane

Cranes have been seen as symbolic and significant for centuries, in a number of cultures around the world. This is due at least in part to their magnificent size, forms, and graceful mating dances. In Greek and Roman myths, these dances are often portrayed as symbolic of joy and the love for life, and the birds were sometimes associated with Apollo and Hephaestus and the vitality of the sun's fire. Throughout many Asian countries, they are seen as symbols of happiness, good fortune, and eternal youth.

In modern witchcraft, cranes are sometimes associated with abundance; the astral realms; balance and cycles; concentration and focus; connections to the otherworld or past lives; creativity; death and endings; divination; endurance; grace, patience, and honour; guardians; healing, wellbeing, and longevity; independence; introspection and knowledge of the self; justice; learning, knowledge, and the mind; magic; the otherworld and the underworld; peace; the protection of children; transformation, rebirth, and renewal; reversal; keeping secrets; and travel.[295]

Eagle

"Eagle" is something of a catch-all name for many different birds of prey, mostly from the *Accipitridae* family. Most of the sixty-plus species are from Eurasia and Australia. Around where I live, we have wedgetail eagles, which have a wingspan much wider than the outstretched arms of a human. They play an important role in the creation stories of the Kulin nation, five indigenous nations whose lands stretch across most of Central Victoria.

Classical writers such as Pliny the Elder wrote that eagles could look directly into the sun, and encouraged their fledglings to

---

295 Kynes, *Correspondences*, 284.

do just that.[296] Eagles also appear frequently in heraldry, where they are often representative of an empire or dominion. Modern witches and Pagans sometimes associate eagles with activating and awakening; adaptability and change; authority, respect, and leadership; awareness; balance; battle and war; beauty; communication, messages, omens, and cooperation; confidence, strength, and courage; connections between the worlds; creativity, motivation, and inspiration; dignity, peace, and freedom; enlightenment, wisdom, and knowledge; fear; fidelity; goals; grounding; guidance; healing; illumination, sight, psychic ability, hidden truths, visions, and intuition; life and longevity; magic; opportunities; passion; rebirth, transformation, and renewal; connecting with spirits; spirituality; and success.[297]

Firefly

Fireflies, glow worms, and lightning bugs are all names used to describe any of the more than two thousand species of soft-bodied beetles who use bioluminescence (emit light) to attract mates at twilight. It is because of this luminescence that these insects have been related to fire for quite some time. Like many other species, firefly numbers are declining around the world due to climate change and habitat loss.

Modern witches and Pagans sometimes associate fireflies with accomplishment; activating and awakening; communication; creativity and inspiration; light, illumination, dispelling darkness, and guidance through dark places; energy; hope; night magic and spirituality.[298]

---

296 The Medieval Bestiary, "Eagle."
297 Kynes, *Correspondences*, 286.
298 Kynes, *Correspondences*, 304.

Goat

Goats are among the oldest domesticated species of animal. Little wonder, then, that they are considered to be symbolic of so many different things by so many different cultures. As archaeologists excavated the ancient city of Ebla in Syria, they found a bronze throne decorated with ornate goat heads in the tomb of an unknown king or noble, which they dubbed thereafter "the Tomb of the Lord of the Goats." The chariot of the Norse thunder-god Thor is drawn by two goats, and the Greek god Pan has the horns and lower body of a goat. From these examples, we could relate the goat to the fire of power/vitality/leadership, the fire of thunder and lightning, and the fire of passion.

In modern witchcraft and Paganism, goats are sometimes associated with abundance; beginnings; spirits and connections with past lives; fertility; independence, stability, and emotional security; life and vitality; sex, sexuality, and sex magic; rebirth and renewal; and sight.[299]

Hawk

Hawks are medium-sized birds of prey from the *Accipitridae* family. Many hawks are reddish-brown in their colouring, and sometimes live in dry or desert areas, which could account for their early associations with the element of fire. Multiple accounts over the years from Australia's Northern Territory describe hawks, often black kites, using burning sticks from bushfires to spread the fire around, using it to flush out prey. These accounts are consistent with the stories and mythologies of several indigenous groups from the area, whose ceremonies and lore tell of the birds behaving in this way.[300]

---

299 Kynes, *Correspondences*, 272.
300 Wilson, "Ornithologist seeks to prove."

Correspondences for hawks in modern witchcraft and Paganism include the afterlife; the astral realm; awareness and clarity; balance and grounding; battle and war; psychic ability, clairvoyance, and past lives; communication, trust, and leadership; courage, fearlessness, and empowerment; creativity and skills; energy and power; life and life force; guardians; illumination; memory and memories; messages and omens; opportunities; problems; self-work; stimulation; truth; and wisdom.[301]

Hedgehog

"Hedgehog" refers to any of the spiny mammals from the subfamily *Erinaceinae*. There are seventeen species of hedgehog found through continents such as Europe, Asia, and Africa, and in New Zealand by introduction. Hedgehogs' association with the element of fire and its healing and restorative qualities could be rooted in their use as food and medicine. The nomadic Bedouins of the Middle East consider hedgehog meat to be medicinal, and it's thought to cure rheumatism and arthritis. In Morocco, inhaling the smoke of the burnt skin or bristles is an apparent remedy for fever, male impotence, and urinary tract infections/inflammations.[302]

Modern witches and Pagans sometimes associate hedgehogs with concentration and focus; defence; fertility; negativity; nurturing; pleasure and wisdom.[303]

Horse

There are many things that associate horses with the element of fire, most of them bestowed upon them by humans. As domesticated animals, they have been ridden into war, helped work blacksmiths' bellows, and even pulled carts to help extinguish fires before

301 Kynes, *Correspondences*, 288.
302 Qumsiyeh, *Mammals of the Holy Land*, 64–65.
303 Kynes, *Correspondences*, 273.

the advent of cars and trucks. The centaur representing fire sign Sagittarius is half horse, and many of the solar deities explored in chapter 3 ride across the skies in horse-drawn boats or chariots.

There are many common magical correspondences with horses, including abundance and wealth; swift action; the astral realm; awareness; danger, battle, and war; change and changes; clairvoyance and divination; communication, friends, and friendship; cooperation; darkness and obstacles; death and burials; dedication and devotion; desire; destiny; destruction; love and emotions; courage and endurance; energy and life; fertility; freedom; guidance; travellers and travelling; light; magic; nightmares; the otherworld and the underworld; personal power; protection; spiritual quests; rebirth and renewal; secrets and initiation; sex and sexuality; spirits; and youth.[304]

Ladybird

Ladybirds, or ladybugs in the USA, were named after the virgin Mary as areas became Christianised. Before this, many areas of Europe referenced the Norse goddess Freja in the name for these beautiful red-backed insects; *Freyjuhæna* and variants are evident across many countries. Another regionalised name for these creatures is bishop-that-burneth, which might be a reference to their fiery red wings when they take off. The famous children's nursery rhyme also connects the ladybird to this element:

> Ladybird, ladybird, fly away home
> Your house is on fire and your children are gone

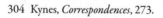

304 Kynes, *Correspondences*, 273.

In modern witchcraft and Paganism, ladybirds are sometimes associated with agriculture; goals; happiness and good luck; messages and omens; problems; and wishes.[305]

Lion

The lion remains one of the most recognised animals in human culture, and one of the most commonly used animal symbols of fire. The Egyptian warrior goddess Sekhmet was often portrayed as a fire-breathing lioness, Leo is the chief fire sign of the zodiac, and lion imagery appears in fire temples and temples for fire deities in different part of Egypt, Europe, and the Middle East. Lion amulets or imagery are often worn as a symbol of rulership, strength, and dominion.

Modern magicians, witches, and Pagans sometimes associate lions with affection; authority, power, and leadership; community, unity, and cooperation; courage and strength; dignity, pride, and integrity; energy; family; jealousy; justice; spirituality and divine knowledge; light; passion; patience; prosperity; protection; rebirth and renewal; release; respect; stress; and wisdom.[306]

Lizard

In many cultures, lizards share some symbolism with snakes, as they represent rebirth and transformation, as does the element of fire. Many First Nations peoples have their own stories about lizards connected to art, creativity, and immortality. Imagery of lizards in ancient Egypt sometimes signified wisdom or abundance.

Lizards are sometimes associated with the following in modern witchcraft and Paganism: agriculture; change and changes; consciousness, the mind, and illumination; intuition, prophecy,

---

305 Kynes, *Correspondences*, 305.
306 Kynes, *Correspondences*, 275.

psychic ability, visions, and divination; sleep and controlling dreams; defence; energy; fear; growth; inspiration; learning; longevity; loss; the otherworld and the underworld; peace; transformation, rebirth, and renewal; and sensitivity.[307]

Ram

Evidence of rams being venerated in some way exists across many cultures and eras, from the ancient near-Eastern religions right up to the Christian, Jewish, and Islamic faiths and beyond. Chrysomallos, the golden-fleeced ram, was the original symbol of the fire sign Aries.

Modern witches and Pagans sometimes associate rams with fertility; generosity; healing; imagination and the mind; inspiration; power and warmth.[308]

Raven

Ravens are associated with fire—especially the theft of fire—in the mythologies of many different cultures. Each culture's story is unique to them, and many tell of the role that fire and a mythological figure of Raven played in the creation of the world.

Ravens feature heavily in many modern witchcraft and Pagan traditions. Some practitioners associate them with the love/affection of a family; battle, war, and battlefields; growth, change, and changes; clairvoyance, messages, visions, omens, prophecy, and divination; clarity and consciousness; communication and connections; courage; the crossroads; death and loss; destiny, quests, and opportunities; gratitude, favour, and favours; guardians and guidance; healing; honouring elders and ancestors; the mind, wisdom, intelligence, and learning; introspection; life; magic and

---

307 Kynes, *Correspondences*, 301.
308 Kynes, *Correspondences*, 280.

manifestation; memory and memories; the otherworld and the underworld; protection; rebirth and renewal; and hearing.[309]

Salamander

Often wrongly labelled as reptiles, salamanders are lizard-like amphibians that live in cool, damp places. Legends have developed around the salamander over the centuries, many related to fire. This connection likely comes from the tendency of many salamanders to dwell inside rotting logs, which are often used for firewood. When the log was placed into a fire, the salamander would attempt to escape, lending credence to the belief that salamanders were created from flames.

Real-world salamanders are easily confused with the elemental creatures of the same name. You can read more about these in chapter 2.

Snake

Snakes are another animal whose associations with fire are centuries old. The Kundalini ("coiled snake") in Hindu Tantra is the vital force believed to be located at the base of the spine, in the *muladhara*. Modern witches and Pagans sometimes associate snakes with the afterlife; assertiveness; cycles, transformation, change, and changes; creativity; cunning; enchantment; energy, life, and life force; fertility; forgiveness; jealousy; mysteries; boundaries and limitations; longevity; lust, sex, and sexuality; magic and manifestation; the otherworld and the underworld; prophecy and psychic ability; quests; rebirth and renewal; storms; wisdom and wellbeing.[310]

---

309 Kynes, *Correspondences*, 293.
310 Kynes, *Correspondences*, 301.

• • • •

Pathworkings: Animals and the Element of Fire

Rose Barkey is a Pagan witch from the tall Mountain Ash forests of Melbourne, Australia. She has been practicing since the 1980s, and has a particular interest in Bronze Age culture, herbalism, horse lore, and English folk magic.

Meeting Your Animal Guide

Find somewhere comfortable and quiet to sit, where you won't be disturbed. If you are able to light a fire—either outdoors or in a fireplace indoors, do; but since that's not possible for everyone, this is written as a pathworking exercise, to be visualised internally. If you have access to a fire, you can adapt this by looking into the actual flames, instead of the flames you have conjured in your imagination. Both are effective in their own way. You can record this pathworking, to play back while you visualise, if it helps. Remember to speak slowly, and allow time for your mind to immerse in the images that come to you. In order to connect more deeply, you can light a candle, or burn some incense with fire associations.

Sit or lie comfortably, with your shoulders wide so you can breathe deeply. Allow yourself to relax, and let the worries of the outside world drift away. Let yourself focus on your intent; you may wish to make contact with an animal spirit to be your working companion in the element of fire, or an introduction to the realms of fire in the Otherworlds. You may wish for insight into the qualities that you associate with this element: courage, action, ferocity, transformation, quickness, passion, healing, or creativity. Whatever your intent, let yourself explore it now, until it is the thing that is foremost in your mind. How does the thought feel? Hold on to that feeling. What questions do you have? What are the lessons you wish to learn? Remember them.

Now, let the image of a fire enter your mind. Let the details gradually fill themselves in. Is the fire indoors, in a cosy stone hearth, provid-

ing warmth? Is it outdoors: a campfire in the forest or the desert, or a bonfire in the centre of a stone circle, or a roaring wildfire? Are you close to it, or far away, or surrounded by it? Is it comforting, inspiring, transformational, terrifying? This is your first insight; the fire of your imagination will give you clues about your needs right now. Spend time with the fire, learn from it. You are safe, it cannot hurt you; the fire you have conjured is here to teach you, inspire you, and guide you. If you can, immerse yourself in the details around you, and the feelings they evoke; the smell and taste of woodsmoke; the crackle of the fire and the dance of flames; the shifting colours in the coals; the warmth or heat on your skin; the landscape around you. Let yourself feel at home with the fire; do you walk closer? Sit down? You may explore as you please, but keep the fire as your focus, let it fill your senses.

Remember your intent, and the feelings it evoked in you. Let that intent fill your mind as you look at the fire before you. Let that intent become desire, a wish. In your mind's eye, stretch out your hands towards the fire, and let that wish become a call, to meet your guide, an animal spirit to teach you the ways of fire. Imagine closing your eyes; you can still hear the flames, and feel the heat on the palms of your hands, smell smoke. Breathe deeply, and sharpen your inner senses; can you feel a change? From the spirit realms, your guide is coming. Perhaps you can feel them against your fingertips, sense them nearby, hear them. Can you feel their breath or their wings against your skin?

Do they make a sound? It may take a while; be patient, they will find you. When you feel them there, open your inner eye and look at them. This is your guide at this time. You may be surprised by the animal that has appeared, but do not be dismayed; fairy tales have taught us that we may learn from the most unlikely of creatures, and all have wisdom to give.

Take a moment in stillness to introduce yourself. You are introducing your spirit to theirs; tell them your name, and thank them for coming to you. Ask them if there is a name they would prefer to be called. Wait for their response. It may not be vocal; look deeply into their eyes, do you see wisdom, understanding, curiosity? Do you see the firelight dancing in their eyes, the shimmer of it on their coat? You have met your guide.

What happens next is up to you, and to them. Ask questions, or request their guidance and companionship in your workings, and pay attention to their responses. Always be courteous to creatures from the other realms. Remember what their presence beside you feels like, so you recognise the feeling in the future if they return. They may return to you again and become a regular working companion, or be present only for this one pathworking. You may revisit the fire you conjured in this visualisation, or invoke the essence of fire differently every time. As with all visualisations, you'll get better at it every time you try— pathworking is a powerful magical technique that gets easier with practice and discipline.

Meeting the Lion of Fire

Prepare for this visualisation as you did the previous one; sit or lie comfortably, making sure you are able to breathe deeply and evenly.

You find yourself on a vast, golden plain. It's midday in summer, and the grass is tall, seeded, just at the height of its growth, and it ripples like water in the breeze. The sun on your face is warm and pleasant; the gold light suffuses everything with warmth, and everything it touches is radiant.

Breathe deeply; you can smell the warm-straw scent of the savannah in the air. You put out your hand, and brush it along the tops of the seedheads that bend gracefully under your touch. There's a path through the long grass; step onto it. You walk calmly and easily along the path, under the clear blue sky above you, bathed in golden light.

Ahead is a clearing. At the entrance to the clearing, there are two torches made from thickly braided grass, wrapped around straight poles, one on either side, unlit. You pause, feeling instinctively there is something here that needs to be done in order for you to enter this space, and wondering what it might be.

A raven swoops in and lands on top of the torch to your left. Intelligence sparkles in those bright black eyes, and the raven dips her head to speak to you.

"You wish to enter this space and learn of fire?"

You nod courteously, knowing that you are speaking to the spirit of the raven that brought fire to humanity so long ago.

"You must bring your own fire with you, and offer it in payment."

You are confused; you don't have any fire, not even a lighter, but the bird is looking at you with conviction and expectation, and you know you possess the answer, or you wouldn't have made it this far. You cast your mind over the reasons you are here, and the lessons you wish to learn; what fire means to you.

The spark of life, which animates you.

The passion you bring to your endeavours.

The initiative and courage that has brought you this far along the path.

The warmth and comfort you offer to those you love.

The "Fire in the Head" of inspiration and creativity.

The bright burning fury that blazes when called, and which you are still learning to control.

The power of transmutation; the transformation of one thing to another.

All of this you consider, and you know that all of this is contained within you, though it is part of your ongoing journey to fully realise it. In this moment you understand that you and fire are kindred; it is part of you, part of your essence.

CHAPTER 8

At that moment you know what to do. You reach your hand up, and touch the torch on your right. You feel the answer tingle through your fingertips, and the torch flares to life, dancing with flames. "Well done," says the raven to your left, and takes to the air, so that you may light the torch on which she stood. Your elation adds to the warmth flooding through you as you light the second torch. You know you are welcome to enter now, and worthy to attempt the lesson to come.

You enter the clearing. Behind you, you can hear the breeze teasing the flames of the torches, and smell the sweetness of the smoke. The earth is soft and warm underfoot, and all around you, the savannah stretches like a great, gold sea. There is a large, flat-topped stone in the centre, on which the raven lands. The sun blazes brightly above you, and within the circle you feel the vibration in the air—of potential, action, a quiver of excitement. On the opposite side of the circle, the grass is moving; the stalks quivering like snakes. Something is coming.

Out of the grass steps a lion. A magnificent creature, he paces towards you, meeting your eyes with his steady, golden gaze. You watch the muscles shifting in his shoulders, the flex of his great paws as they land on the warm earth. His coat is tawny, sleek, and unmarred, and his mane ... his mane is like living flame. It flickers and dances as he moves, in shades of gold and orange, bright-tipped and beautiful. He is all the grace and power of wild things; dangerous and terrible and lovely beyond words. His tail flicks behind him, tipped in flame. His eyes do not leave yours.

"You have called him," says the raven, on the stone behind you. "How do you answer?"

And how DO you answer? You are drawn to such beauty and afraid of it. Like fire, you realise. Like wild things. Like inspiration and fury and love.

You take a step towards him, and he growls, deep in his throat, with narrowed eyes. You pause, and bow, a hand instinctively extended, in the age-old gesture of reassuring wild creatures that you come in peace. And he comes to you, hot breath searing your out-stretched fingertips, not quite pain but almost, and you see the flames on his mane lick over his shoulders as his chest moves with his breath. You almost step away, but stand your ground. This is the courage of the fire within you, answering the challenge.

Behind you, you hear the raven let out an audible breath, relaxing, and you know you have passed another test.

The lion moves away, brushing against you and swinging his head to indicate that you should follow, so you walk together to the stone on which the raven sits. There's no fear in the raven's eyes as the lion huffs a greeting, but the bird hops back nonetheless.

"You came here to learn of fire," says the raven. "Fire consumes; it burns away what can be destroyed. It is hunger. It is transformation, but you must be strong enough to master it. You have come here to learn of fire, and to do that, you must offer yourself up to be burned."

You should be afraid, you know, and yet, this is what you came for. The lion leaps onto the stone and with his face at the height of your own, comes close, until his breath is hot and sweet on your skin. You know, somehow, that you must reach up your hands, and touch that rippling mane, bury your fingers in living flame, find the courage to surrender. And you do. It is soft, not as hot as you feared, and the joy of that fills your chest to bursting as you wrap your fingers in the flickering cascade, combing and stroking. With wonder you meet the lion's eyes, and they see deep into you ... and the mane you touch becomes hotter, and those eyes see deeper. They see your fears, and the shadows in you that hide from firelight; fear of inspiration, of action, of love, of healing. The flames burn your hands, and those deep yellow eyes burn your soul and you cannot pull away, despite it. And in those fathomless eyes, and spreading outwards from your hands, gold turns to green, and the smell of sulphur fills your nostrils as you are laid bare before the lion of flame.

Some part of you knows this is part of fire; not the comfortable warmth of hearth and candle, but the cleansing, purifying blaze that turns metal to liquid and landscapes to ash, and you are here to know the power of fire. And so you feed the flames with your fear, as the lion blazes bright and green, and you feel the fire within you flare up and illuminate all the shadowed corners of yourself.

With a roar, the lion tips back its great head, as you stagger backwards, and you see its jaws silhouetted around the sun, high above you. And then those jaws close, and everything is dark. The sun is gone, and in the dim light of the torches that still burn at the gateway to the circle, you see the lion; a suggestion of lean muscle and grace and glinting eyes, sitting on the stone. You are not afraid; all of your fear was consumed in that bright blaze, and instead, you feel... yourself. Awed and humbled, but centred and strong, and sure of your path. You cross the warm earth to the stone, and reach out a hand to stroke the long mane, now fur beneath your fingers. You have submitted every darkened crevice of your soul to this beast, and been tempered, and now you come forward, transformed and fearless; a witch before a great spirit of the elements. The lion's gaze is gentle, and he lowers his head again, and opens his mouth. Deep in that red cavern, behind curved white fangs, is the sun.

"You must return the sun to the world," says the raven, who has been sitting on the corner of the stone, "or all will be lost to darkness."

You look to the lion for permission, and then reach your hand past those sharp teeth, and close your hand around the sun. Its warmth is in proportion to its size, and you marvel that you can cradle the source of all life on earth in your palm, and not be burned. Gently, you pull the sun out from between those powerful jaws, until you hold it, glowing, in the darkness of the clearing.

"Now!" caws the raven, and you lift it aloft, where it flares into brightness, blinding you with the light of midday and spilling gold

across the fields once more. As your eyes adjust, and you lower your hand, you find something still nestled in your palm. A tiny golden lion sits there; pure and gleaming, made from the base metal of the fears you conquered with fire. This is your talisman, now, and you can conjure it in your mind, when you have need.

The lion jumps down from the stone, and comes to stand by you. You understand that the lesson is over, and it is time for you to return to your world. You stroke his neck once more in thanks; he shakes his head, noble and relaxed, and flowers fall from his mane, taking root in the bare earth and filling the air with a sweet, herbal scent. As feathery green leaves emerge, you notice it is Roman chamomile, the plant that legend says was dedicated to the sun by the ancient Egyptians, its seeds carried to Rome in the manes of lions, and discovered growing in the Coliseum, long after the last games had finished. It spreads in the lion's path as he walks with you to the entrance, between the torches you lit, and there he stops. You have learned what you came for, and you have your talisman. It is time for you to return to the world, carrying this new knowledge with you.

You step between the torches, and into the sunlit plains, towards the world.

Rose Barkey

• • • •

Conclusion

The concept of using animals and animal correspondences in magical and devotional workings is a very old one. And while animal correspondences and symbolism may not be as clear-cut as some would like it to be in modern witchcraft and Paganism, we can still build it into our practice in a considered, mindful, and above all meaningful way.

PART
3
ᴓ

RECIPES, RITUALS & SPELLCRAFT

Fire, Spirit of the Sun,
Wax, thou melted flesh of Earth,
Prove this work that I have done,
Bring me love, and beggar death.
Let me be myself consumed
Not by darkness but by light,
Warmth, not cold, until I spend
My final flame against the night.[311]

—VALERIE WORTH, *THE CRONE'S BOOK OF WORDS*

311 Worth, *The Crone's Book of Words*, 29.

Chapter 9

CANDLES AND CANDLE MAGIC

Candles feature in the ceremonies of religions across the world, including most Pagan and witchcraft traditions. We use candles on our altars to signify fire, the sun, or deity; to mark the quarters; in remembrance; and in magical workings. Candle magic has long been a popular, accessible form of magic to practitioners of many different stripes and walks of life, and most witches consider candles to be one of the staple ingredients of many of their workings. In my rituals, I generally have a single candle in a lantern (we usually work outside) that represents the element of fire and the north quarter. Three other lanterns represent the other quarters at their appropriate place in the circle.

Types of Candle

How long a candle burns depends somewhat on its size, but mostly on the condition of the wick. The size of the flame and hence the rate of a candle burning is controlled largely by the candle wick.

A candle wick works by capillary action, drawing ("wicking") the melted wax or fuel up to the flame. This is the same process that allows the sap of a tree to reach its highest branches. When the liquid fuel reaches the flame, it vaporizes and combusts. The quality of a candle's wick influences how the candle burns. Important characteristics of the wick include diameter, stiffness, fire-resistance, and tethering. Commercial candle wicks are made from cotton that is braided. They are often infused with chemicals to modify their burning characteristics. For example, it is usually desirable that the wick not glow after the candle's flame is snuffed or extinguished.

Taper candles: Long and slender, usually tapered at the top. The eighteen-inch ones have around a ten-hour burn time. The standard size (about twenty centimetres long) ones make a good choice for candle magic.

Tealight candles: Small disc candles that usually come in little aluminium cases. Used in oil-burners, lanterns, etc., or as accent lighting. These have a burn time of around two hours.

Pillar candles: Short, fat candles that come in a variety of sizes. Often less smoky than tapers. Sometimes scented. The burn time of these will depend on how thick and tall they are.

Potted or container candles: These are candles that come in their own fireproof container. These are a good option for soy candles, as soy goes runny when it heats up. Be careful when buying cheap candles in glass containers, as these are not always properly tempered and sometimes explode if they get too hot.

Votive candles: Small, wide candles about fifteen centimetres tall and around ten centimetres thick. These need to be burned in a holder or stand, or on a plate. Often used in churches.

Floating candles: Lightweight candles designed to float on water. These are usually small discs with a base narrower than their top, to prevent them from tipping over as they float.

Birthday candles: Don't laugh. The skinny, colourful candles you see on birthday cakes work great in a pinch, or for rituals on the go. Some people carry one as part of a "mini altar" in their purse or car glovebox, ready to be set up away from home if needed.

Cartridge/chakra/chime candles: These are small candles about as long as your finger. Often used in vigils or as a one-off spell component. A great choice for candle magic.

Spell candles: Candles created for a specific spell or intention (love, luck, money, etc.). These are the ones that are typically found in New Age shops, and they are usually around eight inches long.

Hanukkah menorah candles: These slender candles are made for use in menorahs during Hanukkah. They are often of high quality, and are great for lighting other candles.

Gel candles: These consist of a wick in high-density gel, set in a fireproof container. These are used for decorative purposes but are unsafe to burn for extended periods of time.

Flameless candles: These days, many options exist for realistic candles that emit a flickering "candle" light without the need for actual fire. Either battery or solar powered, these candles are a good alternative for those who can't have actual flames around due to small children, pets, or landlords, or for those like me who live in a country that has fire restrictions almost half the year. You can also use them in hotel settings, or other indoor spaces that don't allow open flames.

Buying Candles

Candles can be bought reasonably cheaply from many mundane stores if you're after the basics. There are also a lot of handmade options available online and at markets. Try witchy retailers if you're after something specific, but be prepared to pay a little more. Candles are relatively easy to make, too, if you're that way inclined.

Cheap wax candles are often smokier, smellier, and not especially good for you. When you buy candles, look for a good, strong wick that sits in the exact centre of the candle. A wick that is too thin or sitting at an angle will mean your candle will not burn as long as it should. If scented candles are your thing, try to go for good quality and subtle scents. Too much cheap oil or chemicals can leave your space smelling like a perfumery and your ritualists with migraines.

Painted candles, candles with herbs and crystals inside, or with fancy decorated wrappings might seem more "witchy," but they are completely impractical when it comes to serious ritual use. Often those decorated candles you can buy online are painted in cheap paint that can release toxic fumes once heated (see later in this chapter for more tips on buying candles for ritual use).

Always remove any paper or plastic from a candle before you light it. Yep, that decal of a skull/moon/anatomically correct heart looks cool, but I'm speaking from experience when I say that they lose any aesthetic appeal *very* quickly when they ignite during a quiet part of the ritual, causing absolute chaos and stress for everyone present!

How Candles are Made

Early candles were made from beeswax or tallow, which was rendered from animal fat. From the mid-1800s they were also made from spermaceti, a waxy substance derived from the sperm whale, and stearin, which was initially manufactured from animal fats but these days is produced almost exclusively from palm waxes. Today, most candles are made from paraffin wax, a by-product of the process of refining petroleum, though beeswax (a by-product of honey collection) candles are also pretty readily available. You might also see candles made from microcrystalline wax, gel (a mixture of polymer and mineral oil), or some plant waxes. Plant waxes are usually soy based, but can also be derived from palm, carnauba, or bayberry.

Many modern candle production methods rely on extrusion moulding. This is an automated process that squeezes a long length of material—in this case, usually paraffin wax—out in a malleable form, which is then moulded into a long thin tube and cut into lengths ... kind of like what you might have done with play-dough as a kid. More traditional candle-making methods melt the solid fuel by the controlled application of heat. The liquid is then poured into a mould, or a wick is repeatedly immersed in the liquid to create a dipped tapered candle. In both processes, fragrance oils, essential oils, or aniline-based dyes are often added.

To Make Your Own Candles

Soy candles are probably the easiest to make. You can buy candle-making soy wax or even candle-making kits in craft and hobby stores, and online too. As well as wax, you'll need a wick, a spatula, and a heat-proof container that will hold your candle. A double-boiler saucepan is also a must, as you will need it to melt your wax.

To begin, measure out how much unmelted wax fills your container, then double that. This is how much wax you'll need once it is melted. Put the wax into the top part of your double boiler (you should have water boiling in the bottom one) and allow it to melt for ten to fifteen minutes, stirring regularly. As the wax is melting, use this time to attach your wick. Do this by dipping it in the melting wax then quickly sticking it to the bottom of the empty container. Let the wax sit five minutes so it can harden.

If you want to add any fragrance oils to your candle wax, this is the time to add them. DO THIS SPARINGLY ... only a few drops if you must use them at all. Remember that an overly perfumed candle can be distracting in ritual and a trigger for allergies and asthma.

Before you pour the wax into your container, let it cool for three to five minutes or so. Then, slowly pour the wax into your container. As you pour, hold the wick in place, but don't pull on it because it will come loose from where you secured it. Leave a small amount of wax in the boiler for finishing off your candle later.

Use two sticks, pencils, or skewers balanced across the opening of your container to hold the wick in place as the wax cools. Leave your candle to sit and harden for five to eight hours at room temperature. One of the benefits of working with soy wax is that it can easily be reheated and reset if your candle sets wonky or with an uneven top.

When your candle has hardened and you're happy with it, trim the wick to half an inch long before you light it.

Candle Safety

All ritual workings conducted carry some kind of risk, and working with any type of open flame holds perhaps the more immediate and obvious ones. Most of these can be minimised with a bit of common sense and forward planning.

Always employ common sense when working with candles. They are easily overlooked as a safety risk as they are so commonplace, especially in the lives of witches, Pagans, and occultists. Nevertheless, candles are the cause of thousands of house and structure fires around the world every year.

From 2012 to 2016, fire departments in America responded to more than eight thousand house fires started by candles every year. On average, these fires caused around 80 deaths, 770 serious injuries and $264 million in damage per year in the US alone.

To minimise risks when working with candles, keep the following in mind:

- **Do not leave candles burning unattended** or if there is a chance you'll fall asleep or otherwise lose consciousness. If you are doing a working that involves meditation, trance, or any other form of altered consciousness, the safest option is to ensure the candle is secured inside a fireproof vessel such as a lantern, or at least sitting in a ceramic dish of sand or earth.

- **Never leave children unattended around lit candles.** This might seem like a no-brainer, but is easy enough to forget when both kids and candles are part of your day to day.

- **Keep curtains and blinds well away from lit candles.** Often tying a curtain up out of the way is not enough— remember that the area above a candle gets very hot as well, and in time will easily singe or even combust fabric, even if it is several feet above the flame. It's better to keep windows closed and remove long or flowing curtains completely if you're placing a candle in a windowsill— and don't forget a fireproof dish.

- **If a ritual or working involves more than one person lighting candles** (for example, a candle lighting service or lighting candles around a circle of people), always have the person holding the unlit candle be the one tipping their candle to light it from a lit candle, rather than vice versa. Once a candle is lit, it should be held as upright as possible.

- **Be mindful of those with respiratory or sensory issues.** Avoid heavily scented candles as they can be a trigger for those suffering from asthma or other conditions. Strong, synthetic scents can also be distracting if you are doing work that involves participants' full concentration.

- **When extinguishing candles, be considerate of others.** If you're working in a small indoor space like a living room, take candles outside or to another part of the house so that you can your fellow ritualists aren't breathing in candle smoke for the next twenty minutes.

- **Always use enclosed, fire-safe containers when using candles outdoors.** My group uses little metal lanterns with glass panels that hold tealight candles and have doors that latch shut, allowing maximum light and meaning we don't have to keep fussing over them when they blow out or struggle in the open air. We picked them up reasonably cheaply from a homewares store.

Candles and Divination

Candles have been used for divinatory purposes for centuries. Two of the most common methods are ceromancy and lychnomancy.

Ceromancy: Divination with Candle Wax and Water

Ceromancy refers to divination with melted candle wax. Fill a bowl with very cold water, light and hold a candle, and focus on an issue or question before tipping it to let the wax fall into the bowl and watching for auspicious signs.

Lychnomancy: Divination with Candle Flame

Lychnomancy is scrying performed with a candle flame. You can do it by centring yourself and focusing on the flame quietly. This is sometimes done with the flames of three candles arranged in a triangle. Some of the common associations made in lychnomancy are:

Blue flickers in the flame: Bad news ahead, unwanted visitors, the presence of spirits.[312] See "Other Fire Omens."

Letters or Writing: Messages, favourable news, unexpected visitors, family[313]

Soot on the Wick: A stranger; someone new[314]

Wick Glows Brightly at the Tip: A lover, spouse, or sweetheart[315]

Candle Magic

Wiccan author Julia Philips once described candle magic as "one of the most common and effective types of magic used."[316] I'm inclined to agree. It is definitely a quite accessible form of magic to learn as it can be learned relatively easily and doesn't require loads of expensive or rare tools or components to do. It's also pretty effective, once you know what you're doing.

Shorter, thicker candles are better than skinny tapers for candle magic, but use what you have on hand before going out and buying something fancy. Candles used for candle magic are best left to burn naturally rather than blowing or snuffing them out (do make sure you read the section on candle safety this chapter if you plan on doing this).

Generally, candle magic usually involves picking a candle or candles of the appropriate colour; charging, dressing, or anointing them with oil; and sometimes carving them with certain symbols, names, or sigils.

---

312 Opie and Tatem, *A Dictionary of Superstitions,* 54.
313 Opie and Tatem, *A Dictionary of Superstitions,* 56.
314 Opie and Tatem, *A Dictionary of Superstitions,* 56.
315 Opie and Tatem, *A Dictionary of Superstitions,* 56.
316 Philips and Philips, *The Witches of Oz,* 53.

Candle Colours and Correspondences	
Issue or Intention	*Candle Colour*[317]
banishing and defensive magic; change and changes; death and the afterlife; receiving or attracting energy; witches and witchcraft	Black
the astral realm; dream work and sleep; emotions; receptive energy	Blue
compassion; gentleness; harmony	Blue (aqua)
impulsiveness; changeability; occult power; night magic	Blue (dark)
ancestors; balance (general, spiritual); clarity; clairvoyance; communication with spirits	Blue (indigo)
calming; emotional growth; patience and understanding; tranquillity	Blue (light)
confidence; happiness; increase; influence; loyalty; psychic ability; strength	Blue (royal)
balance; creativity; growth; healing; peace; prosperity	Blue (turquoise)
agriculture and gardening; balance; grounding; nature and earth magic	Brown
attraction; confidence; the sun and solar energy; increase; influence	Gold
abundance; fertility; growth; luck; spirits (especially nature spirits)	Green
ambition; jealousy	Green (dark)

317 Kynes, *Correspondences*, 425–434.

Issue or Intention	Candle Colour[318]
harmony; influence	Green (sea)
cancellation; challenges; neutrality; the otherworld and the underworld; stability; stagnation or stalemate	Grey
adaptability; attraction; courage; encouragement; stimulation	Orange
adaptability; beauty; communication; confidence; encouragement; happiness; strength	Orange (peach)
honour; life; love and romance; morality; passion; peace	Pink
activating and awakening; enlightenment; friends and friendship; honour; love; morality; passion; patience; peace; romance; wellbeing; youth	Pink (rose)
ambition; manifestation; power; skills; success in business; transformation	Purple
death; grief; magic	Purple (dark)
dignity; gentleness; growth (spiritual); intelligence; psychic ability	Purple (lavender)
happiness; spirits	Purple (lilac)
love; sex and sexuality	Purple (mauve)
the astral realm; concentration and focus; connections (higher self); creativity and the arts	Purple (violet)
health and vitality; sex and sexuality; strength	Red

318 Kynes, *Correspondences*, 425–434.

Issue or Intention	Candle Colour[319]
empathy; grief	Red (Crimson)
moon magic; enchantment; energy (general, psychic); protection (psychic, spiritual); spirituality	Silver
beginnings; clarity; consecrating and blessing; healing	White
friends and friendship; happiness; the home; imagination; memory and memories; peace	Yellow
anger and arguments; cowardice; discord; illness; jealousy	Yellow (greenish-yellow)

Candle Anointing Oil

You can buy different anointing oils for different purposes, or you can have a go at making your own oils for specific ritual purposes by adding essential oils or steeping the relevant herbs in a carrier oil such as olive, sunflower, or almond oil. Remember to always use multiple sources to research any ingredient before you let it come into contact with your skin.

To make a generic oil that will suit most candle magic, try:

INGREDIENTS:

⅛ cup carrier oil (olive, almond, sunflower, etc.)

4 drops sandalwood oil

2 drops orange oil

2 drop patchouli oil

---

319 Kynes, *Correspondences*, 425–434.

To mix oils together, always swirl gently rather than stir or shake. You may wish to consecrate this oil in a way you see fit before you use it, but it's a matter of personal preference whether you do or don't. Store oils in a tightly sealed or stoppered jar/bottle made of glass or ceramic. Label them carefully and store them in a cool, dark place.

If the idea of making your own oils appeals to you, take a look at books and articles on the subject by authors such as Amy Blackthorn, Patti Wiginton, Sandra Kynes, Celeste Rayne Heldstab, or Scott Cunningham.

Candle Magic Ritual

There are loads of different ways to perform candle magic. The one I am including here is no more or less valid. Read up on some alternatives, experiment, and use what works for you.

INGREDIENTS:
   A candle (in a colour appropriate to your working)
   Tools and other items needed to cast a circle (if you plan on using one)
   A cloth or surface to work on
   Candle anointing oil
   Incense (optional)
   A toothpick or skewer for inscribing your candle
   Matches or lighter

1. **Set your intention.** Think carefully about who this magic is for, whom it will affect, what the ideal outcome will look like. Always get someone's consent before performing magic for them. I like to spend a good couple of days mulling all this over—visualising, considering, and daydreaming. This seems to work best when my mind is

half-focused on something mundane, like doing dishes or sorting laundry.

2. **Gather the components for your working.** Different coloured candles have different correspondences. A white or black candle will usually do for most cases, if coloured candles aren't available. Gather any herbs and oils, and any other ritual bits and pieces you might need for casting a circle, if you plan on using one.

3. **Set the scene.** Make sure where you will be working will be safe to burn candles. If you're working indoors, tidy up the room, removing as much clutter as possible. Many people find it beneficial to give the floors and surfaces of a room a good clean before they begin a magical working. Make sure the space is quiet, that electronic devices are off, moved away, or placed on silent. Ensure you have a space to work; an altar is ideal, or just a clear surface like a coffee table that you're okay with perhaps dribbling wax on if accidents happen. Put down a non-treasured cloth, etc., if you're really worried.

4. **Prepare yourself.** Different traditions give different instructions for readying oneself for ritual. One simple and generally agreed-upon method is just to make sure you are rested, clean, and fed. Bathe or take a shower. Put on clean clothes (or go skyclad [naked], or wear ritual garb if that's what you're more comfortable in). Make sure you are fed and comfortable. You will concentrate much better if your basic needs are met.

5. **Begin.** Many folks like to burn incense or light a "working" candle to get into a ritual mindset at this point. You might like to do the same. Quite a lot of the candle

magic workings printed in modern witchy books require incense to be burned alongside your working, so if this is something you plan on doing semi-regularly it might be worth investing in a censer or thurible, which will allow you to burn raw incense blends on charcoal disks, which is just lovely; once you get the hang of this, you won't want to go back to premade sticks and cones!

If you're so inclined, cast a circle or set up your sacred space in a way that works for you. Centre yourself with a few deep breaths while you remember the actions and intentions you thought about and visualised in step one. When you're ready, verbalise this intention. Speaking words out loud gives them power.

6. **Dress your candle.** This involves anointing it in oil, rubbing it in from the centre to the ends. Oil, obviously, is flammable; don't use too much. Concentrate hard on the issue or intention of this working as you do so.

   After dressing a candle, some practitioners like to roll it on the altar while focusing on the intention of the ritual. For workings to bring energy to you or the subject of the working, roll the candle towards yourself. If you are performing this working to banish or disperse something, roll it away from you.

7. **Inscribe your candle.** This could involve carving a certain sigil, rune, or even your subject's name onto the candle. In doing this, you are charging the candle with your intention. For workings that involve burning the candle for a little time each day/night, some folks like to put notches down the candle indicating how much should be burned at a time.

8. **Light the candle.** Omit this step if you are preparing the candle to give to somebody else. If you plan to burn the candle yourself, place it in a fire-safe container and light it. Many workings will require you to leave the lit candle burning until there is nothing left. Only do this if it's safe.

9. **Finish.** Thank and make offerings to any deities or spirits you need to. Close down your sacred space and ground yourself. Leave the candle burning if it is safe to do so.

Conclusion

In religions and spiritualities the world over, candles play an important part in ceremonies more often than not. Witches are no exception to this. As well as altar candles, quarter candles, and candles for deity and spirit, many witches employ the art of candle magic in their regular work. The information above should set you up to get started in candle magic. Read it, practice, and go off and read more if this is something that interests you. You'll find that once you grow accustomed to using candle magic, it is handy in a range of circumstances and for a variety of intentions and issues that might come to your door.

Chapter 10

YOUR RITUAL FIRE

If you're lucky enough to have the space and land for a bonfire, you'll probably agree there is something wonderfully hypnotic and homely about a lit fire. The crackle-pop of a little bonfire is like the punctuation of my group's rituals. They just wouldn't be the same without the light, the warmth, and the cosiness that a fire brings, but that doesn't mean it's something we take for granted or become lax in supervising.

The aim of this chapter is to provide you with enough information to confidently, safely, and legally use fire in rituals, whether you are working alone, with a few friends, or in a larger group setting.

Types of Ritual Fire

You can build fires of different sizes for different settings and ritual contexts. Your space, time, and resources will probably dictate a lot around what sort of fire you build.

Hearth fire: Build these indoors, in an open fireplace that has been properly prepared. Some campgrounds also have chimneys or fireplaces where you can build an outdoor hearth fire. These are great for solo work, families, or small, intimate groups.

Ritual fire: These are usually smaller bonfires/campfires built outdoors. A ritual fire adds power (and warmth!) to solo and group rituals held outdoors.

Bonfire: Larger-scale bonfires are often the highlight or focal point of large group rituals, festivals, or events. They take a bit more work to organise and set up, but are well worth it if you can manage it.

Woods and Kindling

When selecting wood for your fire, always make sure it is dry and properly seasoned. Seasoned wood is wood that has had enough time—usually around eight months or more, depending on the type of wood—to lighten and dry off any excess moisture that was present when it was part of a living tree. Seasoned wood is usually lighter to lift that green wood, and will be an even colour all the way through. Its bark should be completely dry or flaking off, and it shouldn't produce moisture when burned. Burning green or improperly seasoned wood produces a lot of smoke and not much heat. It's difficult to ignite and often won't burn very well either.

If you're someone who uses firewood regularly, consider finding a sustainable option if there's one around. We have a little "pot-belly" fire at our place, and get our wood from a local bluegum plantation, who trim and season their offcuts to sell as firewood. By using plantation timber, we know that we're not contributing to the removal of large dead trees in the bush, which provide essential habitat for a range of different species of birds and animals.

Common Types of Firewood	
Ash	Burns reasonably hot; easy to split
Birch	Quick burning; decent heat
Cedar	Burns slow and hot without much flame; a more expensive option in most places
Eucalyptus	Australian hardwoods; most are slow burning; heat differs between species (redgum, jarrah, or sugargum are best)
Oak	Burns hot if seasoned correctly; difficult to split

Other Woods You Might Come Across	
Acacia (wattle)	Burns hot when properly seasoned
Apple	Slow burning and hot; prized for smoking meats and other food
Bay laurel	Smoky and smelly; burn outdoors only
Hawthorn	Not recommended; see chapter 6
Juniper	Produces a lot of smoke and not much heat; burn outdoors
Olive	Hot and slow burning
Pine	Produces a lot of smoke and sap; burn outdoors only
Rowan	Slow burning; produces decent heat

Woods to Avoid	
Treated or painted wood, building offcuts	Releases toxic fumes when burned
Driftwood	A high salt content means lots more carcinogens

Magical Considerations with Wood

As well as the practical considerations discussed above, Pagans and witches might consider the following when choosing and collecting wood for ritual fires:

- Fallen wood collected from the ground or dead trees is going to have a better feel in ritual that wood collected from cutting down—killing—a living tree. Fallen wood won't always be practical or even possible to obtain, but it's worth keeping in mind and minimising harm where and when you can.
- All woods have magical correspondences. Research them, and keep them in mind when you are warming yourself with the heat of your fire, or standing in its smoke.
- There are folkloric taboos about burning some woods. Hawthorn is one of the most "famous." Look into them and keep them in mind before you go about burning woods willy-nilly.

Fire Safety and Other Considerations

There's a Terry Pratchett quote I like to keep in mind when I am building and tending fires for others:

"Give a man a fire and he's warm for a day, but set fire to him and he's warm for the rest of his life."[320]

Things can go wrong very quickly with fire, and it's important to take as many precautions as you can when building, feeding, maintaining, and extinguishing your ritual fire.

Building Your Fire

- **Only light a fire if the conditions and space are appropriate.** NEVER light a fire on days of total fire ban, or if local laws disallow it.

- **Do your research before building or lighting a fire in a public place.** Many parks and nature reserves have rules around where you can and can't light fires.

- **NEVER light fires indoors,** unless it's in a fireplace that is clean and fit for use, with a clean and safe chimney. This should go without saying, but in my twenty-plus years of Paganism, I've seen some really dangerous things attempted and ultimately fail with catastrophic consequences.

- **Choose a spot that is clear and flat** if you're building your fire on the ground. This will prevent burning logs and sticks rolling out at inopportune times.

- **Define your regular fire spot,** if circumstances allow and you have permission to do so. Dig a shallow indentation in the earth rather than a hole in the ground; your fire won't ignite or burn well if air cannot pass through its base. Rings of stone around the outside of a fire might look cute in cartoons, but surrounding your fire with rocks can be very dangerous; many different types of

---

320 Pratchett, *Jingo*.

rock have tiny pockets of air, water, or soil/minerals all through them, and these can cause the rocks to split or explode in the extreme heat produced by hot coals. If you especially want a defined border around your fire, use a square-mouthed shovel to "chip in" around the diameter.

The Care and Feeding of a Fire

- **Always supervise fires.** This might seem like a no-brainer, but I've seen things go wrong pretty quickly when all ritualists are otherwise occupied. Sometimes it's unclear whether participants are "allowed" to mess with the fire if something goes wrong. Whether your ritual has four or four hundred participants, make sure there is someone who, during your working, knows it's okay to monitor the fire, keep it burning, push in any burnt ends, and keep a watch out for any stray sparks or embers that could become a safety hazard.

- **Keep smoke to a minimum.** Always burn good quality wood that is properly seasoned. "Green" wood—wood that has been freshly cut from a living tree or that has not had time to season and dry all the way through—is difficult to ignite, does not burn well, or give off much heat. It also produces a LOT of extra smoke.

- **Never burn rubbish on a bonfire.** If it's a ritual fire, burning your garbage on it is pretty bloody disrespectful. Even if it isn't a ritual fire, burning man-made items releases toxic smoke and harmful chemicals. Just no.

- **Remember: not all wood is suitable for burning.** Never burn building or carpentry offcuts, as these are often painted, varnished, or in the case of "raw" timber treated with highly toxic pesticides that are released into the air around you as they are burnt. Similarly, treated pine, fence palings, and any wood that has been painted or varnished should be avoided.

Don't Be Those Pagans. Please?

It's very tempting sometimes to take the road of "it's better to ask for forgiveness than permission"—to ignore the rules, have a fire however you like, and deal with any consequences later. This school of thought is not only immature but pretty selfish, too. In all likelihood, you are not, will not be, and have not been the only Pagan/occult/witchy/whatever group to use a particular public place for ritual purposes. If we—and here I mean all of us under the big Pagan umbrella/tent—get a reputation for being careless or disrespectful of public land, it will not fare well in the eyes of officials for years to come.

We owe it to ourselves, to the land, and to our community not to be the reason that restrictions are tightened up even further than they already are, perhaps to a point where we as Pagans are viewed with distrust by land management authorities, or even the reason that all open fires are banned in a venue completely.

Please don't be the reason we can't have nice things!

Hearth Fires

If you're building a fire indoors in an open fireplace, it's important to make sure it is swept clean before you begin. Make sure the chimney is in good condition and has also been professionally cleaned recently; chimneys that are not used regularly can become blocked either partially or completely with debris, cobwebs, birds' nests, etc. These can create respiratory hazards if the smoke can't properly escape, and debris such as leaf matter and birds' nests become very dangerous if they catch fire inside the chimney.

Ritual Fires for Small Groups or Solo Practitioners

If you work as part of a group, preparing the ritual fire before the ritual itself can be a great exercise in friendship and camaraderie. Before building or lighting a fire anywhere, ask yourself the following questions:

What are the current fire restrictions for this area? In many regions there are set times of the year when it is forbidden to light fires in the open. Many built-up areas forbid them altogether. Different shires and local councils sometimes have different definitions of what constitutes a "fire in the open."

Am I allowed to light a fire here? Many public parks and reserves require you to light fires in designated fireplaces only. Some allow portable fireboxes or fire drums, which affords you some flexibility of location if you bring one of these along. If you're planning a working that involves a fire, do your homework. If you can't find the information about a venue online, call them directly and have a chat. If you don't want to go into specifics and your fire isn't going to be a big one, keep things general and ask about "campfires."

Do I have enough wood? Many parks and reserves do not permit collection of firewood. It is never appropriate to cut firewood from living trees or plants, and often fallen sticks and branches form an important part of a delicate ecosystem, and they are better left. Before visiting a place for the first time, check whether you need to BYO firewood.

Fires for Larger Groups

I can still remember the first big public Samhain ritual I ever attended, and most of my memories of that weekend are anchored in some way to fire. The bonfire was enormous, at least ten metres across, and built by all the festival attendees throughout the day.

At its centre stood a huge wicker man, who we'd also put together that day. He was made up of a huge iron skeleton, whose pieces locked together and came apart for travel and storage. Together, we bundled up thick bunches of dry sticks and secured them around his legs, arms, and torso to beef up his skinny frame. Someone even made him a big gold phallus from papier mâché. The atmosphere and energy of the ritual was absolutely electrified with anticipation, and the feeling of release when the bonfire and the man were finally lit was nothing short of, well, magic.

Big bonfires require a bit more work and planning than smaller fires, but if done properly they can be truly spectacular and a memorable focal point of your ritual or celebration.

Before you start planning your event, do your homework and research your intended venue, or look at a few different options. Make sure a venue's rules, as well as any local/state/national laws, allow you to build and light a bonfire on your proposed date. For large events you will probably need some kind of public liability insurance, and at least one qualified first-aider.

Make room. As well as all the additional safety info I've added at the end of this chapter, the thing to remember about big bonfires is that the radiant heat from them is always more severe than you expect. You need to leave a LOT of space around a big fire for people to stand at a comfortable and safe distance. Building your bonfire on a treeless field or oval is ideal, as continuous radiant heat causes damage and stress to trees and buildings alike.

A bonfire is more than a heap of wood you set fire to. Exercise care in how you build your fire. Too much dry, light material like dead branches with leaves attached, reeds, loose paper, or light, flaky bark will send large floating embers across a wide area and potentially shower your attendees in burning debris. Too much dense wood will leave you with a slow-burning fire that will be difficult to light and extinguish, will take ages to burn, and will lack the "wow factor" of a fire that takes hold quickly.

Other Types of Ritual Fire

In the part of Australia where I live, it often won't rain for five or six months over summer and into autumn. These dry conditions, coupled with long stretches of very hot weather, produce tinderbox conditions in the bush and grasslands around here and across a large part of the country. Lighting any kind of flame in these conditions would not just be illegal but quite possibly deadly, too—if you have experienced any kind of bushfire event, you'll know just how fast a wildfire moves and how devastating they can be.

Even if you don't live on a dry continent like Australia, sometimes it just isn't practical or safe to have a ritual fire. You might be working indoors, on an apartment balcony, in a courtyard, or on rented or shared land. But don't despair, fireless friends. There are options.

Correspondences

Sometimes a fire can be replaced with *representations* of fire. Use a suitable decorative (or at least brightly coloured) dish to hold as many representations as you like. Look into fire correspondences (hint: there are a bunch of them in the previous few chapters) and use what works for you.

Solar Lights and the Sun

Okay, okay. I'll admit to being sceptical about this the first time I attended a working that used these. It was a full moon rite in the height of summer, the middle of bushfire season. Instead of the usual bonfire, a large cauldron had been placed in the centre of the circle. It glowed red and yellow, and it took me a moment to realise that it had around a dozen handheld solar lights sitting inside it, each one covered with coloured fabric (I found out later they had t-shirts, etc., stretched over them and secured with rubber bands) in varying shades of red, yellow, and orange. It looked amazing, but the stuffy traditionalist side of me that I still can't always escape wasn't sure … until it was pointed out to me where, exactly, these lights got their energy from.

By using solar energy, we are utilising the power of the sun—unfiltered, sustainable, concentrated fire energy. What could be more natural or more magical than a *literal vessel of sunlight* on your altar or in your circle?

Solar powered lanterns can be purchased fairly cheaply these days. My preference is the ones with more yellow-coloured globes; I find the yellow light is nicer than the more artificial white. If white is all that's available, you can alter their colour and brightness by wrapping them with some coloured tissue paper, cellophane, or thin fabric. This also opens your options up to having different coloured lights for different occasions.

Torches

What's almost as groovy as a big fat bonfire? A torchlight procession, that's what! Here I have to acknowledge some of our Australian Wiccan and Pagan elders—Trevor, Peter, Linda, Michel, Gabrielle, Adrienne, Julie, Andrew, and others—for the many, MANY lessons and sermons I have received about making and using torches safely.

Best-Ever Ritual Torches

Kerosene is stinky. Work outdoors and away from any flames, including people smoking. Make these torches around twenty-four hours before you need them. Torch-making workshops can be great for building community cohesiveness before a ritual.

Chapter 10

INGREDIENTS:

Straight, strong "greenish" (recently cut from a living tree/not fully seasoned) sticks, about a metre long, one for each torch.

Old cotton or linen bedsheets, cut/torn into strips about five centimetres wide and around a metre long. You can also buy calico or cotton from a fabric store, but reusing old sheets is much kinder on the environment than buying something new, and this "aged" fabric seems to burn really well for some reason.

A plastic bucket about half full of kerosene for soaking the torches in.

Somewhere outdoors that you can hang or place the torches to dry.

1. Take a strip of the fabric and tie it tightly to the end of a stick so that the stick is in the middle of the strip, with two equal "tails." Cross the two tails over and tie them firmly again on the other side of the stick, so that the knot is just below but opposite the first. Repeat until you have gone about twenty centimetres down the stick, knotting the tails **every** time you cross them.

2. Keep going up and down this twenty centimetres adding more strips when you run out of tail, knotting **every** time you cross strips. Do this for three to four strips worth of wrapping, or until you're happy with the size of the torch's head.

3. The tighter and more frequently you wrap and knot the fabric, the less likelihood of burning debris coming loose and burning your torch bearer or bystanders when they're lit.

4. When all the torches are wrapped, place them upside down in the bucket, so that all the fabric is soaking in the kerosene. **From this point on it is important to keep the torches upside down**, to keep kerosene from getting on the handles and creating a fire hazard for torch bearers.

5. However tempting it might be, do not decorate torches with dangling feathers, fabric, or other bits and pieces that will present a hazard to torch bearers. Do not paint or treat the torch handles with oils or varnish as these are flammable and release toxic fumes when burned or sometimes just heated. Less is more.

6. Leave the torches to soak for three to five hours. Then, keeping them upside down, remove them from the bucket and hang them upside down from a line or place them heads-down against a tree, chair, etc., where they can drip off excess kerosene.

7. Leave the torches like this for another eight hours at least. Do not omit this step as it saves you from dripping, dangerous torches once they are lit.

8. To light a torch, hold it well away from you and others, angled upwards but not completely vertical. Always carry and handle torches at this angle; holding them horizontal or angled down causes the flames to lick up the stick and burn you.

9. Be sensible and mindful of others when holding a flaming torch. Do not wave it around excessively or allow it too close to others. Always walk when your torch is lit and hold it well out of harm's way. At Mount Franklin, we teach torch bearers to always keep their flames at around head height to protect people's clothing, etc.

10. To extinguish a torch, plunge its head into a fireproof bucket of sand or loose dirt, or water if there is no other option.

Conclusion

Whether they're for a sabbat or moon celebration, spell or magical work, or initiations, ritual fire adds energy and gravitas to any working, and helps bring practitioners together if you are working in a group. Building a fire yourself helps to set the intention for magical workings, especially if you exercise care and attention to what goes on it.

By following the advice in this chapter, you should be able to create a ritual fire that gives your outdoor rituals more power and poignancy, and encourage the warmth of human connection for anyone present in your circle.

Chapter 11

FIRE SPELLS AND RECIPES

For many, fire magic is one of most effective ways to work your will. The workings, recipes, and chants in this chapter should provide a good starting point for working magic geared towards the intentions of fire.

A good habit to get into before you turn to magical workings is to make sure all the "mundane" boxes are ticked first. A spell to find work will probably be more successful if you've had a look over your résumé and started to look at job ads or make enquiries. Workings to smooth things over between you and a family member who are rowing will likely have more oomph if you've tried the boring communication stuff first. Never turn to witchcraft when you should be seeing a healthcare professional or law enforcement authorities.

Censing Bundles: For Setting
Intentions and Creating Sacred Space

Use natural fibre like cotton or twine for bundling fresh leaves and herbs. You need to tie them reasonably tightly (but not chokingly tight) as fresh herbs shrink as they dry. Hang your finished bundles somewhere warm and dry and out of direct sunlight. Depending on the weather, they will usually take between two to six weeks to fully dry and be ready to use.

For concentration and focus: Use at least four of the following—cinnamon stick, basil, bergamot, fern, geranium, hibiscus, honeysuckle, iris, lavender, lemon balm, lilac, peppermint, rosemary. Bundle with red or white twine/thread.

For healing: Use four, seven, or nine of the following—apple leaf, holly, juniper sprig, amaranth, angelica, basil, blackberry leaf, carnation, chamomile, clover, comfrey, daisy, dandelion, fennel, feverfew, geranium, heather, heliotrope, honeysuckle, jasmine, lavender, lemon balm, marigold, peppermint, rose petals, rosemary, rue, thyme, vervain, yarrow. Bundle with white twine/thread.

For inspiration: Use at least five of the following—wattle/acacia flowers, willow leaf, angelica, grape leave, honeysuckle, jasmine, lavender, lilac, rose, rosemary, rue, vervain, cinnamon stick, vanilla pod. Bundle with silver or light blue twine/thread.

For love: Use at least three of the following—apple leaf, carnation, red chrysanthemum petals, columbine, heather, heliotrope, honeysuckle, marigold, rose petals, thyme, valerian, violet, yarrow, wormwood. Bundle with red or pink twine/thread.

For magical workings: Use at least three of the following—carnation, peony, rosemary, rue, vervain, cinnamon stick, nettle, mistletoe, mullein. Bundle with purple or silver twine/thread.

For protection: Use at least four of the following—acacia/wattle flowers, ash leaf, hawthorn berries, holly leaf, magnolia petals, oak leaf, rowan berries, pine sprig, angelica, basil, blackberry leaf, chrysanthemum, heather, jasmine, lavender, lilac, peony, primrose, raspberry leaf, snapdragon, spearmint, thyme, valerian, vervain, violet, yarrow, bamboo leaf, thistle, coriander, cloves, wormwood. Bundle with white or silver twine/thread.

For transformation, rebirth, and renewal: Use at least three of the following—cypress sprig, juniper sprig, fir sprig, maple leaf, walnut leaf, grape leaf, ivy, marigold, violet, flax, lotus, worm-wood. Bundle with orange or purple twine/thread.

To break a bad habit: Use at least two of the following—apple leaf, cypress sprig, dill, heliotrope, rosemary, rushes. Bundle with yellow or white twine/thread.

To build confidence: Use at least three of the following—oak leaf, basil, carnation, geranium, heather, honeysuckle, passionflower, rose petals, rosemary, thyme, yarrow. Bundle with gold or royal blue twine/thread.

To calm the mind: Use at least two of the following—clover, passionflower, apple leaf, borage, violet. Bundle with blue or black twine/thread.

To encourage truthfulness: Use at least seven of the following—cypress sprig, bay leaf, magnolia petals, pine sprig, carnation, chrysanthemum, daisy, snapdragon, valerian, cloves, mint, raspberry leaf, apple leaf. Bundle with violet or white twine/thread.

To enhance divination: Use at least four of the following—apple peel, cherry blossom, juniper sprig, angelica, basil, daisy, hibiscus, honeysuckle, lavender, marigold, peppermint, strawberry leaves, rose petals, thyme, yarrow, cinnamon stick, mullein, wormwood. Bundle with gold or silver twine/thread.

To find a lost item: Use at least two of the following—peony, rosemary, rue, vervain, cinnamon stick, vanilla pod, sunflower petals. Bundle with white or yellow twine/thread.

To promote communication: Use at least three of the following—blackberry leaves, yellow carnation, chamomile, daisy, dandelion, fennel, geranium, lavender, marigold, rosemary, valerian, white violets. Bundle with orange or blue twine/thread.

To promote justice: Use at least four of the following—bay leaf, carnation, dill, honeysuckle, jasmine, vervain, violet, cinnamon stick, nettle. Bundle with purple or red twine or thread.

To purify: Use at least three of the following—juniper sprig, oak leaf, bay leaf, angelica, chamomile, dill, fennel, fern, geranium, heather, hyacinth, lavender, jasmine, rosemary, peppermint, thyme, white violets, star anise, thistle, cinnamon stick, nettle, thistle, wormwood. Bundle with white or undyed twine/thread.

To manifest your desires: Use at least four of the following—cinnamon stick, dittany, galangal, vanilla pod, red rose petals, strawberry leaves, juniper sprig. Bundle with red twine/thread.

To regain authority: Use at least three of the following—borage, carnation, daisy, heather, honeysuckle, marigold, thyme, yarrow, mullein. Bundle with black or gold twine/tread.

To soothe anger and diffuse heightened environments: Use at least three of the following—valerian, peony, juniper, holly, chamomile. Bundle with black or purple twine/thread.

Incense Blends

These loose blends are for burning on a charcoal disc in a censer. Make them out of dried herbs rather than fresh.

Cheer up, Charlie: 1 part honeysuckle, 1 part cloves, 2 parts frankincense, 1 drop rose oil

Crafternoon: 1 part cloves, 1 part dried orange peel, 1 part hawthorn berries, 2 parts sandalwood

Consecration of an Athame: 1 parts cedar chips, 1 pomegranate seed, 2 parts sandalwood, 2 parts frankincense

Divination Nation: 2 parts sandalwood, 1 part cinnamon, 1 part dried orange peel

Eine Kleine Nachtmagie: 2 parts sandalwood, 1 part rose petals, a drop of jasmine or rose oil

Fighting Trousers: 1 part allspice, 2 parts sandalwood, 1 part rosemary, 1 part juniper berries

For What Ails You: 1 part juniper berries, 1 part rosemary

GTFO: 3 parts frankincense, 1 part myrrh, 1 part dill seed, 1 part dragon's blood, 1 part sandalwood

Hexbuster: 1 part bay leaves, 2 parts sandalwood

Study Skills: 1 part frankincense, 1 part cedar chips, 1 part sandalwood, 1 part rosemary

Kindling Bundles for Every Occasion

If you live where you have access to lots of different woods, you can collect and bundle certain combinations for your ritual fire. This makes a great group activity. When these bundles are dry, they can be tossed onto an already burning fire, or used as part of the kindling. There are tips on drying and burning woods in chapter 10.

Beltane Bundle: Use at least three of the following—apple, ash, cherry, chestnut, elder, elm, juniper, magnolia, maple, olive, pomegranate, rowan. Bundle with red and white ribbon or twine.

Dance Magic Dance: Use at least three of the following—apple, blackthorn, elder, hazel, laurel, rowan, willow. Bundle with purple or silver ribbon or twine.

Defence Against the Dark Arts: Use at least three of the following—birch, cypress, fir, hazel, holly, juniper, laurel, oak, palm, pine, rowan, gorse. Bundle with black or silver ribbon or twine.

Esbat Bundle: Use at least three of the following—ash, willow, elder, laurel, hazel, poplar, rowan. Bundle with white or silver ribbon or twine.

For Tough Times: Use at least two of the following—aspen, cedar, holly, laurel, oak, palm, pine, poplar, willow. Bundle with red or brown ribbon or twine.

Let it Go: Use at least three of the following—birch, cedar, cypress, elder, juniper, laurel, maple, palm, pine, wormwood, rose petals. Bundle with black or purple ribbon or twine.

Meeting of the Minds: Use at least two of the following—blackberry vine, beech, cedar, hazel, holly, olive, walnut, rosemary sprigs. Bundle with blue or black ribbon or twine.

Out With the Old, In With the New: Use at least two of the following—alder, blackthorn, rowan, rue. Bundle with red ribbon or twine.

Pants Party: Use at least five of the following—acacia/wattle, apple, magnolia, palm, vanilla pod, oak, rose petals, pinecones, palm, mistletoe, cinnamon stick. Bundle with red or white ribbon or twine.

Scrying Soiree: Use at least four of the following—acacia/wattle, alder, apple, ash, birch, cedar, cherry, fir, hazel, horse chestnut, juniper, laurel, maple, pomegranate, poplar, rowan, willow. Bundle with silver or gold ribbon or twine.

Fire and Divination

Tephramancy: Divination with Coals

To divine with hot coals, sit and gaze at a fire when it has started to die down. Some folkloric associations in tephramancy are:

Hot coals amidst cold ash: Several records of superstitions from Yorkshire, England, hold that to find a hot, red coal amidst otherwise cold ash when cleaning out a cold fireplace signifies that you will soon receive news of a death.[321]

---

321 Opie and Tatem, *A Dictionary of Superstitions*, 150.

Large spark flies straight up the chimney: Superstitions from Wiltshire and Shropshire in England hold that seeing a large, bright spark going straight up the chimney indicates you will soon receive an important message or news.[322]

"Strangers" on the grate: One commonly held belief in England and elsewhere was that soot flakes landing on the fire grate indicated a stranger would soon visit. One particularly creepy rhyme collected and written down at the end of the 1800s goes:

> If the stranger on the bar goes in the fire,
> Your friend will come nigher;
> If the stranger goes in the ash,
> Your friend will come nonetheless;
> If the stranger goes up the chimney,
> Your friend will come, but you'll not see him.[323]

Other Fire Omens

The behaviour and appearance of fire and flames have also long been considered to be omens by many.

Blue flames: An old Scottish belief holds that blue flames indicate the presence of hearth spirits. In Scots Gaelic, these spirits are called the *Corracha cagalt*. An abundance of blue flames was often thought to signify bad weather ahead.[324]

Fire burns on one side: Several different superstitions exist about a fire that obstinately burns to one side of the fireplace only. These are conflicting in places, but the common theme seems to be that this is a bad sign: of a failing marriage, an unwanted visitor, or even an imminent death in the household. It was

322 Opie and Tatem, *A Dictionary of Superstitions*, 151.
323 Opie and Tatem, *A Dictionary of Superstitions*, 151.
324 Opie and Tatem, *A Dictionary of Superstitions*, 150.

thought by some that this omen could be negated by spreading the fire back to fill the entire fireplace.[325]

Fire won't burn or is difficult to light: There are folkloric accounts from around England during the mid-1800s that claim a difficult-to-light fire or one that will not stay lit indicates someone in the household is in a foul mood. One 1855 account stated that a fire that burns black and gloomy was a sign of dissent or ill-will from a faraway place.[326]

Fire spits and roars: Many accounts from all over England as far back as the 1600s claim that a fire that spits and roars is a sign of an argument or scolding ahead. Some thought that spitting back at the fire would counteract this.[327]

Fire still burning in the morning: Folkloric accounts from several parts of England hold that a fire still burning in the fireplace by morning is a sign you'll soon receive bad news.[328]

Fire suddenly blazes or flares up: Several accounts from folklore around Devon, Dorset, and Sussex in England claim that if a fire suddenly blazes brightly without warning, it is a sign that a stranger is coming. An old saying recorded in a collection from the 1930s goes "When it burns without blowing, you'll have company without knowing."[329]

Log burns hollow: An old English folkloric belief is that a log that burns and leaves a hollow in the middle is a sign of a coming death or parting of ways. It was considered good practice to poke down "hollow fires" as soon as they were spotted.[330]

---

325 Opie and Tatem, *A Dictionary of Superstitions*, 150.
326 Opie and Tatem, *A Dictionary of Superstitions*, 150.
327 Opie and Tatem, *A Dictionary of Superstitions*, 151.
328 Opie and Tatem, *A Dictionary of Superstitions*, 150.
329 Opie and Tatem, *A Dictionary of Superstitions*, 150.
330 Opie and Tatem, *A Dictionary of Superstitions*, 150.

Peppermint Tea to Get You Moving

Do you have trouble getting started on cold mornings? Do you feel frazzled by the mid-afternoon? Make a pot of peppermint tea according to the tea's instructions (bonus witch points if you make your own tea, but totally not necessary). Before you pour, turn the pot three times clockwise. Use your finger to draw the alchemical symbol for fire in above it and pour yourself a cup. As you drink, visualise the tea warming you right through, invigorating your muscles, and refreshing your tired mind.

A Children's Bonfire Wishing Rhyme, circa 1800

A girdle o' gold,
a saddle o' silk,
a horse for me as white as milk![331]

A Silver Ring and Thistledown: Your Heart's Desire

Next time you see a floating thistledown, catch it before it touches the ground. Try to keep it as intact as possible, and store it somewhere until the next full moon. An empty matchbox is ideal for this. At the full moon, stand or sit where you are bathed in moonlight; have the thistledown and a silver ring with you. Cast a circle if you need to, then hold the ring and the thistledown in your cupped hands. Focus on something you have wished for for some time. Say:

Thistle of fire, hear my words and know my heart.

My greatest wish for you is _____.

Thistle of fire, I beseech you, ride warm
winds over mountain, land, and sea.

---

331 Opie and Tatem, *A Dictionary of Superstitions*, 152.

CHAPTER 11

Take these words, know my heart,
carry this true desire to me.

Look up at the moon and let the thistledown blow away on the breeze. Wear the ring until your wish is fulfilled, or until you no longer need it.

Bay Leaves: For Banishing

An oldie but a goodie. Write the name of issues (or people) you want to be done with on dry bay leaves and burn them in a fireproof receptacle. For extra firepower (ha!), sprinkle their ashes somewhere desolate, where the light is weak and nothing grows.

Basil and Bay: To Improve Divination Skills

Dress three golden candles in oil infused with both bay and basil (see the chapter on candle magic on how to do this). Have these three candles burning whenever you perform divination. These candles could be used in the practice of lychnomancy.

Nine Geranium Petals: For Courage

Dress an orange candle in oil infused with at least one of the following: allspice, basil, borage, ginger, mullein, nettle. See chapter 9 for advice on how to do this. Collect the petals from a geranium, the brighter the better, and burn nine of them in the flame of this candle, one by one, saying:

Courage to dream, courage to try
Courage to dare, courage to see

Salt and Red Ribbons: For Success in the Workplace

Put some lengths of red ribbon in a jar. Cover them with sea salt (table salt will do the trick too) as you verbalise your intent: to get a promotion, to find a job, etc. Set the jar in direct sunlight for a few weeks before removing the ribbons and attaching them to your desk/workspace or wearing them on your person.

Chalk and Coal: To Assist the Healing Process

This one is inspired by folkloric customs from Yorkshire, which claimed that writing a patient's name in chalk on the hob would cure them of ague (fever, chills, or even malaria) once the fire had blackened the chalk enough that it could no longer be seen.[332]

If you are lucky enough to have an actual hob or chimney you can chalk a name onto directly, go for it. If not, try using white chalk to write a name on a stone or token. Go over the name three times with a piece of charcoal, ideally charcoal from a fire this person has recently sat by. Place the token outside off the ground where it will face the full impact of sun, wind, and rain. Do not move it until the name has worn away.

---

332 Opie and Tatem, *A Dictionary of Superstitions*, 151.

Chapter 12

FIRE HOLIDAYS AND RITUALS

Fire festivals are by no means exclusive to the Pagan and witchy community. Long-standing traditions like Guy Fawkes Night in England, the Onyo fire festival on Japan's Kyushu island, South Korea's Jeongwol Daeboreum Deulbul festival, and countless others illustrate just how much this primal and powerful element is a part of our collective psyche as humans, no matter how modern we think we might be.

The Wheel of the Year

The Wheel of the Year is how most witches and Pagans refer to one year's worth of seasons and the festivals that mark them and, by extension, the continuing cycle of life, death, and rebirth. The changes that occur throughout one turning of the wheel—one year—can most easily be seen in nature, especially trees and flowering plants.

The wheel is made up of eight sabbats, or holy days, including two solstices, two equinoxes, and four "cross quarter" days, sometimes called "lesser" sabbats. It's important to remember that these days are to celebrate a seasonal time of the year that lasts for several weeks as it fades and overlaps with the next season. I find it helps if you think of the celebration days only marking the *turning point* in each sabbat season.

Some Pagan and witchcraft traditions consider the year to begin and end at Samhain. Others mark the year's beginning and end at the winter solstice or the spring equinox. The eight-sabbat structure is a common way to celebrate the seasons throughout the year, but not all witches celebrate every sabbat, nor is there a "right" way to mark these occasions, if you choose to mark them at all.

The Winter Solstice

Also known as: Yule, Midwinter

Southern Hemisphere: June 21 (approx.)

Northern Hemisphere: December 21 (approx.)

Depending which Pagan you speak to, the Winter Solstice is sometimes considered to be the Pagan New Year. This is the longest, and often the darkest, night of the year. After the autumn equinox, days are shorter and nights are longer, culminating in the solstice in June (or December for our friends in the Northern Hemisphere). After the solstice, the light slowly begins to return and the daylit periods will get a little longer each day for the next six months.

The winter solstice has been marked with celebrations of some kind for centuries. In the Northern Hemisphere many customs associated with it have been adopted into secular and Christian New Year and Christmas traditions. Many witches call the winter solstice *Yule*, named after Yule (or Jol, Jul, or *Julmonat*), the traditional holiday season in Germany and Scandinavia, and the origins of some of the most well-known midwinter customs.

In some traditions, the triumph of light over darkness is symbolised by the struggle between the Oak King and the Holly King. This seasonal myth—originating in part in Robert Graves's *The White Goddess* and explored more deeply by traditional Wiccans Janet and Stewart Farrar—tells of the Oak King and the Holly King, two brothers who are locked in a constant battle for dominion over the world and its seasons, and they fight for the throne every six months. Some traditions include stories of the two kings growing stronger or becoming weaker at each sabbat, and they enact battles at the two solstices. Sometimes a goddess figure is also present in these stories, to mourn a fallen king or to join with a victor in celebration.[333]

Fire and the Winter Solstice

MIDWINTER FIRES

Midwinter is often seen by modern witches as the rebirth of the sun. Because of this, modern Yule and midwinter rituals, celebrations, and festivals involve light and fire in many cases—lots of glowing candles and lanterns, bonfires, etc., to combat the long darkness.

In a habitually tinder-dry country like Australia, the winter months are often the only time when it's safe enough to have a huge bonfire. The contrast of the glowing coals in the frigid air brings about feelings of safety and community for me. One of my fondest midwinter memories is doing a private ritual outdoors with a friend, our boots crunching through the frost and the fire crackling merrily.

The ashes of a Yule or midwinter ritual fire are considered significant by many modern witches.

---

333 Mankey, *Wheel of the Year*.

YULE LOGS

Yule logs are a folk custom from England and Europe that made their way to places like North America and Australia as they were colonised. Though their exact origins are unclear, it is thought that this tradition of having a long-burning log to symbolise the return of the sun might have its roots in early Germanic paganism.

Traditionally, Yule logs are kindled with an unburned portion of the previous year's log, and an unburned piece saved to be used as a symbol of protection before being used to light the new log the following year.

Winter Solstice Fire Projects and Activities

- At least once in your lifetime, make the time to sit up all night one midwinter, ideally with some of your closest likeminded friends. Keep televisions off, phones and other electronic devices to a minimum. Sit and talk and watch the coals in your fire. Connect with each other and think about the year that's passed. Make a toast to your gods, if you have them, for the year ahead. Watch the new sun rise on a new year before you go to bed. A night like this will warm you down to your soul's bones, and will become a memory to treasure for years to come.

- Decorate your home with evergreen boughs or leaves to celebrate the wintertime and to be burned at Imbolc to banish the cold. You can burn these on ritual fires later in the year to symbolise the return of the light.

- Make a Yule log (see below) for yourself or your group. Remember to save an unburned portion to light next year's log!

- Collect the cold ashes from your midwinter or Yule ritual fire. Store them in a glass bottle and use them in workings for prosperity or protection. Alternatively, sprinkle them on your garden to encourage fertility for the coming year.

- Candle magic at this time of year often features gold, green, red, silver, or white candles, and often focuses on the long darkness, divination/messages/omens for the year ahead, the return of the light, purification, rebirth/renewal, or other transformations.
- Woods commonly associated with this time of year include apple, birch, cedar, chestnut, fir, holly, juniper, oak, or pine.[334]

How to Make a Yule Log

Usually, a Yule log is selected earlier in the year and set aside for use. Around Samhain or earlier, choose a dense, seasoned log to be your Yule log for the following year. Oak is traditionally used, but other dense, slow-burning wood like redgum, rowan, etc., will do the trick.

As the midwinter season approaches, decorate your home or altar with evergreen foliage such as pine, fir, holly, etc., if it is practical to do so. Include the Yule log in your decorations. Some folks who follow the Oak/Holly King myth use leaves of both to decorate their log. Others wind it in ivy vines or use sprigs of yew to symbolise the death of the sun god or of the old year. Top this off with a big red bow.

As part of your midwinter festivities, include the placing and burning of the Yule log on your ritual fire. Use the remainder of last year's log, if you have it, to light the new one. You may want to say a chant or prayer (I've included some ideas below), or sing carols.

---

334 Mankey, *Wheel of the Year*.

Remember to save an unburned portion of your log. You can place this somewhere around your home for protection and good fortune before using it to light next year's log.

Imbolc

Also known as: Candlemas, Brigid, February Eve
Southern Hemisphere: August 1 (approx.)
Northern Hemisphere: February 1 (approx.)

Relatively little is known about the ancient Irish festival of Imbolc, after which modern Pagan and witch celebrations are named. We do know that they took place in early February in Ireland and in some other areas where this date would have been the beginning of spring. While it is still a fire festival, the focus of Imbolc is on light rather than warmth.[335] For modern witches who follow the seasonal cycle of the goddess in her journey from maiden to crone, Imbolc is sometimes when the goddess is honoured as the corn maiden, with workings focused on prosperity and increase.

One thing we do know about the origins of this festival is that the goddess Brigid was connected in some way. Or *a* goddess Brigid—several Brigids were venerated throughout the British Isles, and it's unclear whether she was a universal deity or more localised to smaller areas.[336]

Some witches like to use this time of year to do some spring cleaning: cleaning, repairing, or replacing working tools; replenishing altar supplies; cleaning and cleansing ritual spaces, etc.

---

335 Farrar and Farrar, *A Witches' Bible*, 61.
336 Mankey, *Wheel of the Year*.

Fire and Imbolc

IMBOLC VS. CANDLEMAS

While they sometimes share a similar date and the name was used by many witches in the 1950s and 1960s and is still sometimes used today, Candlemas is actually a different holiday altogether. It is a Christian holy day which owes its origins at least in part to similar ceremonies held in ancient Greece. In some Christian countries, Candlemas ceremonies are still held on the second of February to mark the end of the Christmas-Epiphany period.

IMBOLC CANDLES

Many witches and Pagans also celebrate the return of the light at Imbolc. This is why candles feature so prominently in rituals for this season. Some Imbolc ceremonies have a chain of candles—sometimes one held by each ritualist—lit gradually to represent the sun's slow return.

Imbolc Fire Projects and Activities

- Collect up the greenery that you used to decorate your home and burn it in your Imbolc ritual fire to banish the winter cold.

- Start a tradition of a thorough spring cleaning every Imbolc. I know many covens who use this time to officially retire the pillar candles they've used all year and replace them with fresh ones as part of the Imbolc ritual itself. You might even like to have a go at performing sainings/smoke cleansings on ritual space, tools, or ritualists.

- Imbolc is about newness. Take this opportunity to craft or consecrate working tools. Burn small amounts of dried angelica, basil, marigold, cinnamon, galangal, or frankincense and use the smoke as part of a consecrating rite of your choosing (or use the one in chapter 11).

- Candle magic at this time of year often features green, pink, yellow, or white candles, and often focuses on awakenings; animals; banishings and new beginnings; divination and prophecy; fertility and childbirth; healing, hope, and inspiration; light and illumination; prosperity; purification; transformations; wellbeing; and youth.

- Woods commonly associated with this time of year include blackthorn, rowan, and sycamore.[337]

TO MAKE A CROWN OF CANDLES

One tradition that is mentioned in *Buckland's Complete Book of Witchcraft* [338] is that of a candle crown, or crown of lights, worn by a priestess to symbolise the goddess in her very young form.

As someone with thick, coarse hair that floats around my head and sticks out with a mind of its own, the idea of wearing a crown of burning candles on my head fills me with more anxieties than I can list here.

There are instructions for a slightly less alarming one in Janet and Stewart Farrar's *Witches' Bible* that uses birthday-cake candles and an inner cap of tinfoil to protect the wearer's scalp, but I prefer using electronic candles, gold tinsel, or a garland of the new season's flowers in yellows, oranges, or reds. Here in Oz, blooming wattle is just perfect for this.

COLLECT AND DRY SACRED WOODS

With warmer days finally on the horizon, it's time to plan for the future. Collect, wildcraft, beg, or trade for cuttings of different

---

337 Kynes, *Correspondences*, 395–396.
338 Buckland, *Complete Book of Witchcraft*, 101.

woods and store them somewhere warm and dry. If you stick to gathering pieces no thicker than your thumb, these should be dry enough to light your ritual fire at Beltane.

If you're feeling especially clever, look into woods with certain correspondences (such as good fortune, health, prosperity, etc.) and bale the appropriate ones accordingly with some coloured cotton or natural twine to make a fire-starting bundle for future use.

Some sacred woods you might want to start with could be: oak, ash, birch, rowan, willow, holly, or hazel. See chapters 6 and 10 for more on preparing firewood and the magical associations of some common woods.

Spring Equinox

Also known as: Ostara, Eostre

Southern Hemisphere: September 21 (approx.)

Northern Hemisphere: March 21 (approx.)

After Yule, the days begin to grow longer. By the spring equinox—a precise moment in time on a specific day when the sun is perfectly lined up with the earth's equator—day and night are more or less equal. Many witches and Pagans call the season around this day Ostara and celebrate balance, life, fertility, and springtime. While it is less common these days, some Pagan and witchcraft traditions do consider the Spring Equinox to be the beginning and end of the year, due to the equal amounts of light and dark.[339]

In Paganism and witchcraft, the name *Ostara* was first coined and used for the spring equinox by poet and witch Aidan Kelly in

339   Campanelli, "The Wheel of the Year" in *Llewellyn's Magical Sampler*, 329–335.

1974. Until a few decades ago it was a name used only by American witches and authors for the most part, although as the community has become more global, and more Pagans from farther afield consume US authors' content, it has become more widely used around the world. That said, many witches do still prefer to use pre-1970s names like Vernal Equinox and Spring Equinox.

Some modern witches use this season for both magical and mundane spring cleaning; rites of abundance/fertility/growth; returning to the outdoors after the winter cold; gardening; "small-c craft" such as egg painting, flower crown making, and flower pressing; and divination for the year ahead.

Fire and the Spring Equinox

BALANCE AND THE RETURN OF LIGHT

In the solar calendar, the Spring Equinox is when the length of daylight matches the length of night. After this day, the balance shifts in favour of the growing sunlight and the days will slowly get longer. Many workings and rituals at this time focus on balance, or on leaving darker days behind.

THE GODDESS OF THE DAWN?

The name Ostara is derived from Eostre, the name of an old Germanic goddess of the dawn and the spring. Details about the goddess were reconstructed by Jacob Grimm—one half of the famous Brothers Grimm—in his book *Deutsche Mythologie* ("German Mythology") in 1835.

When Grimm was writing about Eostre, he was referencing a much earlier work by the Venerable Bede, an English Benedictine monk who lived from 672 to 735 CE. Bede was considered by many to be the "father" of English history. He is thought to be the single most influential and important scholar of antiquity during the early Middle Ages. He wrote extensively on many traditions and histories of Christian denominations, but his main area of interest was *computus*, or the mathematical pinpointing of dates for holy days and celebrations.

In his work *De Temporum Ratione* (Latin: "The Reckoning of Time"), Bede wrote about the Germanic holiday season *Eosturmonath* ("Eastern month"), which he claimed was named after an ancient goddess named Eostre.

But there's a bit of a problem here. This goddess seems to only have been written about in any depth or detail by Bede. No mention of her or her worship exists in any other written history or mythology. We can't be one hundred percent certain, but as time goes on and more research is done, it's looking more and more like Bede might have made her up, embellishing on the name *Eosturmonath*.

The closest researchers have come to evidence of a goddess Ostara/Eostre is mention of a proto-Germanic goddess called *Austrō*, a proto-Indo-European goddess of the dawn called *Ausṓs*, and the Romano-Germanic Matronae called Austriahenae, but these are separate deities from completely different time periods; if anything, it would be the names only that evolved into Eostre/ Ostara, and even then this is just a theory.

Many of the "ancient" symbols of Ostara/the equinox were not associated with the goddess or celebration until the mid-1800s; things like hares, eggs, chicks, etc., were never mentioned by Bede or by Grimm. The earliest mention was actually a fairly offhanded comment made by author Adolf Holzmann in 1874. As with the identity of the goddess Ostara, this one innocent quote was picked up and used by several authors, who were cited by other authors, and so on and so on, until it appeared as "fact" in many of the Pagan and witch books you might have on your shelf right now.[340]

Regardless of where they came from or how ancient (and therefore somehow better) they're seen to be, modern symbols of Ostara and the spring equinox include painted or fresh eggs, fresh spring flowers, hares/rabbits, and baby animals.

The Strengthening of the Sun

Robert Graves, the Farrars, and others write about the sun "arming" itself at the spring equinox. Some rituals involve symbols of the sun in the form of solar discs or wheels, or even personified by someone in a mask or bright robe/dress. For the 2019 Wiccan Conference here in Australia, we had someone dressed as the sun, wearing a gold cape and a grand mask. As part of the ceremony, this person was handed a spear in a show of strengthening against the darkness.

Spring Equinox Fire Projects and Activities

- As the plant life continues to wake up, use vines or flowers with red and yellow ribbon to weave a solar disc, a wreath or solid circle to represent the sun.

- This is a great time of year for gardening, and in many areas "potted colour"—punnets of easy-to-grow annual seedlings—is available. Plant a round tub or a small manageable garden bed of marigolds, nasturtiums, yellow pansies, and wildflowers to celebrate this time of growth and growing light.

- If you collected sacred woods to bundle for ritual fire-lighters in the cooler months, now is a good time to set

---

340 O'Connor, *Ostara*, 20.

them outside when the weather is fine to soak up some rays and aid the drying process.

- Candle magic at this time of year often features light blue, green, pink, or yellow candles, and often focuses on gardening and farming, balance, beauty, fertility, growth, and new life, light, love, and rebirth/renewal.

- Woods commonly associated with this time of year include ash, birch, and maple.[341]

MAKE A SUN WHEEL

Sun wheels—also called solar wheels, sun crosses, and solar crosses—are a symbol of the sun, made up of an equilateral cross inside a circle. They are a symbol that has appeared in many cultures, dating back to prehistoric times. In modern witchcraft and Paganism, it's a symbol used to represent the sun or the wheel of the year.

To make a sun wheel, you need to cut thin, green branches that are bendy enough to fashion into a wheel. In the past I've done this with the long leggy branches I've cut from climbing or hedging plants. Use a couple of branches at first to get the roundness and size right, then wind more branches around it. Save two straighter bits to form the cross, poking each end in at the wheel's quarters. Use a piece of red string or cotton to hold the centre of the cross in place, or use a glue gun. Finish your wheel by winding red fabric around the edge. Hang it up somewhere inside or outside your home for good luck and protection, and burn it at the summer solstice.

I've seen some really groovy sun wheels woven from willow or even fashioned from papier mâché, but equally effective for

---

341 Kynes, *Correspondences*, 396.

a spring equinox altar is to set out tealight candles in the shape of the wheel on a brightly coloured plate or decorative tray. You could start with half of the wheel lit and the rest in darkness, lighting (or getting participants to light) the remaining candles at the height of the ceremony when you welcome back the sunlight.

Beltane

Also known as: May Day, May Eve
Southern Hemisphere: October 31 (approx.)
Northern Hemisphere: May 1 (approx.)

Beltane in modern witchcraft and Paganism is a name borrowed from a traditional Irish celebration/fire festival that later spread throughout the British Isles. It's likely that the name comes from the Irish word *bel*, meaning "bright" or "fortunate." Some have tried to attribute them to certain deities, but these links are tenuous at best, and little historical evidence exists to support them.[342] Traditionally, this was a time that farmers and herdsmen would seek protection and blessings for their herds and harvests through the coming summer. Beltane as we know it in modern witchcraft and Paganism is derived mostly from the English celebration May Day, a celebration from which we get traditions such as maypoles, may queens, jack-in-the-green, green men, etc.

Many superstitions and folkloric beliefs around Beltane and May Day had to do with fire. One of my favourites is around never letting anyone come and take a piece of your kitchen fire to light their own on May Day. Anyone who did this was considered to be a witch, and would steal your butter for the rest of the year if you let her light her fire from yours.[343] It was also considered in many

---

342 Mankey, *Wheel of the Year*.
343 Opie and Tatem, *A Dictionary of Superstitions*, 152.

parts very bad luck to let a hearth fire go out on May Day morning. If this happened in parts of Ireland, the fire could only be relit with a burning sod brought from a local priest's house. Once the fire was lit, the ashes of this turf was often sprinkled on the floor and threshold of the house.[344]

> This evening being May Eve I ought to have put some birch and witan (ash) over the door to help keep out the "old witch." But I was too lazy to go out and get it. Let us hope the old witch will not come in during the night. The young witches are welcome.
>
> —Diary of English Clergyman Reverend
> Francis Kilvert, 30 April, 1870.[345]

In modern Paganism, many consider Beltane to be a celebration of life and fertility. Celebrations sometimes include an enactment of the young Horned God courting the maiden Goddess, though the idea of a male/female gendered "chase" and its fuzzy lines around consent is slowly falling out of favour as the community and our values change. Maypoles, Morris dancing, and bonfires are also a part of many rituals today. Many Morris sides I know like to "dance up the sun" at dawn on Beltane.

Fire and Beltane
Protective Beltane Fires

Traditional Beltane celebrations often involved big bonfires and using fire/smoke for protection. In some areas, farmers would pass their livestock through the smoke of the fires to protect them from evil.

This was also the reasoning behind lighting great big bonfires in Germany; Walpurgis Night (*Walpurgisnacht*) is observed at

344 Opie and Tatem, *A Dictionary of Superstitions*, 152.
345 Costley and Kightly, *A Celtic Book of Days.*

around the same time of year as Beltane in the Northern Hemisphere. Named after a Christian saint, *Walpurgisnacht* was thought by some to be a night when witches were especially active, only to be driven off by smoke/fire. Because of the distance between Germany and Ireland, it's unlikely this festival is directly related to Beltane, though.[346]

Beltane in Australia

I help organise the Mount Franklin Pagan Gathering, which takes place here in Australia at Beltane. Beginning in 1981 and held in the crater of a dormant volcano, this is now among the oldest Neopagan gatherings anywhere in the world. It's a relaxed weekend of camping that feels more like a big family reunion, with a community Beltane rite, maypole dancing, and most importantly, fire. We have a bonfire that burns all night, and sometimes begin the ritual with torchlit processions around the inside of the tree-lined crater.

Beltane Fire Projects and Activities

- Get together with some friends and "dance up the sun" on Beltane morning. There are lots of simple Morris steps you can learn on YouTube for this purpose, or you can make up your own. If Morris is too tricky, even a simple circle dance would do the trick. Make sure your friends consent to being dragged out of bed at stupid o'clock first, though.

- Other centuries-old Beltane traditions include rising before dawn to wash your face in dew—especially dew collected from a hawthorn bush—to promote youth, beauty, and vigour. Churning butter at sunrise was also

---

346 Mankey, *Wheel of the Year*.

thought to bring good fortune. I don't know many who still churn their own butter, but I've seen modern versions of this that involve a big pancake breakfast cooked at dawn!

- If you collected and dried wood for ritual fire-starting bundles in the colder months, now is the time to use them. Place them around the base of the bonfire proper, or light one as part of your Beltane ceremony and carefully place it on the main fire. See chapter 10 for more on building and lighting the perfect bonfire.

- Hold a torchlight procession as part of your Beltane festivities, using the lit torches to light your Beltane bonfire. I've included some tips about torch making in chapter 10.

- Candle magic at this time of year often features green, orange, pink, red, yellow, or white candles, and often focuses on gardening and agriculture; creativity; fertility; lust, sensuality, sexuality, and pleasure; marriage; the otherworld and the underworld; psychic ability and visions; purification; warmth and youth.

- Woods commonly associated with this time of year include apple, ash, blackberry/bramble, cedar, elder, fir, hawthorn, juniper, linden, oak, pine, poplar, rowan, and willow.[347]

Caudle and Oatcake

One interesting account of Beltane festivities comes from Scotland during the 1700s. Welsh naturalist and traveller Thomas Pennant describes villagers building a huge fire and mixing up a caudle—a sweet, hot drink—and using it to pour libations onto

---

347 Kynes, *Correspondences*, 397.

the earth. Once this was done, the people all took an oatmeal cake decorated with nine square knobs, "each dedicated to some particular being, the supposed preserver of their flocks and herds, or to some particular animal, the real destroyer of them."[348]

Each person faced the fire in turn, breaking off a knob, throwing it over their shoulder, and saying variations of: *this I give to thee, preserve thou my (horses/sheep/etc).*

This process would then be repeated for animals that might cause livestock to come to harm: *this I give to thee, O fox (crow, eagle, etc)! Spare thou my lambs!*

You could perform a modern ceremony down similar lines, with a focus on protection (for self/family/community/whatever), or even as a devotional to your gods or spirits. The caudle described in Pennant's account sounds a bit like modern egg-nog: eggs, milk, butter, and oatmeal. But if that's not your bag, mugs of warm honeyed chai or hot chocolate would do the trick.

There are loads of recipes floating around out there for oat cakes. I've found this one simple and effective:

> INGREDIENTS:
> ½ cup (125g) butter
> 1 tablespoon sugar
> 1 cup plain flour
> 1 teaspoon bicarb soda (baking soda)
> 1 teaspoon cream of tartar
> 1 cup oatmeal
> warm water

---

348 Costley and Kightly, *A Celtic Book of Days.*

1. Preheat oven to moderate (180 C/350 F).
2. Using clean hands and a dry bowl, rub the butter into the sugar. Sift in the flour, soda, and cream of tartar.
3. Add enough warm water to mix everything into a stiff dough.
4. Roll out thinly and cut into desired shapes. You might like to replicate the cakes described in Pennant's account by making squares scored with a knife to make the nine segments.
5. Bake for 10 to 15 minutes, until golden brown.

Summer Solstice

Also known as: Litha, Midsummer, St. John's Night
Southern Hemisphere: December 21 (approx.)
Northern Hemisphere: June 21 (approx.)

The solstice may not be the middle of the calendar summer in all places, but many witches view Beltane as the beginning of the summer season, the Solstice as the middle, and Lammas as the first harvest and summer's end.

Midsummer has long been connected to the Fae, partly because of William Shakespeare's play *A Midsummer Night's Dream*. This was among the first works to present the Fae as anything other than malevolent and wicked,[349] and is certainly the most popular.

Modern Pagan midsummer celebrations sometimes include offerings and acknowledgements of the Fae; Oak/Holly King rituals; bonfires (or at least representations of fire in Australia where we have fire restrictions all summer); prayers and offerings to solar

349 Mankey, *Wheel of the Year*.

deities; solar wheels/discs, etc. Some also like to do divination for the year ahead on this auspicious date.

Fire and the Summer Solstice

Throughout the centuries, many records exist of people across Europe building huge bonfires to celebrate midsummer, or St. John's Night, the birthday of John the Baptist. In some northern countries, this was considered the chief celebration of the year. Fires were to honour the sun on its strongest day, in celebration of its many powers—including the power to keep the "fair folk" at bay. The smoke from midsummer fires was considered by some to have protective properties, and with this in mind bonfires were built alongside crops and orchards. In some areas these protective fires were separate from the "main" bonfires and contained animal bones.[350]

In Ireland and parts of England, fires were lit at midnight in honour of the sun. One Englishman's account from 1795 described fires in Ireland being lit exactly at midnight for miles around "with religious solemnity."[351]

BUSHFIRES AND DEAD GRASS

Because this is the driest inhabited continent on Earth, summer is the barren season in many parts of Australia. Here in Central Victoria we sometimes go for four to six months or more with no proper rain, and the dust, the dead grass, and the bare baked ground are the antithesis of the greenery, plump fruits, and beautiful blossoms that we read about in witchy books from America and Europe.

---

350 Mankey, *Wheel of the Year.*
351 Costley and Kightly, *A Celtic Book of Days.*

Many of these texts' ideas of modern midsummer traditions for Pagans are so far from doable that they're almost laughable—especially the ones that involve a roaring bonfire. In these parts, fire restrictions start in October (Beltane) and last until March or April (Samhain). During extreme heat waves, the roads melt and it is too hot to go outside during the day. Remember, midsummer occurs in December in my part of the world. Many non-Pagans celebrate Christmas at this time, which often involves eating salads and barbecue, going to the beach, or having a big nap in the shade after lunch. We also have roast meat, a fully clothed Santa Claus, and fake snow everywhere. It can sometimes feel…jarring, to say the least.

What this means for Pagans here is that we've had to adapt much of the witchy material from overseas to suit our needs. Many folks who work in traditional Wicca have come up with some ingenious ways of representing fire when needed in their midsummer rites. I discuss some of these in chapter 10. In recent times, I have seen several community midsummer events geared towards breaking drought, bringing rain, or even healing the land or mourning human and animal lives lost after bushfire disasters.

Summer Solstice Fire Projects and Activities

- If you live somewhere that you can safely and legally have a ritual bonfire, go for it! Check out chapter 10 for instructions on how to build a marvellous fire that will burn long into the night.
- If you crafted a burnable sun wheel out of paper or vines at the equinox, now is a great time to set it alight (if it's safe to do so)! Secure it to the top of your ritual fire for maximum drama.

- If, like me, you live on land whose midsummer looks nothing like the one presented in the witchy books, have a go at making it work for you and the land around you. Try fire alternatives or signifiers if you need them. Instead of abundance and fertility, it's perfectly fine to change the focus of your ritual to suit your region and the creatures who live there. If you need inspiration, look into some of the popular motifs that are important at this time of year, such as the Oak/Holly King myth cycle, or the notion of a cauldron of inspiration, etc.

- Decorate your ritual space, altar, or home with summer flowers, especially yellow, orange, or red ones to symbolise the strength and power of the sun at this time. Think sunflowers, marigolds, geraniums, and others.

- Candle magic at this time of year often features blue, gold, green, or red candles, and often focuses on gardening and agriculture; changes and endings; divination; fertility and new life; light; manifestation and success; power and strength; and unity.[352]

Midsummer Herbs

Midsummer is a great time for gathering herbs and setting them to dry. I've included some tips and instructions on growing, wildcrafting, and preparing herbs—as well as details about many of the herbs listed below—in chapter 6.

Woods commonly associated with the sun/midsummer: acacia; ash; bamboo; beech; birch; cedar; chestnut; elder; hazel; holly; horse chestnut; juniper; laurel; linden; oak; olive; palm; rowan; walnut; witch hazel

---

352 Kynes, *Correspondences*, 398.

Herbs and plants commonly associated with the sun/midsummer: angelica; broom; carnation; chamomile; chrysanthemum; daffodil; daisy; eyebright; galangal; ginseng; gorse; heather; heliotrope; lavender; lotus; lovage; marigold; mistletoe; peony; rosemary; saffron; St. John's wort; sunflower; vervain[353]

FAREWELL THE SUN

The day of the solstice is the height of the sun's power, but that power starts to slowly ebb away the very next day as the days begin to shorten again. Just as many midwinter celebrations begin at sunrise, so too do midsummer celebrations start at sunset. Consider building your ritual around seeing out the last of the longest day, or getting some friends together to light a flame (or electronic candle?) and sing out the strongest light.

Lammas

Also known as: Lughnasadh, Loaf-mass
Southern Hemisphere: February 1 (approx.)
Northern Hemisphere: August 1 (approx.)

Historically, the ancient Irish festival of Lughnasadh took place at sundown on the 31st of July, with festivities running into the next day. Lammas was an Anglo-Saxon festival that took place at around the same time of year. It's not clear whether the two were related. Lammas later became a festival in the Catholic Church, where it was sometimes called "loaf-mass." It was a celebration of grain harvests and the loaves of bread that came from them. It was usually celebrated on the first of August, although some witches observe the second of August, which is the date given in Robert

---

353 Kynes, *Correspondences*, 383.

Graves's *The White Goddess*. Some witches observe the two holidays separately.[354]

In Ireland and Scotland, Lammas celebrates the beginning of the cereal harvest. Lammas in modern Paganism is still often associated with bread and grain harvests. Some traditions include making corn dollies, which are generally seen as representing the Goddess in her role as the Earth Mother. You can make these with whatever grains or grasses are at hand. I have a friend who makes some absolutely beautiful ones with native Australian grasses in beautiful reds, yellows, and greys.

Rituals around this time of year often honour the harvest in its many forms, and they are sometimes localised to specific harvests relevant to that area. In central Victoria, lavender, grape, and apple harvest festivals are a common event on the secular calendar at this time. Some groups and individuals celebrate their own harvests and incorporate the sharing, cooking, and eating of homegrown produce into Lammas rituals. Others celebrate metaphorical "harvests," schemes coming to fruition, the achievement of goals, important transitions, etc.

Fire and Lammas

LUGH AND LUGHNASADH

Lughnasadh in Ireland was not really a fire festival in the same way that Beltane and Samhain were. Some modern witches and Pagans associate Lughnasadh with the god Lugh and make him (and mythology about him) a focal point for their celebrations, although it's unclear whether he was worshipped as a solar deity by the Celts.[355]

---

354 Mankey, *Wheel of the Year*.
355 Mankey, *Wheel of the Year*.

JOHN BARLEYCORN: WASTED O'ER A SCORCHING FLAME

"John Barleycorn" is a British folk song first written down during the 1500s (but it's probably much older) which has made its way into the liturgy of quite a few modern witchcraft and Pagan traditions. The song tells the story of the life cycle of John Barleycorn, a personification of the barley harvest and everything that comes from it, especially whiskey and beer. Throughout the song, John faces humiliation, misfortune, and "death" in different verses that correspond to the different stages of the barley harvest.

As with all traditional songs, there are a few different variations kicking around. Scottish poet and lyricist Robert Burns mentions the important part that fire plays in the processing of barley in his version:

> They wasted o'er a scorching flame
> the marrow of his bones;
> but a miller us'd him worst of all,
> for he crush'd him between two stones.[356]

Some witches and Pagans who like to keep a grain harvest theme in their Lammas rituals will often bake a humanoid John Barleycorn figure out of bread dough and include it in their celebrations.

Lammas Fire Projects and Activities

- If the focus of your celebrations is less about the grain harvest and more about sharing the harvest, consider hosting a communal cooking afternoon, where everyone contributes ingredients either homegrown, borrowed, or purchased.

---

356 Burns, "John Barleycorn: A Ballad."

- If you can have a campfire at this time of year, a great group activity could be baking potatoes, sweet potatoes, pumpkins, or other hard marrowy veggies. Just wrap each one in tinfoil and leave it in the fire (but not in the hottest centre part) for twenty minutes or so.

- Candle magic at this time of year often features reddish brown, gold, orange, purple, or yellow candles, and often focuses on the achievement of goals; gardening and agriculture; challenges and facing the darkness; death, release, and endings; transformations.

- Woods commonly associated with this time of year include acacia, apple, blackberry/bramble, gorse, myrtle, oak, and rowan.[357]

SIMPLE BREAD RECIPE

This is a good way to celebrate fire's ability to create and transform while you eat lots of butter and jam. This recipe makes either one loaf or a dozen or so bread rolls. You could also fashion it into a John Barleycorn figure.

Whether you're baking a loaf or a John Barleycorn figure for ritual, using a standard electric oven, or something fired by wood or gas, take some time to read and reflect on the physical and chemical changes brought on by heat/fire throughout this process.

INGREDIENTS:

2 cups plain flour

2 cups wholemeal flour

2 cups stoneground flour (or another flour of your choice)

½ teaspoon salt

357 Kynes, *Correspondences*, 399.

2 cups warm water

1 teaspoon honey

½ tablespoon dried yeast

milk

1 tablespoon sesame seeds

1. Sift flours and salt together. Put into a warm bowl in a warm place.

2. Mix ½ cup of the warm water with the honey and add yeast. Leave for 10–15 minutes or until the mixture froths.

3. Add the yeast mixture to the warm flour. Add the rest of the warm water and mix just enough to combine the ingredients.

4. Turn onto a floured board or benchtop and knead well for about 10 minutes (this is great as a group activity if you take turns).

5. Return to the bowl and cover with plastic wrap or a clean tea towel. Leave in a warm place until the dough has doubled in size. This usually takes around 40 minutes, sometimes longer in cooler climates.

6. Preheat oven to 220 C/425 F.

7. Return dough to the floured board/benchtop and knead again. Shape it into your desired shape: a loaf, some rolls, a John Barleycorn, whatever.

8. Place onto oiled trays (use a loaf tin if you're making a loaf). Cover again and return to the warm place to rise some more. This is usually another 40 minutes or so. If you're using a loaf tin, the dough should now come to the top of the tin.

9. Glaze with a little bit of milk and sprinkle with sesame seeds.

10. Bake in a preheated very hot (220 C/425 F) oven for 10 minutes. Then reduce the heat to moderate (180 C/350 F). Cook for a further 30–40 minutes.

SOME TIPS ABOUT BAKING BREAD

- Yeast is a living organism. To grow, it needs warmth, moisture, and food. It will not work properly unless all these three needs are met. The carbon dioxide released as it grows is what causes bread to rise.

- Always put bread dough in a warm place to rise. Cold slows or sometimes stops yeast from growing. Too much heat will kill it.

- The most commonly available form of yeast is dried yeast. Store this in a cool dry place. Once opened, keep in an airtight glass container in the fridge.

- Most flour is made from wheat, but more and more alternatives are available all the time as people's needs and diets change. Once you've made a few simple loaves, try experimenting with different flours. Heavier flours like multigrain or wholemeal generally need a little extra liquid and yeast than lighter flours.

- Utensils and ingredients should be warm when working with bread dough, so that the yeast can grow uninterrupted.

- Very thorough kneading is essential to a good loaf of bread. It's a pretty good arm workout, too.

- Always cover dough you've left to rise.

- A hot oven is also essential in the initial cooking of any yeast mixture. Always put the raw mixture into a very hot oven, then reduce the heat as needed after 10 minutes or so.

- Bread is cooked when it has shrunk slightly from the side of the tin, and you can tap on the crust and get a hollow sound.

Autumn Equinox

Also known as: Mabon

Southern Hemisphere: March 21 (approx.)

Northern Hemisphere: September 21 (approx.)

> Don't try to cling to the incoming spiral once it is over—look onward to the outgoing.[358]
>
> —Janet and Stewart Farrar, *Eight Sabbats for Witches*

There are no records of specific autumn equinox celebrations held in ancient times, but there is evidence in several different countries of harvest festivals held roughly at this time of year. Common themes and motifs of modern Pagan and witchcraft celebrations at this time of year acknowledge the end of the harvest, and the continued waning of the sun.

Mabon is another name coined by Aidan Kelly and first published in various American Pagan and witchy books throughout the 1970s. The name comes from the Welsh mythological figure Mabon ap Modron, who appears in some Arthurian myths and in the Welsh collection of literature known as *The Mabinogion*. In the myths, Mabon is most certainly a very minor figure and is not associated with the equinox or the harvest in any real way. He generally appears as a young man, and some scholars have connected him to the Celtic Maponus, who was a god of youth.[359]

358 Farrar and Farrar, *A Witches' Bible*, 117.
359 Mankey, *Wheel of the Year*.

Many modern witches and Pagans treat the autumn equinox as a second harvest festival. As with Lammas, what constitutes a harvest is often localised or personalised, and varies from area to area. In areas where there are no grain crops grown, witches might celebrate the local apple harvest, etc. In recent times, some witches have also done rituals and offerings dedicated to Persephone. Some Americans treat the holiday as being synonymous with Thanksgiving, as it happens at a similar time of year there.

Fire and the Autumn Equinox
Balance and the Waning Sun

The light and the dark face each other as equals on the day of the equinox, but the darkness prevails. After the equinox, the nights will be a bit longer than the days, and will grow longer and longer until the longest night of the winter solstice.

Things often get a bit wonky at this time of year. As Wiccan author Julia Philips points out, this can be a difficult time of year for many, because humans largely fear darkness and death above all else.[360] In the process of learning to accept those first signs of death and decay we see around us at this time of year—the dying leaves, the finishing blooms, the harvest, the fading light—some believe there is solace and learning.

Autumn Equinox Fire Projects and Activities
- The days will get colder from here on in. If you have a fireplace or wood heater, this is a great time for putting into motion plans for a cosy winter in months to come. Chop and stack firewood, sweep hearths, clean chimneys, and start collecting up stores of kindling to save you working in the cold and wet later on.

---

360 Philips and Philips, *The Witches of Oz*, 79.

- Harvesting and collecting seeds is a great activity for this time of year. Store dry seeds for future planting in airtight jars or sealed in paper envelopes in a dry place. Use an oven on a low setting to dry out edible nuts and seeds spread out on a tray; you could even add some oats and have a go at making your own granola.

- Burning leaves and garden cuttings at this time of year feels witchy as fuck, but check your local laws first and be mindful of your neighbours and their laundry.

- Candle magic at this time of year often features blue, brown, gold, maroon, orange, violet, or yellow candles, and often focuses on the achievement of goals, bountiful harvests, balance and grounding, and gratitude.

- Woods commonly associated with this time of year include aspen, blackberry/bramble, cedar, hazel, maple, myrtle, and oak.[361]

DIVINATION WITH APPLES AND FIRE

One of the most common folkloric divinations associated with apples you'll see in modern witchcraft books involves an unbroken apple peel spelling out the name of a lover. But there are lesser-known customs out there that involve apples and fire for the purpose of divination.

Try this one, from an 1849 collection of English popular rhymes. It encouraged young women to say the following as they tossed apple pips into a fire and thought of someone they were interested in romantically:

> If you love me, pop and fly
> If you hate me, lay and die

361 Kynes, *Correspondences*, 399.

If the pip made a noise and burst from the heat, it was said that the woman's love was reciprocated. A pip that lay still and burned silently was thought to signify the absence of any romantic feelings. Variations of this superstition are evident in the folklore of many parts of England, and in Scotland and Ireland, too.[362]

Autumn Equinox Herbs

This is a great time of year to make and dry bundles for censing and saining.

Use natural twine, cotton, or wool to tie your bundles. Dry them for six to ten weeks in a warm, dry spot out of direct sunlight before you use them. Herbs and plants commonly associated with the autumn equinox include grains, thistle, aster, chrysanthemum, fern, grape vine leaves, ivy, marigold, and sage.[363]

Samhain

Southern Hemisphere: May 1 (approx.)

Northern Hemisphere: October 31 (approx.)

Samhain (pronounced "Sow-in") was an ancient Irish harvest celebration, though records on just how it was celebrated are patchy; most "Halloween" traditions we associate with it only date back as far as the Christian era. In contemporary witchcraft, this is a holiday that takes place just as the coldest and darkest nights of the year begin to set in. Many witches and Pagans see this as a season for the dead, but there are no historical records to suggest that this was originally the case. The connection of Samhain with spirits and the dead wasn't until Sir James Frazer and *The Golden Bough* in the 1890s. Because of Samhain occurring so close to All

---

362 Opie and Tatem, *A Dictionary of Superstitions*, 3–4.
363 Kynes, *Correspondences*, 399.

Souls' Day, Frazer wrote of the ancient festival being watched over by "the souls of the departed hovering unseen."[364]

Some think of Samhain as the "Celtic New Year," but there is very little evidence that this was the case back in the day. Many modern witches and Pagans use Samhain season as a time to remember the dead, especially those who have passed over the last twelve months. At the same time, Samhain is sometimes still treated as the harvest celebration it was in days gone by, a time for bringing in the last of the crops and for hunkering down as the days keep darkening and winter sets in. It has also become tradition for some in recent decades to do workings and rituals connected to the myth of Persephone and Demeter at Samhain.

Fire and Samhain
ANZAC DAY, DAWN SERVICES, AND THE ETERNAL FLAME

Interestingly, Samhain in the Southern Hemisphere falls very close to ANZAC Day, a holiday that commemorates the anniversary of the first major military action fought by Australian and New Zealand forces during the First World War, and those who have served in wars since. ANZAC stands for the Australian and New Zealand Army Corps. The soldiers in those forces in WWI are known as the Anzacs. Many of these soldiers died or were injured during the Gallipoli campaign, which killed or injured almost four hundred thousand troops from around the world in less than a year (April 1915-January 1916).

ANZAC Day is a national day of remembrance here. Commemorative services are held at war memorials across the nation at dawn, the time of the original landing. Dawn vigils have been the basis for commemoration since the end of the First World War, when they were instigated by veterans, clergy, and civilians from

364 Mankey, *Wheel of the Year.*

all over the country and farther afield. These ceremonies typically include the laying of wreaths, the reading of hymns, a minute's silence, and a bugler playing the Last Post, a military tradition that marks the end of the day, done to bid farewell to the dead and to symbolise the end of their duty so that they may rest in peace.

Just as in many European countries, the Australian National War Memorial and many others around the country have an eternal flame—a perpetually burning brazier—to represent remembrance and to symbolise the idea of an undying soul. This tradition was first started in France during the 1920s, and it seems to be inspired by the idea of a perpetually tended flames from classical history, like that of the Vestal Virgins (see chapter 3). While this is by no means a Pagan holiday, motifs like these are certainly familiar to many Pagans.

It took me years to realise the significance of ANZAC Day occurring near Samhain in the Southern Hemisphere. The rest of the year, non-Pagan society celebrates with the Northern Hemisphere; secular Easter occurs nowhere near our spring equinox, for instance. Many Australians are donning Halloween costumes as we Pagans head into the forest for Beltane, and don't get me started (again) on "Yule" logs, fake snow, and wreaths in the height of summer!

But at this time of year, as we are watching a new ending every day in the garden and thinking of those who are no longer with us and those who fell long before their time, Australia is, to some extent, thinking in the same way.

Samhain Fire Projects and Activities
- If you have a garden, gather up the dry, dead flowerheads and finishing plants and, after collecting any seeds you want, include them in the kindling for your Samhain fire.

- If it's practical to do so, consider setting out a small offering to ancestors or spirits by the fireside or a small candle.

- Candle magic at this time of year often features black, orange, red, or white candles, and often focuses on the crossroads and introspection; darkness, the otherworld, and the underworld; death, release, and honouring ancestors; and divination, visions, and wisdom.

- Woods commonly associated with this time of year include apple, beech, blackthorn, pomegranate, willow, and witch hazel.[365]

Carve a Neep Lantern

Long before the gaudy, weirdly symmetrical jack-o-lanterns so popular during the American Halloween, folks carved swedes or turnips—called "neeps" in parts of Scotland—into lanterns. The pale white flesh and purpley blush of the turnip makes for a scary little face once it's hollowed out, and they're just the right size for a tea-light candle.

Use turnips or swedes around the size of a fist, no smaller than a tennis ball. Think of it as carving a pumpkin but in miniature. Carefully cut a round "lid" in the top and set it aside. Scoop out the insides until you have a shell about a centimetre thick. Cut out two little triangle eyes and a jagged mouth. Use a skewer to put a hole in either side for a handle and place a tealight candle inside. We usually use string to make a longish handle so we can hang the neeps around our outdoor ritual site.

Wicked little neep faces get even creepier as they wither and dry out. Leave them in the sun then burn them at midwinter or at Samhain the following year.

---

365 Kynes, *Correspondences*, 400.

Conclusion

As witches, Pagans, polytheists, and other dirt-worshipping folks, we build bonfires to celebrate the stages of the sun, line our processions with torchlight, and dot our altars and circles with candles for almost every imaginable occasion. Whether literal or metaphorical, fire and flame play a big part in the way many witches and Pagans celebrate the Wheel of the Year and continuing cycle of life, death, and rebirth.

CONCLUSION

In many ways, fire is an element that brings us closer. It's there we are sitting around a campfire, locked in a passionate embrace with a lover, sharing warmth and cooked food with family, or sharing our ideas and passions to create something bigger than ourselves. In this way, it is a very human element.

But it goes above and beyond us, too. Fire is the heat and light of the sun that sustains life on this planet. It governs us, from our seasons and ecosystems right down to our individual daily schedules and routines. So much hinges on the sun and its journey through the year, there is little wonder that it has formed the centrepoint of veneration for so many, for so long.

Now that we've explored the many faces and facets of fire throughout the ages, I hope that you have found something useful or relevant to your practice in some way. I hope that you have found something that makes you *want* to do something, too, whatever that might be—to stop dreaming about that passion that burns inside you and get on with the work!

May you always find your spark in the darkness.

Josephine Winter
Imbolc, 2020

ACKNOWLEDGMENTS

This book is dedicated to my grandmother Josephine and to Simon Hannan and Justin McGeachin, beside whose fire I first stepped into myself.

Heartfelt thanks and love to my mum Fiona; to Mark, Tim, Alithea, Aunty Chris, and Aunty Sue, who support me in all my weird jaunts and schemes; and to Kylie Moroney, Ryan McLeod, Sarah Morgan, Paul Donovan, Jason Tremain, Seumas MacLeod, Dean Forest, Dorian Manticore, Eryk Adish, David Waldron, Andrew and Julie, Fran, Keegan, Shaz, Ang and Callum; to Trevor Curnow, Linda and Michel Marold, Gabby C., Adrienne Pigott, Peter Mc, Tree, Kundra, and all the other "doers" in the Pagan community in Oz, and anyone else who taught me how to make torches without burning my arm off.

Appendix

FIRE CORRESPONDENCE CHART

Keywords	Passion, will, transformation, strength
Direction	South
Time of Day	Midday
Astrological Signs	Aries, Leo, Sagittarius
Planets	Sun, Mars, Jupiter
Tarot	Wands, The Emperor, Strength, Devil, The Tower, The Sun
Chakra	Solar plexus
Tools	Athame, wand
Incense	Cedar, frankincense, pomegranate
Elementals	Salamander, djinn
Colours	Crimson, gold, orange, pink, red, white, yellow

Gems	Amber, obsidian, ruby
Plants	Fennel, marigold, rosemary
Trees	Hawthorn, juniper, rowan
Natural Objects	Volcanic stones and glass
Animals	Lion, horse, goat
Deity	Brigid, Agni, Freya, Hephaestus
Sense	Sight
Symbol	Flames, or the alchemical symbol for fire
Runes	Dag, Ken, Rad, Sigel
Archangel	Michael
Magical Lesson	To Will

BIBLIOGRAPHY

Adler, Margot. "A Time for Truth." *Beliefnet.* 2000. Accessed April 2020. https://www.beliefnet.com/faiths/pagan-and-earth-based /2000/09/a-time-for-truth.aspx.

Andersen, Johannes. *Myths and Legends of the Polynesians.* Rutland, Vermont: Tuttle Publishing, 1986.

Arthur Yates & Co. *Yates Garden Guide: Centennial Edition, 1895– 1995.* Pymble, New South Wales: Angus & Robertson, 1995.

Atkin, Emily. "Do You Know Where Your Healing Crystals Come From?" *New Republic.* May 11, 2018. Accessed April 2020. https:// newrepublic.com/article/148190/know-healing-crystals-come-from.

Australian War Memorial. "Red Poppies." *Australian War Memorial website.* Accessed February 27, 2020. https://www.awm.gov.au /commemoration/customs-and-ceremony/poppies.

"Averni." In *Cyclopædia, or an Universal Dictionary of Arts and Sciences*, edited by Ephraim Chambers. London: James and John Knapton, et al., 1728.

Bloodofox. "The Snaptun Stone." *Ancient History Encyclopedia.* November 17, 2017. Accessed April 2020. https://www.ancient .eu/image/7640/the-snaptun-stone/.

Boardman, John, Jasper Griffin, and Oswyn Murray. *The Oxford History of the Classical World.* 3rd. New York: Oxford University Press, 1993.

Brasileiro, Adriana. "Brazilian mines produce world's priciest gems under fire." *Reuters*. June 19, 2016. Accessed March 2020. https://www.reuters.com/article/us-brazil-tourmaline-mines/brazilian-mines-produce-worlds-priciest-gems-under-fire-idUSKCN0Z30O5.

Buckland, Raymond. *Buckland's Complete Book of Witchcraft*. St. Paul, Minnesota: Llewellyn, 1986.

Burns, Robert. "John Barleycorn: A Ballad." *robertburns.org*. Accessed June 2020. http://www.robertburns.org/works/27.shtml.

Caesar, Julius. *Caesar's Commentaries on the Gallic Wars*. Translated by T. R. Holmes, London, 1908.

Cart, Julie. "Hawaii's Hot Rocks Blamed by Tourists for Bad Luck: Goddess said to curse those who take a piece of her island." *Los Angeles Times*. May 17, 2001. Retrieved July 2020. https://www.sfgate.com/news/article/Hawaii-s-hot-rocks-blamed-by-tourists-for-bad-2920041.php.

Cartwright, Mark. "Agni." *Ancient History Encyclopedia*. May 18, 2015. Accessed April 2020. https://www.ancient.eu/Agni/.

Chauran, Alexander. *Faeries & Elementals for Beginners: Learn About & Communicate With Nature Spirits*. Woodbury, Minnesota: Llewellyn, 2013.

Classic Folktales from Around the World. London: Leopard, 1996.

Costley, Sarah, and Charles Kightly. *A Celtic Book of Days*. London: Thames & Hudson, 1998.

Craig, R. D. *Dictionary of Polynesian Mythology*. New York: Greenwood Press, 1989.

Cunningham, Scott. *Cunningham's Encyclopedia of Crystal, Gem & Metal Magic*. St. Paul, Minnesota: Llewellyn, 1988.

Cunningham, Scott. *Cunningham's Encyclopedia of Magical Herbs*. St. Paul, Minnesota: Llewellyn, 1985.

Daimler, Morgan. *Brigid: Meeting the Celtic Goddess of Poetry, Forge, and Healing Well.* Arlesford, UK: Moon Books, 2016.

Daimler, Morgan. *The Dagda: Meeting the Good God of Ireland.* Arlesford, UK: Moon Books, 2018.

Davis, F. H. *Myths and Legends of Japan.* New York: Dover Publications, 1992.

Day, Ed, ed. *Llewellyn's Magical Sampler.* Woodbury, Minnesota: Llewellyn, 2015.

D'Este, Sorita, and David Rankine. *Practical Elemental Magick: Working the Magick of the Four Elements in the Western Mystery Tradition.* London: Avalonia, 2008.

Dorsey, Lilith. "Feast for Chango and Santa Barbara." *Patheos Pagan.* Accessed July 2020. https://www.patheos.com/blogs/voodoo universe/2015/12/124-feast-for-chango-and-santa-barbara/.

Dorsey, Lilith. "Orisha Ogun: Lord of Iron, God of War." *Patheos Pagan.* Accessed July 2020. https://www.patheos.com/blogs /voodoouniverse/2013/11/orisha-ogun-lord-of-iron-god-of-war/.

Dorsey, Lilith. *Orishas, Goddesses and Voodoo Queens: The Divine Feminine in the African Religious Traditions.* Newburyport, Massachusetts: Weiser Books, 2020.

Drury, Nevill. *The Watkins Dictionary of Magic.* London: Watkins Publishing, 2005.

Drury, Nevill, and Gregory Tillett. *The Occult Sourcebook.* London: Routledge & Kegan Paul, 1978.

Dublin, Trinity College, MS 1319. *Cath Muige Tuired Cunga.* pp. 90–110 [s. xv] pp. 90a–99b. Translated by Fraser, J. "The First Battle of Moytura." *Ériu* v.8 (1915), pp. 1–63. Accessed July 2020. https://loraobrien.ie/first-battle-of-moytura-cath-muige -tuired-cunga/.

BIBLIOGRAPHY

Dunwich, Gerina. *Dunwich's Guide to Gemstone Sorcery: Using Stones for Spells, Amulets, Rituals, and Divination.* San Francisco: Weiser, 2003.

Dunwich, Gerina. *The Wicca Garden.* Secaucus, New Jersey: Citadel, 1998.

Earthworks. "How the 20 tons of mine waste per gold ring figure was calculated." *Earthworks.org.* Accessed April 2020. https://earthworks.org/cms/assets/uploads/archive/files/publications/20TonsMemo_FINAL.pdf.

Elsie, Robert. *A Dictionary of Albanian Religion, Mythology and Folk Culture.* London: C. Hurst & Co., 2001.

Encyclopaedia Britannica. "Cacus and Caca." *Encyclopaedia Britannica.* Accessed April 2020. https://www.britannica.com/topic/Cacus-and-Caca.

Etymology Online. "Fire." Accessed April 2020. https://www.etymonline.com/search?q=fire.

Fobar, Rachel. "Frankincense trees—of biblical lore—are being tapped out for essential oils." December 13, 2019. Accessed February 20, 2020. https://www.nationalgeographic.com/animals/2019/12/frankincense-trees-declining-overtapping/.

Ford, David N. "Dinas Emrys: Vortigern's Hideout?" *David Nash Ford's Early British Kingdoms.* Accessed April 2020. http://www.earlybritishkingdoms.com/archaeology/emrys.html.

Frazer, James G. *The Golden Bough.* 3rd ed. London: McMillan & Co., 1955.

Gardner, Lily. "The Nine Sacred Trees." In *Llewellyn's Magical Sampler*, edited by Ed Day, 70–75. Woodbury, Minnesota: Llewellyn, 2015.

Goren-Inbar, Naama, Nira Alperson, Mordechai E. Kislev, Orit Simchoni, Yoel Melamed, Adi Ben-Nun, and Ella Werker.

"Evidence of Hominin Control of Fire at Gesher Benot Ya`aqov, Israel." *Science*. April 30, 2004: 725–727. Accessed April 2020. doi:10.1126/science.1095443.

Gray, Eden. *The Tarot Revealed*. London: Penguin, 1969.

Green, Marian. *The Elements of Ritual Magic*. Shaftesbury, UK: Element Books, 1990.

Grimassi, Raven. *Encyclopedia of Wicca and Witchcraft*. St. Paul, Minnesota: Llewellyn, 2000.

Groundspeak. "Seafarers and Killed in the Sea Monument and Eternal Flame—Helsinki, Finland." Wayfinders.com. Accessed July 2020. http://staging.waymarking.com/waymarks/WMG1R3 _Seafarers_and_Killed_in_the_Sea_Monument_Eternal_Flame _Helsinki_Finland.

Gupta, Shakti M. *Plant Myths and Traditions in India*. Leiden, Netherlands: E. J. Brill, 1971.

Gwydion MacLir, Alferian. *The Witch's Wand: The Craft, Lore, and Magick of Wands & Staffs*. Woodbury, Minnesota: Llewellyn, 2015.

Hall, Judy. *The Crystal Bible*. Cincinnati, Ohio: Walking Stick Press, 2003.

Hazen, Walter. *Inside Hinduism*. Dayton, Ohio: Milliken, 2003.

Holmyard, Eric John. *Alchemy*. Middlesex, England: Penguin Books, 1957.

Hughes, Kristoffer. *From the Cauldron Born: Exploring the Magic of Welsh Legend and Lore*. Woodbury, Minnesota: Llewellyn, 2012.

Hughes, Kristoffer. *The Journey into Spirit: A Pagan's Perspective on Death, Dying and Bereavement*. Woodbury, Minnesota: Llewellyn, 2015.

Human Rights Watch. "The Hidden Cost of Jewelry: Human Rights in Supply Chains and the Responsibility of Jewelry Companies."

HRW website. February 8, 2018. Accessed March 2020. https://www.hrw.org/report/2018/02/08/hidden-cost-jewelry/human-rights-supply-chains-and-responsibility-jewelry.

Hutton, Ronald. *Blood and Mistletoe: The History of the Druids in Britain.* New Haven, Connecticut: Yale University Press, 2009.

Hutton, Ronald. *Triumph of the Moon: A History of Modern Pagan Witchcraft.* Oxford, UK: Oxford University Press, 1999.

Illes, Judika. *The Element Encyclopedia of 5000 Spells.* London: Harper Element, 2004.

Illes, Judika. *The Encyclopedia of Spirits: The Ultimate Guide to the Magic of Fairies, Genies, Demons, Ghosts, Gods, and Goddesses.* New York: Harper Collins, 2009.

Jones, Gwyn. *A History of the Vikings.* Oxford, UK: Oxford University Press, 2001.

Jones, Gwyn, and Thomas Jones, transl. *The Mabinogion.* London: J M Dent & Sons, 1993.

Jung, Carl. *Man and His Symbols.* London: Aldus Books, 1964.

Khan, Inayat. "Abstract Sound." *The Mysticism of Music, Sound and Word.* Accessed July 2020. https://wahiduddin.net/mv2/II/II_8.htm.

King, Hobart M. "Igneous Rocks." *Geology.com.* Accessed March 2020. https://geology.com/rocks/igneous-rocks.shtml.

Kirton, Meredith. *Dig Deeper.* Crows Nest, New South Wales: Murdoch Books, 2014.

Kirton, Meredith. *Harvest.* Millers Point, New South Wales: Murdoch Books, 2009.

Kryuchkova, Elena and Olga Kryuchkova. *The Illustrated Encyclopedia of Slavic Gods and Spirits.* Translated by Inna Rutkovska. Babelcube Inc., 2019.

Kynes, Sandra. *Llewellyn's Complete Book of Correspondences.* Woodbury, Minnesota: Llewellyn Publications, 2016.

Little, Brenda. *The Complete Book of Herbs and Spices.* Frenchs Forest, New South Wales: Reed Books, 1986.

Lochtefeld, James G. *The Illustrated Encyclopedia of Hinduism: A–M.* New York: The Rosen Publishing Group, 2002.

Lurker, Manfred. *The Routledge Dictionary of Gods and Goddesses, Devils and Demons.* London: Routledge, 2005.

MacCulloch, J. A. *The Celtic and Scandinavian Religions.* London: Hutchinson & Co., 1948.

MacGregor, Trish. *The Everything Astrology Book.* Avon, Massachusetts: Adams Media, 1999.

Mackenzie, Donald A. *Myths of Babylon and Assyria.* London: The Gresham Publishing Company, 1915.

Mankey, Jason. *The Witch's Athame: The Craft, Lore & Magick of Ritual Blades.* Woodbury, Minnesota: Llewellyn, 2016.

Mankey, Jason. *Witch's Wheel of the Year: Rituals for Circles, Solitaries & Covens.* Woodbury, Minnesota: Llewellyn, 2019.

Mierzwicki, Tony. *Hellenismos: Practicing Greek Polytheism Today.* Woodbury, Minnesota: Llewellyn, 2018.

Mitchell, Alan. *A Field Guide to the Trees of Britain and Northern Europe.* London: Collins, 1974.

Moss, Vivienne. *Hekate: A Devotional.* Alresford, UK: Moon Books, 2015.

Murrell, Nathaniel Samuel. *Afro-Caribbean Religions.* Philadelphia, Pennsylvania: Temple University Press, 2010.

Norton, Holly. "Honey, I Love You: Our 40,000 Year Relationship with the Humble Bee." *The Guardian.* May 24, 2017. Accessed August 2020. https://www.theguardian.com/science/2017/

may/24/honey-i-love-you-our-40000-year-relationship-with
-the-humble-bee.

Nowak, Claire. "The Fascinating History of the Birthday Cake."
Readers' Digest website. Accessed May 2020. https://www
.rd.com/culture/origin-of-birthday-cake/.

O'Connor, Kerri. *Ostara: Rituals, Recipes & Lore for the Spring
Equinox*. Woodbury, Minnesota: Llewellyn, 2015.

Ono, Sokyo. *Shinto: The Kami Way*. North Clarendon, USA: Tuttle
Publishing, 1962.

Opie, Iona, and Moira Tatem. *A Dictionary of Superstitions*. New
York: Oxford University Press, 1992.

Patinkin, Jason. "World's Last Wild Frankincense Forests Are Under
Threat." *Yahoo Finance*. December 25, 2016. Accessed February
24, 2020. https://finance.yahoo.com/news/worlds-last-wild
-frankincense-forests-084122152.html.

Paxson, Diana L. *Essential Asatru: Walking the Path of Norse Paganism*.
New York: Citadel, 2006.

Paxson, Diana L. *The Way of the Oracle: Recovering the Practices of the
Past to Find Answers for Today*. San Francisco: Weiser, 2012.

People's Daily Online. "Archaeologists Find Crocodile is Prototype
of Dragon." April 29, 2000. Accessed June 2020. http://
en.people.cn/english/200004/29/eng20000429_40001.html.

Philips, Julia, and Matthew Philips. *The Witches of Oz*. Chievely,
UK: Capall Bann, 1994.

Pollack, Rachel. *Seventy-Eight Degrees of Wisdom: A Book of Tarot*.
Wellingborough, Northamptonshire: The Aquarian Press, 1980.

Pratchett, Terry. *Jingo*. London: Corgi Books, 1997.

Qumsiyeh, Mazin B. *Mammals of the Holy Land*. Lubboch, Texas:
Texas Tech University Press, 1996.

Ravenwolf, Silver. *American Folk Magic.* St. Paul, Minnesota: Llewellyn, 1996.

Readers' Digest Association. *Folklore, Myths and Legends of Britain.* London: Readers' Digest, 1977.

Reilly, Michael, Suzanne Duncan, Gianna Leoni, Lachy Paterson, Lyn Carter, Matiu Rātima, and Poia Rewi. *Te Kōparapara: An Introduction to the Māori World.* Auckland, New Zealand: Auckland University Press, 2018.

Riegler, Dan. "Co-Ops—Do we support ethical frankincense harvesting?" March 21, 2014. Accessed February 20, 2020. https://apothecarysgarden.com/2014/03/21/co-ops-do-we -support-ethical-frankincense-harvesting/.

Save Frankincense. "Certifiable Resin Supply Chain." Accessed February 20, 2020. https://www.savefrankincense.org /certifiable-resin-supply-chain.

Save Frankincense. "Frankincense Decline." Accessed February 20, 2020. https://www.savefrankincense.org/frankincense-decline.

Scot, Reginald. *The Discoverie of Witchcraft.* London: William Brome, 1584. Accessed March 8, 2020. https://www.gutenberg .org/files/60766/60766-h/60766-h.htm.

Solas Bhride Centre and Hermitages. "Lighting the Perpetual Flame: A Brief History." Solas Bhride. Accessed July 2020. http:// solasbhride.ie/the-perpetual-flame/.

Stromberg, Joseph. "Where Did Dragons Come From?" *Smithsonian Magazine.* January 23, 2012. Accessed June 2020. https://www .smithsonianmag.com/science-nature/where-did-dragons-come -from-23969126/.

Skinner, Stephen. *The Complete Magician's Tables.* London: Avalonia, 2006.

Squire, Charles. *Mythology of the Celtic People.* 3rd ed. London: Bracken Books, 1996.

Symes, Alison. *Willow.* London: Reaktion Books, 2014.

The German Way & More. "Fasching and Karneval." Accessed February 13, 2020. https://www.german-way.com/history-and -culture/holidays-and-celebrations/fasching-and-karneval/.

The Medieval Bestiary. "Eagle." *The Medieval Bestiary website.* Accessed July 2020. http://bestiary.ca/beasts/beast232.htm.

The University of Auckland. "Basalt." *Geology: Rocks and Minerals.* Accessed March 2020. https://flexiblelearning.auckland.ac.nz /rocks_minerals/rocks/basalt.html.

Thompson, Janet. *Magical Hearth: Home for the Modern Pagan.* York Beach, Maine: Samuel Weiser, Inc., 1995.

Tourist Office of Brocéliande. "The Fountain of Barenton." *Tourist Office of Brocéliande website.* Accessed February 2, 2020. https:// tourisme-broceliande.bzh/en/lieu/fontaine-de-barenton/.

Tudeau, Johanna. "Girra (god)." *Ancient Mesopotamian Gods and Goddesses.* Oracc and the UK Higher Education Academy. Accessed July 2020. http://oracc.museum.upenn.edu/amgg /listofdeities/girra/.

Tuan. "The Working Tools of the Witch: The Sword." *Esoterica* (1995), 42–44.

Valiente, Doreen. *An ABC of Witchcraft Past and Present.* London: Robert Hale, 1973.

Valiente, Doreen. *The Rebirth of Witchcraft.* London: Robert Hale, 1989.

Virgil. 29–19 BCE. *The Aeneid (1697 translation).* Translated by John Dryden. Accessed April 2020. http://www.gutenberg.org /files/228/228-h/228-h.htm.

Waite, Arthur Edward. *The Pictorial Key to the Tarot: Fragments of a Secret Tradition under the Veil of Divination (1993 edition).* London: Parragon, 1993.

Waldron, David. *The Sign of the Witch: Modernity and the Pagan Revival.* Durham, North Carolina: Carolina Academic Press, 2008.

Watts, D. C. *Elsevier's Dictionary of Plant Lore.* London: Elsevier, 2007.

Weber, Courtney. *Brigid: History, Mystery, and Magick of the Celtic Goddess.* San Francisco: Weiser, 2015.

Willard, Pat. *The Secrets of Saffron.* Boston: Beacon Press, 2002.

Wilson, Courtney. "Ornithologist seeks to prove theory NT desert hunting birds spread fire to flush out prey." *ABC News.* March 3, 2016. Accessed July 2020. https://www.abc.net.au/news/2016 -03-03/smart-bushfire-birds/7216934.

Wiseman, Eva. "Are Crystals the New Blood Diamonds?" *The Guardian.* June 16, 2019. Accessed March 2020. https://www .theguardian.com/global/2019/jun/16/are-crystals-the-new-blood -diamonds-the-truth-about-muky-business-of-healing-stones.

Woodbury, Sarah. "Dinas Ffareon (Dinas Emrys)." *Sarah Woodbury: Mystery, Fantasy and Romance in Medieval Wales.* Accessed April 2020. https://www.sarahwoodbury.com/dinas-ffareon-dinas-emrys/.

Worth, Valerie. *The Crone's Book of Words.* St. Paul, Minnesota: Llewellyn, 1971.

Yeats, William Butler. "The Song of Wandering Aengus." *The Wind Among the Reeds.* Accessed April 2020. https://www.poetry foundation.org/poems/55687/the-song-of-wandering-aengus.

Zai, Dr. J. *Taoism and Science: Cosmology, Evolution, Morality, Health and more.* Ultravisum, 2015.

Zakroff, Laura Tempest. *Weave the Liminal: Living Modern Traditional Witchcraft.* Woodbury, Minnesota: Llewellyn, 2019.

△

INDEX

INDEX

H

T

Tradition is not the worship of ashes,
but the preservation of fire.

GUSTAV MAHLER